RONALDO

About the author

Luca Caioli is the bestselling author of *Messi*, *Neymar* and *Suárez*. A renowned Italian sports journalist, he lives in Spain.

RONALDO

THE OBSESSION FOR PERFECTION

Updated Edition

LUCA CAIOLI

ICON

This updated edition published in the UK in 2015 by Icon Books Ltd

Previously published in the UK in 2012 by
Corinthian Books, an imprint of
Icon Books Ltd, Omnibus Business Centre,
39–41 North Road, London N7 9DP
email: info@iconbooks.com
www.iconbooks.com

Sold in the UK, Europe and Asia
by Faber & Faber Ltd, Bloomsbury House,
74–77 Great Russell Street, London WC1B 3DA or their agents

Distributed in the UK, Europe and Asia
by TBS Ltd, TBS Distribution Centre, Colchester Road
Frating Green, Colchester CO7 7DW

Distributed in Australia and New Zealand
by Allen & Unwin Pty Ltd,
PO Box 8500, 83 Alexander Street,
Crows Nest, NSW 2065

Distributed in South Africa
by Jonathan Ball, Office B4, The District,
41 Sir Lowry Road, Woodstock 7925

Distributed in India by Penguin Books India,
11 Community Centre, Panchsheel Park,
New Delhi 110017

ISBN: 978-190685-093-7

Typeset in New Baskerville by Marie Doherty

Printed and bound in the UK by
Clays Ltd, St Ives plc

Contents

Chapter 1
Me

'I love being Cristiano Ronaldo.'

'I love what I do, I love my life, I'm happy.'

'I consider myself a winner. I win more often than I lose. I always try to stay focused. I know it's not easy, but nothing in life is easy. If it was, we wouldn't have been born crying.'

'I'm a competitive person and that's never going to change. Obviously I'm growing up and becoming more mature. But the way I think doesn't change.'

'I have faith in my abilities. I always have done.'

'I am who I am. The way I act, what others see – that's the real me.'

'I have never altered my behaviour for anyone. If they like me, great. If not … they can stay away. They don't have to come to my games.'

'Those who know me know who I really am, my personality, my character.'

'I'm very close to my family. I was close to my dad and I'm still close to my mum and siblings. My family is my rock. They've been incredibly supportive; they're always there for me when I need them. They have helped me so much, and I try to be there for them as they have for me.'

'The people who know me well love me. The few people who live with me, the people I train with every day, those who work with me … they think highly of me because they know what I'm like. Of course, other people have a very different opinion because they don't know me. I can understand that.'

'I always speak my mind. I tell it like it is. That might be what others don't like about me.'

'I don't pay any attention to what people say about me. I don't read the newspapers or magazines. Everyone's entitled to their opinion.'

'There have been lots of lies spread about me ... that's the price of fame.'

'I think people are jealous of me because I'm rich, good looking and a great footballer. There's no other explanation.'

'I'm always ready to learn, to hear different opinions.'

'I'm someone who is very easy to live with. And I feel very lucky because if I ever need to talk about anything, I have the best friends in the world.'

'I'm a normal guy and I have feelings just like anybody else.'

'I'm the kind of person who loves a challenge – I always have. My entire life is geared towards finding new challenges.'

'I'm generally quite a positive and well-balanced person.'

'To me, getting on with people is more important than money.'

'Having a good quality of life is more important than money.'

'I've had a great education. My parents taught me to be myself, not to change for anyone. If people like me, fine. If not, it doesn't bother me.'

'I like seeing the people around me happy, smiling, content.'

'You don't win anything in this life without overcoming the kinds of obstacles that I've encountered.'

'I used to cry every day when I was a little boy growing up in Lisbon. I still cry – I cry a lot of tears, both happy and sad. It's good to cry. Crying is just part of life.'

'I have no time for people who lie to me – to me lying is one of the worst traits. It makes me really angry.'

'Talking incessantly is not my style. Talking too much isn't good for your image.'

'I don't like talking about my private life. I don't like drawing attention to it but I don't hide anything either. Let people gossip if they want to. If people want to sell their story, that's up to them. I'm not interested.'

'I'm a smart kid – but no one's perfect and that includes me.'

'There are days when it's not easy being Cristiano – days when I'd love to do something normal and I can't. But I know how to handle it and to be honest I'm not uncomfortable with this kind of life.'

Chapter 2

Football

'If you love football, then there's no doubt you'll love watching Cristiano Ronaldo.'

'I get to do the thing I love most in life – play football.'

'I've already won everything there is to win, but I'll never stop trying to win until the day I retire. That's just who I am. I believe in a bad run of form, but not in letting it get you down. Mental focus is paramount when it comes to achieving your goals. And the key is to keep setting those goals.'

'My aim, my ambition, is to be the best. Ultimately, if I come within reach of being the best, then great – although what I'd really love is to go down as one of the best players in history. I'm grateful to God that I've won the trophy for best player in the world, but I'd like to win it again, this year or next. I'm definitely going to get that Ballon d'Or again.'

'I believe I'm a well-rounded footballer, although there are always countless ways to improve. I'm not referring to specific elements of my game, I just mean generally. You have to grow as a complete player. You can't just focus on shooting or dribbling.'

'Dribbling and dodging is the way I play. I've played like that since I was little. I love dodging and feinting, getting past the opponent. I know that people get annoyed when I dodge past them, or when I bicycle kick or backheel the ball. But I'm not trying to make fun of my opponents, that's just my style. I didn't change it when I was in England and I'm not going to change it whether I'm in Spain or Brazil.'

'My goal-scoring technique is a secret I'll never divulge. I just think about which side I'm going to go for, I look at the goal, the goalie and the defenders, and I shoot. When I take the shot I say to myself "Make it a good one Cristiano".'

'I always try to score goals, play well and help the team. But I never think I have to score in every game. If you think that way you end up not scoring at all. Where there's talent, ability and technical quality, the goals come naturally. So I don't get too worried if I don't score. If I play well, if the team plays well, the goals will come.'

'It doesn't matter where we play or who we play, in every match I go out onto the field to give it my all, play the way I know how, and do everything possible to ensure we win.'

'When I get home after losing a game, I don't talk to my mum or any of my family. They know what I'm like and they know how I react. I've been known to cry after certain losses.'

'What's my biggest weakness? I don't know … I like to be great on every level, not just physically but mentally too. There's no single aspect that I work on more than others. I just want to keep getting stronger.'

'Footballers are people too and naturally the things that happen in our lives affect us as much as the next person. But the higher level you are professionally, the stronger you have to be to ensure it doesn't affect your performance. That's what we're paid to do.'

'During the season, my life is quite calm and focused – it's all about football. Sometimes it's about enjoying life and on other occasions it's about working hard. During the holidays I might like to let off steam with my friends, but when I'm working, nobody can fault my attitude. I try to set an example as a professional, and that shines through when I play. If you go out partying every weekend, there's no way you can give it your all on the pitch.'

'I like to look after my body, it's an important part of my life and my profession. I don't have any particular routine, I just train. I eat whatever I want but in moderation. I have good genes so I don't put on weight, but I do have to work hard to maintain my fitness.'

'When I'm on the pitch or training I'm happy because I love playing football. It's my passion, it's what I enjoy.'

'I consider my team-mates to be friends because I'm with them every day. The team is my second family. Apart from the people I live with, they're the people I spend the most time with.'

'I love it when there's a lively atmosphere in the changing room, when everyone's enjoying themselves and feeling positive.'

'When I step onto the pitch I'm fearless. The opposition defenders don't bother me; they're just out there to do their job. I don't believe any player intends to cause injuries. Ninety-nine per cent of players are honest and just want to do the best they can for their team. Of course, some of them will try to stop me by fouling me – if they didn't, they wouldn't be able to stop me. But I try not to worry about it too much.'

'I think the footballing industry should protect and nurture the players who try to make it fun and creative, who try to give the fans a fantastic show. That's the most important thing, because there would be no football without the fans. It's thanks to their fans that teams like Real Madrid, Man United and Barcelona are world renowned.'

'I try to ignore provocation because there's no place for it in football. People who try to stir things up are just looking for trouble. What people say really doesn't bother me, I just ignore it.'

'When people say bad things about me it falls on deaf ears. I only hear those who shout about how great that Portuguese boy is. I don't need insults to motivate me.'

'The ones who insult me are always the first to ask for my autograph when they see me in the street. I don't understand why they're so negative, I really don't. I can understand if they're afraid of me, but not if they're rude. People love you in the airports and then they hate you on the pitch – that's what my team-mates always say, and it really rings true.'

'I'm not the kind of person who spends the whole afternoon at home watching four or five matches. It's not that I don't like football, I just don't like watching it on TV. I prefer to play. When I'm not on the pitch I only watch Real Madrid games, and the really big matches.'

'If I weren't a footballer, I would have liked to go back to studying. But I was training with the Sporting Lisbon first team from age sixteen so I couldn't stay in school. I would have studied marketing or been a PE teacher.'

'I'd like to be remembered as a role model, as a footballer who always gave a hundred per cent, who put on a good show – and who won absolutely everything.'

Author's note

These quotations are extracted from interviews with the following media: RTVE, Antena 3, Telecinco, Intereconomía TV, Cadena SER, Cadena COPE, Real Madrid TV, Marca, As, A Bola.

Chapter 3

'Abelhinha'

*'On the one hand I had a happy childhood; on the other hand
it was unusual because I left my family and moved to Lisbon at
the age of twelve.'*

The three-bedroom concrete council house where Cristiano
was born no longer exists. In 2007, the house at 27A Quinta
do Falcão, in the Santo António neighbourhood of Funchal,
capital of Madeira, was demolished to avoid problems with
squatters.

The Aveiro family had long since moved on by this point.
Cristiano's mother Dolores now lives in a big white house
overlooking the Atlantic in São Gonçalo, at the other end of
Funchal – a beautiful home bought for her by her son, near
the homes of his brother Hugo and sister Katia.

The once impoverished Quinta do Falcão, with its clus-
ter of council blocks on the mountain slope, has undergone
a transformation in recent years thanks to investment from
the European Union. New housing complexes have sprung
up and the area has become acceptable to the Portuguese
middle classes, many of whom have been horrified by the
house prices on the coast.

At the end of a narrow little road where the footballer's
house used to stand, there is now an empty patch of over-
grown scrubland, a five-a-side football pitch, and a bar. But
it's not unusual for fans to find their way down here, and

for a few Euros the cabbies take them on a tour – his birthplace, where he grew up, his school, where he first played football ... in Portugal's collective imagination he has succeeded in eclipsing such illustrious visitors to Madeira as Winston Churchill, Empress Elizabeth 'Sissi' of Austria, Charles I of Austria, George Bernard Shaw, the poet Rilke, Christopher Columbus and Napoleon.

Madeira is an Atlantic archipelago some 860 kilometres from Lisbon, comprising two inhabited islands – Madeira and Porto Santo – and three minor, uninhabited islands. Hailed by the tourist guides as the 'garden of the Atlantic', Madeira island sits on a volcanic rock 57 kilometres long by 22 wide, a mountain range which rises up from beneath the sea to a summit of 1,862 metres at Pico Ruivo, its highest peak. The capital, Funchal, has a population of 110,000.

It was here that Cristiano was born, at 10.20am on Tuesday 5 February in the Cruz de Carvalho Hospital. He was 52 centimetres long at birth and weighed nearly nine pounds. A fourth child for Maria Dolores dos Santos and José Dinis Aveiro, younger brother to Hugo, Elma and Katia. It was an unplanned pregnancy, nine years after the birth of Katia, and now there was the issue of what to name him.

'My sister, who was working in an orphanage at the time, said that if it was a boy we could name him Cristiano,' recalls Dolores. 'I thought it was a good choice. And my husband and I both liked the name Ronaldo, after Ronald Reagan. My sister chose Cristiano and we chose Ronaldo.'

Cristiano Ronaldo dos Santos Aveiro is duly baptised in the Santo António church – a day which coincidentally is marked by football. In his spare time, José Dinis helps out as a kit man for amateur football club CF Andorinho in Santo António. He asks team captain Fernão Barros Sousa to take on the role of godfather to his new baby. The ceremony is booked for 6.00pm, but first there's a match at 4.00pm – Andorinha are playing Ribeiras Bravas.

Reverend António Rodríguez Rebola is getting nervous. He has already baptised the other children and there is still no sign of either father or godfather. Dolores and the godmother-to-be are following him around the church, baby in tow, trying to keep the priest calm. Eventually Fernão and Dinis arrive, half an hour late, and the ceremony can finally get underway.

The first photos in the family album show baby Cristiano, big eyes staring straight at the camera, dressed in a little blue and white outfit and white booties, with gold bracelets on both wrists, a gold ring, and a long chain with a crucifix around his neck. As he gets older, the photos show his hair forming into a little tuft of curls and his smile becomes gappy after losing his front teeth.

Dinis is the town hall gardener, while Dolores works hard as a cook so that she can put food on the table for her own children as well. Like thousands of Portuguese citizens, Dolores had emigrated to France at the age of twenty, where she spent three months cleaning houses. Her husband was going to join her, but when he wasn't able to she returned to Madeira. They already had two children.

Life isn't easy for the Aveiro family – it's difficult for anyone who lives far away from the luxury hotel industry which has colonised the coast. It's a small home for a family of six – and whenever there's a storm the house leaks in dozens of places. Dolores fetches bricks and mortar from the town hall to try to keep the problem under control.

But today, Cristiano remembers that time as a happy childhood. At two or three years old, playing in the yard or on Lombinho Street, he began to discover his best friend – the football.

'One Christmas I gave him a remote controlled car, thinking that would keep him busy,' recalls his godfather Fernão Sousa, 'but he preferred to play with a football. He slept with his ball, it never left his side. It was always under his arm – wherever he went, it went with him.'

Cristiano goes to nursery at the Externato de São João da Ribeira, a school run by Franciscan nuns. At six, he joins the local primary school. For secondary school he attends Gonçalves Zarco, better known as the Barreiros school because of its proximity to the Barreiros stadium, where renowned Portuguese team CS Marítimo play. Cristiano is not the studious type. He doesn't fare too badly but he's no bookworm either – he is happy just to scrape a pass.

One of his class teachers, Maria dos Santos, remembers her former pupil as 'well behaved, fun and a good friend to his classmates'. When asked about his favourite pastime, she says: 'From the day he walked through the door, football was his favourite sport. He took part in other activities, learnt songs and did his work, but he liked to have time for himself, time for football. If there wasn't a real ball around – and often there wasn't – he would make one out of socks. He would always find a way of playing football in the playground. I don't know how he managed it.'

It was football in the playground and football in the street. 'When he got home from school, I used to tell him to go to his room and do his homework,' says Dolores. 'He always told me he didn't have any. So I would go and start the cooking and he would chance his luck. He would climb out the window, grab a yoghurt or some fruit, and run away with the ball under his arm. He'd be out playing until 9.30 at night.'

As if that wasn't enough, he began to skip classes to go out and play. 'His teachers told me I had to punish him, but I never did. He had to practise as much as possible to become a football star.' As her son would later acknowledge: 'I was always playing football with my friends, that's what I loved doing, that was how I spent my time.'

He plays in the street because there is no football pitch in the neighbourhood. One particular street, Quinta do Falcão, proves to be a challenge when buses, cars and motorbikes want to get through. They have to remove the stones marking out the goalposts each time and wait for the traffic to pass before resuming the game. The games they play are intense battles between households, between gangs of friends. They are games that never end. The only hiccup is when the ball lands in one of the neighbours' gardens – and if it's old Mr Agostinho's garden he always threatens to puncture the ball and tell Dolores and the other mothers to keep their children in check.

There's a well where Cristiano spends hours on end kicking the ball against the wall alone. The well and the street are his first training grounds. It's here, between the pavement, the asphalt and the cars, playing against kids young and old, that Ronaldo learns the tricks and techniques which will make him great and become his signature style. 'He used to spend all day in the street, doing authentic tricks with the ball. It was as if it was attached to his foot,' recalls Adelino Andrade, who lived near the Aveiro family.

'When it came to football he was truly gifted,' maintains Cristiano's sister, Elma. 'But we never dreamed he would be where he is today.'

At six years of age, Cristiano has made his first foray into the footballing world. His cousin Nuno plays for Andorinha and Cristiano has been to the ground a number of times with his father. Nuno invites him to come and see him play, and asks him if he would like to join one of the teams. Cristiano joins the practice and decides to give it a go. Dolores and Dinis are happy with their youngest son's decision – they have always loved football. Dinis and his older son Hugo are Benfica fans, while Dolores adores Luís Figo and Sporting Lisbon.

In the 1994-95 season, nine-year-old Cristiano Ronaldo dos Santos Aveiro is awarded his first sporting licence, number 17,182, from the Funchal football association, and dons the light blue strip for Andorinha. It's a local club with a long history, founded on 6 May 1925. The name Andorinha is Portuguese for a swallow, which according to legend derives from one particular footballer's superb shot which was followed by the flight of a swallow.

Primary school teacher Francisco Afonso, who taught Cristiano's sister Katia, has dedicated 25 years to coaching in the Madeira junior leagues. He was Ronaldo's first coach and he has never forgotten the first time he saw him on the Andorinha pitch, age seven.

'Football was what Cristiano lived for,' he says. 'He was fast, he was technically brilliant and he played equally well with his left and right foot. He was skinny but he was a head taller than other kids his age. He was undoubtedly extremely gifted – he had a natural talent that was in the genes. He was always chasing the ball, he wanted to be the one to finish the game. He was very focused, he worked equally hard regardless of where he was on the pitch. And whenever he couldn't play or he missed a game he was devastated.'

Club president Rui Santos tells a juicy anecdote about a match during the 1993-94 season: Andorinha versus Camacha, who at that time were one of the strongest teams on the island. At half time Andorinha were losing 2-0 and

'Ronaldo was so distraught that he was sobbing like a child who's had his favourite toy confiscated. In the second half he came onto the pitch and scored two goals, leading the team to a 3-2 victory. He definitely did not like to lose. He wanted to win every time and when they lost he cried.'

'That's why he was nicknamed 'cry-baby' explains Dolores. He cried and got angry very easily – if a team-mate didn't pass him the ball, if he or someone else missed a goal or a pass, or if the team wasn't playing how he wanted. The other nickname he acquired was *abelhinha*, 'little bee', because he never stopped. Like a busy bee, he was always zigzagging across the pitch. Years later in Madrid, Cristiano would christen his Yorkshire Terrier with the same name.

'A footballer like Ronaldo doesn't come along every day,' adds Rui Santos. 'And suddenly when he does, you realise he's a superstar – different from all the other kids you've seen play.' Unfortunately Andorinha was one of the weakest teams in the league, and when they faced the likes of Marítimo, Camara de Lobos or Machico, the matches were something of a whitewash. Ronaldo didn't want to play because he already knew they would lose. But his father would come home, cheer him up and persuade him to put his kit and boots on and join his team on the pitch. Only the weak give up, he would say – and it was a lesson that little Ronaldo would never forget.

In a few short years his name becomes known across the island. The two big island clubs, Nacional da Madeira and Marítimo, begin to take an interest in the little bee. Talk of a kid who knows how to play ball reaches the ears of Fernão Sousa, Cristiano's godfather, who is coaching the young Nacional da Madeira team. 'I was delighted to discover that they were talking about my godson,' he says. 'I knew he was playing football but I had no idea he was so good. He was streets ahead of the rest. He handled the ball beautifully and he definitely had a bright future ahead of him. I immediately realised that this kid could be a godsend to his family.' Without the slightest hesitation, he decides to bring him to Nacional. 'I talked to his mother. I told her it was the best thing for him, and we reached an agreement with Andorinha.'

But it wasn't all as simple as Sousa makes out. Dinis would have preferred his son to go to Marítimo. The club's historic Almirante Reis ground is close to the family home. Plus the kid bleeds green and red – his heart beats for Marítimo. No one can agree, so Rui Santos arranges a meeting with both clubs to discuss possible offers. The Marítimo youth team coach doesn't turn up to the meeting with the Andorinha president, so Cristiano goes to Nacional in return for twenty balls and two sets of kit for the junior team.

It's a deal which isn't worth much at the time, but Andorinha will go down in history as the first club of a Ballon d'Or winner, and will later receive funding from the municipality. Today, the old ground has been replaced with an artificial surface complete with floodlights. And that's not all. The deal with Nacional is sealed in Madeira's history books – just as Raúl's transition to Real Madrid from the Atlético Madrid youth team became legendary across Madrid, purely because (the story goes) the Red and Whites didn't want to pay the bus fare for the kid to get to training.

Cristiano is just ten years old when he arrives at Nacional – and his mother is more than a little concerned. 'My husband was always encouraging him to play with older kids. I was worried he could hurt himself or break a leg, but Dinis always said, "Don't worry, they can't catch him, he's too fast."'

The fact that he is somewhat skinny and bony doesn't escape the attention of the Nacional coaches, who are quick to recommend that he eats more to help him fill out a bit. But when it comes to assessing his credentials, they are in no doubt. 'We saw immediately that he was fantastic,' says António Mendoça, Cristiano's coach during his two seasons playing in black and white. 'His skills were already highly developed: speed, dribbling, shooting, lightning execution. Street football had taught him how to avoid getting hit, sidestep the opponent and face up to kids much bigger than he was. It had also strengthened his character – he was extremely courageous.'

Now it's up to Mendoça and the other coaches to help him understand that football is a team sport. Ronaldo is capable of getting hold of the ball in his own half and heading for the goal – without passing to anyone on his team. His opponents don't bother him. Losing isn't an option; he wants to win everything. He cries and gets angry with his team-mates when something goes wrong. 'They put up with it because he used to score so many goals,' says Mendoça. 'We won all our games nine- or ten-nil.' But his individualism and pride are a problem. He behaves as if superior to the others and it's difficult to give him advice – it has to be in private, never in front of the staff.

In the 1995-96 season at Nacional, Cristiano wins his first regional title in the league for ten-to-twelve-year-olds. Clubs like Porto and Boavista, the big clubs in 'the rectangle' (as islanders call mainland Portugal), begin to take an interest in him.

Fernão Sousa thinks it's about time and only fair to let his godson take the plunge. For the second time, he contacts someone who will change the boy's future: João Marques Freitas, assistant to the district attorney and president of the

Sporting Lisbon club in Funchal. He is the one who tells the powers that be at the Green and Whites about this incredible kid from Quinta do Falcão. Sporting send someone over to talk to the family. Before long, Ronaldo is saying goodbye to his childhood, his family, his friends and his island. It's time for him to make his way to the continent.

Chapter 4
Far from the island

'It was the most difficult time in my sporting career.'

He has never been on a plane – he has never even left the island. This is the toughest challenge he has ever faced and he is so nervous that he cannot sleep the night before.

His godfather Fernão Sousa is accompanying him to Lisbon. It's 1997, it's the Easter holidays and Cristiano is on his way to a trial at Sporting Lisbon

. He would have preferred to go to Benfica, a team both his father and brother love. But his mum has always been a Sporting girl and she has a hunch her son will be as great as Luís Figo. Besides, you can't turn down one of the greatest clubs in the capital. Sporting has the best youth academy in Portugal, counting the likes of Paolo Futre, Figo and Simão among its alumni, while current players include João Pinto, Quaresma, Hugo Viana and Nani.

He's convinced he can do well there. He knows he's good and he thinks he can persuade the Green and White coaches that he's good enough. But he's only twelve years old, and when he finally arrives at the youth team training ground it's incredibly overwhelming.

Coaches Paulo Cardoso and Osvaldo Silva are there to observe him play. They are not particularly impressed by Ronaldo's physique – he's a scrawny little kid. But once they see him in action it's a whole different story. The boy from

Quinta do Falcão gets hold of the ball and takes on two or three opponents. He's relentless – a one man show: feinting, dribbling and driving the ball up the pitch.

'I turned to Osvaldo and I said, "This one's different, he's something special,"' recalls Cardoso. 'And we weren't the only ones who thought so. At the end of the training session all the other boys were crowding around him. They knew he was the best.'

The Sporting coaches are impressed by the trial. They want to see him play again the next day, on the training ground next to the old José Alvalade stadium. This time, youth academy director Aurélio Pereira will be there to observe him.

'He was talented, he could play with both feet, he was incredibly fast and when he played it was as if the ball was an extension of his body,' says Pereira. 'But what impressed me more was his determination. His strength of character shone through. He was courageous – mentally speaking he was indestructible. And he was fearless, unfazed by older players. He had the kind of leadership qualities that only the greatest players have. One of a kind. When they got back to the dressing room all the other boys were clamouring to talk to him and get to know him. He had it all, and it was clear he would only get better.'

On 17 April 1997, Paulo Cardoso and Osvaldo Silva sign Cristiano's player identification document. It reads: 'Player with exceptional talent and excellent technique. Of particular note is his ability to dodge and swerve, from stationary or while moving.' Next to 'enrol' there is a tick in the 'yes' box. He plays as a central midfielder, or 'in the hole' as the coaches say. Cristiano Ronaldo dos Santos Aveiro has passed the test – he can play at Sporting. But first they have to reach a deal with Nacional da Madeira.

After a week in Lisbon, Ronaldo returns home to life on the island. It's up to the coaches now to arrange the final details of the transfer. Nacional owes Sporting 4,500 Portuguese 'Contos' (22,500 Euros) for Franco, a young footballer who has transferred there from Sporting. Cristiano's signing could be an opportunity to waive the debt, but 22,500 Euros for a twelve-year-old kid is an exorbitant price. 'It was unheard of,' agrees Simões de Almeida, the club's former administrator. 'Sporting had never paid anything for a youth player.'

Aurélio Pereira and the other coaches have to convince the administration that it's worth investing so much in one boy. On 28 June 1997 Pereira prepares a new report, adding the following postscript: 'Although it may seem absurd to pay so much for a twelve-year-old boy, he has enormous talent, as proven during his trials and witnessed by the coaches. It would be a great investment for the future.'

These few lines are enough to win over the club's finance director and the transfer is agreed.

In the last week of August, Cristiano Ronaldo leaves Madeira to settle in to the Sporting youth academy. It's an extremely difficult time for a twelve-year-old. He still remembers the emotional day when he had to say goodbye to his family.

'My sisters and my mother were crying. I was crying,' he recalls. 'Even when I was on the plane and we had just taken off, I thought of my family crying about me and I started to cry again.'

Ronaldo will be moving into Sporting's residential accommodation for youth players who have come from other parts of the country. It consists of seven dorms and a living room and is located inside the Alvalade stadium just next to the three training grounds. Ronaldo is the youngest resident and he'll be sharing a room with Fábio Ferreira, José Semedo and Miguel Paixão. Other residents come from Mozambique (a former Portuguese colony), the Algarve and Vila Real. Their schedule is strict: school until 5pm followed by training.

The first day of school is a traumatic experience. He is late to class and the teacher is already taking the register. He is number five. As he stands up and recites his name he can hear some of the students at the back of the classroom making fun of his Madeiran accent. The dialect is very different from the Portuguese spoken in the capital, almost a different language entirely. He sounds strange. He sounds poor. He sounds like an islander, and no one can really understand him. Cristiano loses his temper and threatens his teacher with a chair.

He becomes the laughing stock of the class and he feels like an idiot. A few days later he insults a coach who has asked him to clear up the changing room. 'I'm a Sporting player and I don't have to pick up anything off the floor,' he retorts. It's not a good move. His punishment involves missing a number of games. And of course, he cries – almost every day. He is homesick for his family, his island and his friends.

'It was very hard,' he says. 'It was the most difficult time in my sporting career.' He finds it impossible to get used to the locals, life in the apartment, the rules and the stress of big city life. Everything is different – everything is complicated. Lisbon is another world to him. He calls home two or three times a week.

He buys a 50-unit phone card and goes down to the phone box. It saddens him to hear his mother's voice, it makes him cry and miss her even more. Dolores tries to cheer him up, telling him to ignore the jokers at school.

She often has to console him and convince him that his life and his future are over there in Lisbon, at the Sporting youth academy. In the end she has to fly out to the capital because Cristiano says he can't take it anymore. He wants to quit, abandon his dream and go home to the island so he can be with his family.

'Cristiano's mother was a key factor in determining who he has become today,' affirms Aurélio Pereira. 'She often took our side over her son's. She helped us and she helped Cristiano.' When the boy goes home and doesn't want to return to Lisbon, his godfather also intervenes to ensure that he stays at the academy.

The first year is quite an ordeal. But gradually he begins to adapt. 'In difficult times you learn a lot about yourself,' CR7 will say years later. 'You have to stay strong and focus on what you really want.'

'He had a lifelong dream – he wanted to be somebody,' says Paulo Cardoso. 'He wanted to be a professional footballer with all his heart.'

During those tough early years he has a Madeiran tutor, Leonel Pontes, who accompanies him to training and to school. 'Ronaldo was decisive in everything he did,' he recalls. 'He wanted to be the best at everything – table tennis, tennis, pool, table football, darts, athletics – he wanted to beat every opponent, be the fastest. He had to win no matter what sport he was playing. I think one of the reasons he got to where he is today is because he always wanted more.'

They find him in the gym at 1am lifting weights without permission. He does press-ups and sit-ups in the dorm and trains with weights around his ankles to improve his dribbling. When his team-mates head for the showers after training sessions, he stays on the pitch, practising free kicks against a wall of life-sized targets. He eats two bowls of soup with every meal because they have told him that he plays well but he's too thin.

On Sundays he's the 'ball boy' when Sporting play at home, retrieving the ball when it goes out of play. He gets to see some of the club's greatest players up close, feel the atmosphere at the ground, and earn five Euros. At the end of each match he and his team-mates pool their money and go to the pizzeria. They buy one pizza and get two more to take home.

His first salary at Sporting amounts to ten Contos a month, around 50 Euros. It's enough to cover the text-books, exercise books and backpack he needs for school, as well as clothes and daily spending money. But one day Dolores calls the club to inform them that 'Ronaldo didn't buy his lunch at the canteen, he spent all his money on chocolate.' It's funny because, although he has been forced to grow up quickly and leave his childhood behind, he is still just a kid. 'I regret not having really enjoyed my child-hood,' he will say years later in an interview just before the South African World Cup.

He is expected to behave like an adult, living autono-mously and taking responsibility for all his own washing and ironing. He is there to be a footballing apprentice, not a child. He is also forced to face the reality of his family's problems. At fourteen, Cristiano is aware that his father Dinis is a chronic alcoholic and that his brother Hugo is a drug addict. He is shocked, but he can't let it overwhelm him. His older brother is admitted into a rehab clinic in Lisbon, and after various relapses he manages to get clean. His father, on the other hand, does not.

Luckily, life at the academy begins to improve. 'Thanks to his extraordinary talent and hard work he began to adapt to his new life and become the centre of the team,' says Pontes, his tutor. 'The other players began to pass him the ball because they knew he was the best.'

He's a leader on and off the pitch. In the documentary *Planet Ronaldo*, aired on the Portuguese TV channel Sic, Pontes narrates that on one occasion when Cristiano and three team-mates were mugged by a gang on the street in Lisbon, he was the only one who didn't try to run away, despite being the youngest. He fought back to defend what little money they had in their wallets. The muggers dispersed without any cash.

The Sporting youth academy doesn't just take care of its promising young players on the training ground. It provides them with a tutor so that they can excel in the Crisfal local day school. Ronaldo loves football but going to school is more of a hobby. He likes science but can't stand English. He is a decent student and does the bare minimum, but football, friends and work experience as a ball boy distract him from his school work. In the end, he has to choose between sport and his studies. He speaks to his mother and makes a decision: he will drop out of the ninth grade.

The club's directors try to help young players overcome any issues of acclimatisation, offering counselling with a psychologist. They also maintain a strict discipline policy. Ronaldo has not forgotten what it was like to feel the force of that discipline in his youth team days.

In the final round of the championship Sporting has to face Marítimo, the team from Cristiano's home town. The chance to return to his island, his town, to the stadium where he played his first matches – to see his whole family and his school friends – is more than he could have hoped for.

But Cristiano has been behaving badly at school and the directors decide to punish him where it really hurts. He won't be going with them to Madeira. 'I saw the list and I wasn't on it,' he says. 'I checked it four times and … nothing. I started crying and stormed into the training centre angrily demanding an explanation. It was tough but I learned a very important lesson.'

The academy expects players to adhere to strict guidelines. Along with the team doctor, the directors take charge of each player's physical development. In Cristiano's case, they monitor his bone density to see what his maximum height will eventually be. It looks promising – all being well he should reach 1.85 metres. But at fifteen they discover a serious problem.

'The club informed us that his resting heart rate was too high,' his mother revealed in *The Sun*. 'I had to fill in a mountain of paperwork so that they could admit him and do some tests. Eventually they decided to operate. They used a laser to repair the damaged area of his heart and after a few days' recuperation he was discharged. Before I knew exactly what was going on I was really worried that he might have to give up football.' He had a congenital defect which meant his pulse was higher than the normal rate, but hadn't affected his career. 'A few days after the procedure he was back training with his team-mates,' said his mother. 'He could even run faster than before.'

He not only runs fast, he also moves up the ranks with incredible speed. At sixteen Ronaldo is undoubtedly the academy's star player. He is the only player in the club's long history to play for the Under 16s, Under 17s, Under 18s, second team and first team in a single season. In August 2001 he signs his first professional contract. Four years, 2,000 Euros a month and a 20-million-Euro buyout clause. He moves from living in the academy dorms to a hostel near the Marques de Pombal square, in the heart of Lisbon, just until he is able to find his own apartment where his family can come and visit him more often. The boy has grown up; he's more independent and he decides to find a new manager. He leaves Luis Vega, the man who manages Figo, and places the future of his career in the hands of Jorge Mendes.

In August 2001 the Sporting first team gains a new manager. László Bölöni is a Romanian originally from Hungary, a former star midfielder for Steaua Bucharest who won the Champions League with them in 1986. He has spent eight seasons in the dugout at French team AS Nancy, and after a brief stint as the Romanian national coach he has accepted the job at Sporting.

In his first year he wins the league and the Portuguese cup, and he takes note of players like Cristiano, Ricardo Quaresma and Hugo Viana. He is keen to promote Cristiano to the first team as soon as possible. In fact, CR7 does get to train with the top players on occasion. The medics don't advise him making the leap just yet, as he is still growing, but it's clear that it won't be long before the kid from Madeira makes his debut.

Chapter 5
Seventeen years, eight months, two days

'They've yet to see the real Ronaldo. This is just the beginning.'

A green and white bus is on its way to the Sporting academy in Alcochete. It's 1 July 2002 and it's Cristiano Ronaldo's first day with the first team. Romanian coach László Bölöni has promoted him for the preseason alongside three other B team players: Custódio, Carlos Martins and Paíto.

'I hope to play well and be able to stay with the first team. I want to do my best and try to live up to the coach's expectations,' declares a humble Ronaldo, adding: 'Playing alongside João Pinto and Jardel is a dream come true. They are amazing role models for any footballer.'

The first match is scheduled five days later against Samoquense, a first division team from the Setúbal district. They win it 9-0. The next is against Rio Maior: 5-0 in favour of the Sporting Lions. Ronaldo is on top form, and he scores a goal, but Bölöni decides to proceed with caution.

The kid is used to playing up front, but the manager puts him on the left wing – he can make good use of his speed there, but it's also better because he's not physically up to taking on the opposition midfielders yet. He doesn't disappoint. He is fast, he has good ball control and he creates trouble for his markers.

The coach repeats his tactics on 14 July, at Sporting's official 2002-03 season presentation match in front of all the fans and shareholders at the José Alvalade stadium. Their opponents are Olympique Lyonnais, current French champions. It ends in a one-all draw, but it gives the crowd a chance to watch the jewel in the youth academy's crown.

'This boy is one to watch,' writes *Record*. 'He knows how to lose his opponent, he can dribble, and he has a nose for goals.' It's true – Cristiano scores a goal on his first appearance at a ground where just a short while ago he was a mere ball boy. The referee wrongly disallows it.

Less than a week later it's time for a rendezvous with another French team, Paris Saint-Germain. It ends 2-2, and Cristiano Ronaldo has another surprise in store. After the game, when everyone is expecting him to be gracious and emotional and to say that it's been the happiest night of his life, the Madeiran offers: 'The shareholders have yet to see the real Ronaldo. This is just the beginning.' He is cheeky, irreverent and very sure of himself. Nonetheless, he has played well on the left wing, he has taken three shots, and there is already talk of a new star Lion.

The manager is quick to play down the impassioned outburst. 'Ronaldo is a young man with excellent skills, but he is not yet a fully-fledged player.' In any case, he is only prepared to bring him on in small stints of fifteen or twenty minutes at most, and at the moment it's only in the summer friendlies, like in the Benfica derby on 27 July, or against Pontevedra on 1 August. But gradually the boy starts to become an integral part of the Lions' game and the results are flowing thick and fast.

On 3 August, Sporting face another green and white team, Seville's Real Betis, who have come over to Maia. In the 77th minute László Bölöni makes four substitutions.

Danny comes on for Barbosa, Luís Filipe for Quaresma, Diogo for Niculae and Rui Bento is replaced by number 28, 'Ronaldo Cristiano' as it says in the programme. Quaresma scores in the 27th minute, Alfonso equalises in the 30th, and Barbosa puts them in the lead in the 53rd – 2-1 to the Portuguese team.

In the 84th minute Alfonso nets his second goal of the night, bringing the scores level once again. It feels like the point of no return and two minutes later Casas tries for the victory goal. Only a spectacular dive from César Prates keeps it out. The game goes into extra time and now it's time to see what this seventeen-year-old kid can do.

Defensive mistake from a confident Juanito. His team-mate takes a free kick and he takes it on the chest. But he doesn't control it well enough, the ball bounces away from him and Cristiano is on it like a shot. He steals the ball with a backheel, then brings it back in front of him and heads for the left wing. He dribbles towards Betis goalie Toni Prats, and from an impossibly tight position on the far left corner of the area he spies the open goal and aims for the far corner, evading Rivas whose desperate leap to deflect it is in vain. It's a phenomenal goal, demonstrating ability, technique, control, potential, and instinct in the box.

Cristiano erupts into celebration mode, running round the pitch and blowing kisses into the stands. It's his first goal in the Sporting strip and he deserves the 3-2 victory. The Portuguese press call it 'a work of art'. The goal has cemented his self-confidence and any last trace of fear has vanished. He had previously been nervous when playing with the first team – he felt he didn't quite match up, like he was just a boy among men. Everything has changed now – although people still don't know who he is. The TV network credits the goal to Custódio, and the Spanish press can't stop talking about the incredible goal by Custódio, his team-mate who had come onto the pitch just minutes before him.

'I dedicate this goal to my family, especially my mother Dolores who is here with me in Lisbon,' an ecstatic Cristiano Ronaldo tells Portugal's morning tabloid, *Correio da Manhã*. He thanks his manager for being 'a great coach who has taken big risks on the young players and helped me to integrate into the first team'. And not forgetting the fans: 'I know they care about me and I am going to work hard to live up to their trust in me, to thank them for how they have welcomed me. I will do my best and hopefully I'll succeed.'

Eleven days later on 14 August, the gods are smiling on him once again. It is his debut in an official match, in the Champions League qualifiers at the Alvalade. The opponents are none other than Héctor Cúper's Inter Milan. Ronaldo comes on for the Spaniard Toñito in the 58th minute. He immediately comes up against veterans Javier Zanetti and Marco Materazzi, who between them have more years of footballing experience than Ronaldo has been alive. They make Cristiano's life extremely difficult, but by the end, despite the 0-0 scoreline, he has managed to pull off a stunning performance. His flashes of brilliance, albeit isolated, have the stands buzzing with anticipation. Not bad for a debut.

The criticism from the Portuguese press concerns excessive dodging and feinting and individual one-on-ones on the parts of Ronaldo and Kutuzov, the other junior member of the Lions' attack. In other words, they don't know when to give up the ball. It's a youthful vice which can only be corrected through years of training.

He is certainly capable of entertaining the crowds, and he proves it on his second outing, on 7 October 2002 in the Portuguese SuperLiga. The current title holders are at home to Moreirense FC, who have been promoted from the second division. As matches go it's not particularly special. But Cristiano is in the starting line-up for the first time, and at seventeen years, eight months and two days old he makes history as Sporting's youngest ever goal-scorer. He scores 'a monumental, majestic, unbelievable goal ... there are not sufficient adjectives to describe this young Sporting prodigy's achievement', scream the SportTV commentators.

It's the 34th minute: Ronaldo gets a backheel from Toñito just over the halfway line, he dodges past two defenders, slaloming back and forth for some 60 metres; he follows it up with a bicycle kick on the edge of the area to wrong-foot another opponent and slides it smoothly past Moreirense goalkeeper João Ricardo, who makes a desperate dash out into the box.

Cristiano tears off his shirt, hugs his team-mates and runs towards the stands. Bölöni celebrates with his colleagues in the dugout. He is the one who took the risk and changed Ronaldo's position. It's a risk which has paid off in spades.

Back to the match: number 28's performance is not over yet. Despite the presence of Brazilian striker 'Super Mário' Jardel – last year's Golden Boot, back on the Sporting team sheet after four months of injury – Cristiano is the playmaker, scoring the winner and taking it to 3-0 with a spectacular header. The only thing that mars the occasion is when Cristiano's mother Dolores feels faint in the stands. Perhaps it's the excitement of her son's performance, but in the end it's just a scare.

The following day Ronaldo dominates Portugal's front pages with his 'monumental goal'. The journalists milk the opportunity to tell his story, from his first street games in the 'slums' of Madalena in Santo António. They interview his childhood coaches. They try to get hold of his father. The poor man has only seen the highlights – he followed the match on the radio because Andorinha were playing at the same time. He says that everyone on the island has mentioned his son's success and they joke that he should see if Sporting will loan him to Andorinha so that they can win something for a change.

José Dinis maintains that his son is a force of nature who has played ball day and night since he was a little kid. He hopes he will have a great future and will keep maturing as a person as much as a player. He has no desire to be famous simply because he is the number 28's father, but he definitely won't be missing his son's next match. He's already bought a plane ticket to see him at Belenenses – his first trip to Lisbon in six years.

It's not just the Portuguese press that are interested in the newcomer's profile. Ronaldo is also making waves across Europe, thanks to his goals and his name – let's not forget that the original Ronaldo (Ronaldo Nazário de Lima) is enjoying his umpteenth comeback and has just helped Brazil win the Korea/Japan World Cup on 30 June 2002. He is the tournament top scorer with eight goals. Italy's *Gazzetta dello Sport* is already talking about the 'new Ronaldo' on its front page.

What does the kid from Madeira think about such a comparison? 'I would never dare to think about it. Real Madrid's Ronaldo is a superstar, he's the best player in the world. He's my favourite player.'

Cristiano's performance in the first team has been outstanding. He has become the fans' golden boy. László Bölöni has the utmost faith in him, but competition is fierce, with Jardel, Quaresma, João Pinto, Toñito and Niculae already on the strikers' roster. At the end of the season, Ronaldo has played in 25 games and only started in eleven of them. He has scored three goals in the league and two in the cup.

It hasn't been a great run for Sporting. They are out of the race for the Champions League, having been beaten 2-0 by Inter in the return leg at the San Siro. They are also out of the UEFA Cup, losing 1-3 to Serbia's FK Partizan in Portugal and drawing 3-3 in the second leg. On 1 May they are knocked out of the Copa de Portugal by Naval in the quarter finals. And they fail to hold onto their league title. They finish third, 27 points behind José Mourinho's Porto and sixteen behind Benfica.

Bölöni bows out of the dugout – a moment of great sadness for his number 28. 'I really enjoyed working with him. He was the one who moved me up into the first team,' says Cristiano. 'Without him, I would probably still be in the B team.'

The new manager is Fernando Santos. Cristiano doesn't know him but he has heard that he is good natured, he favours a high level of discipline and he is a god in the footballing world. With his arrival, the rumour mill is rife with speculation about the possible departure of the academy's star player from the first team. Santos is forced to make a statement, declaring: 'Ronaldo is a key player as far as Sporting is concerned.'

Cristiano can only hope that this is the case, and explains that he wants to stay at Sporting. 'I want to channel all my energy into helping the club win the titles that evaded them this year. I have played with Sporting since I was twelve years old and I want to win championships with this team. If I go without winning anything it would leave a bitter taste in my mouth. But that's life. Let's see what the future holds ...'

Chapter 6
Festival

'It wasn't about being the best player in the tournament.'

1985: Jean-Pierre Papin from Valenciennes is the top goal-scorer and wins the trophy for France.

1991: During his time with AS Cannes, Zinedine Zidane's brilliance gets him as far as the final, where the Frenchmen then lose to England. Southampton's Alan Shearer is the star player with seven goals in four games.

1992: Benfica's Rui Costa gives an exceptional performance – player of the tournament and top scorer.

1997: AS Monaco's Thierry Henry is the top scorer and best player, and he wins the title with France.

1998: Juan Román Riquelme from Argentina's Boca Juniors is crowned player of the tournament and the European clubs are outraged.

The Festival International Espoirs de Toulon et du Var, or the 'Toulon Hopefuls Tournament' as it is known in English, began in 1967 as an Under 21 club tournament. In 1974 it switched to national teams only. It is not recognised by FIFA, but it has long been considered a place for talent-spotting the youngsters who years later are confirmed as global superstars.

The 31st tournament, between 10 and 21 June 2003 is no exception. Against all predictions, the player of the tournament is named as Javier Mascherano. The boy who will one day become the star of Barcelona and the Argentine national team is currently at River Plate, and he helps Argentina to third place in the tournament. Two years later he will transfer to SC Corinthians in Brazil, then move on to the Premier League where he will join West Ham and later Liverpool.

Ronaldo, who was tipped for the top prize along with Italy's Pagano and Argentina's Rivas, will have to console himself with the accolade of youngest finalist.

'Winning the player of the tournament prize wasn't what was most important,' declares a modest Cristiano. 'It was more important for the team to come out on top – and we have. We've won the trophy.'

After winning in 1992 and 2001, Portugal lifts the Toulon trophy for the third time, beating Italy 3-1 in the final, and putting on a fantastic all-round performance. Sporting's number 28 is also learning about introspection.

'I have done what I came here to do. In three of the fixtures I think I played well but in the other two I was a bit tired,' he confesses. 'It's not surprising when you consider how many games are squeezed into such a short space of time.'

In each of the national teams, CR7 has always played alongside slightly older team-mates. He was fourteen when he joined the Under 15s and sixteen when he went to the Under 17s. He is eighteen in the Under 20s team in Toulon, where he makes an impression right from the start during the first match against England in Nîmes on 11 June.

Portuguese coach Rui Caçador had promised an attacking formation and he is true to his word. He puts Danny in the hole, Ronaldo and Lourenço on the wings, leaving the giant Hugo Almeida to find gaps in the opponents' defence. After ten minutes of careful observation, Portugal take the reins, and despite the fact that the three goals don't come until the second half, their superior performance throughout crushes their opponents. Cristiano scores the decisive third goal and makes an impression not only on the national team staff, but on the numerous coaches from the top teams who are always out in force at Toulon looking for potential signings.

Barcelona scout Juan Martínez Vilaseca is one of them. After seeing Ronaldo in action he declares that 'He is an extremely interesting player. He has unique characteristics that make him a promising young man. If he stays focused on his career, one day he will be able to play for one of the big European clubs if he puts his mind to it. It won't be long before he's one of the best players in Portugal, no doubt about it.'

This young footballer is no longer an unknown among the footballing powers that be – Vilaseca is not the only one who thinks highly of him. For a while now he has been courted by some of Europe's biggest clubs. Arsenal, Man United, Liverpool, Chelsea, Juventus, Parma, Atlético Madrid, Barça and Valencia have all shown an interest in the boy from Madeira.

Gunners manager Arsène Wenger has extended a personal invitation to Cristiano and his mother to come to London in January 2003 to talk about the future, visit the club and get to know striker Thierry Henry, whom Ronaldo greatly admires. The conversation continues on his return to Lisbon, but Wenger is keen for him to stay there for another year before making the leap into the Premiership.

Inter have the same idea: they're willing to pay the transfer fees but they think the kid should stay and train in Lisbon a bit longer. Inter scout Luis Suárez, winner of the 1960 Ballon d'Or and ex-Inter and Barça midfielder, had received a call from a friend tipping him off about a really good player who was excelling in the Sporting youth academy. He had seen him once or twice before he debuted with the first team and he was convinced they should speak to his family and sign him as soon as possible.

According to inside sources, Valencia have already put 500 million pesetas on the table. And Ronaldo is apparently also in talks with Atlético Madrid who, according to the Spanish press, have joined the Iberian teams in the race to sign the young sportsman.

Even Liverpool manager Gérard Houllier has taken his scouts' words about the Madeiran marvel to heart and has flown over to France to see the new Portuguese phenomenon in person. When he sees him play there is no doubt in his mind: he believes he is one of the most promising youngsters in Europe and he wants to bring him to Anfield. There are murmurings in the press about an offer of a Liverpool player and 7.5 million Euros in exchange for Ronaldo, and there's talk of it being finalised within a few days. Cristiano's agent Jorge Mendes has met with the Liverpool representatives and the Lisbon club is ready to give the go-ahead for the number 28's departure to the birthplace of the Beatles.

Cristiano says that he greatly admires English football (although it's not his favourite style – he prefers the Spanish game). 'Liverpool is one of the top English clubs. It would be a dream for any player,' he concedes. On the other hand, he has no reason to leave Sporting in such a hurry.

But the press want to know how the eighteen-year-old feels about having caught the eye of all the scouts in Toulon and having a whole slew of clubs clamouring for his attention. 'I don't feel pressured by it all,' he replies. 'I am just excited and happy to know that the big clubs and the top names have noticed me. It gives me strength and encouragement to try to improve every day. But I haven't spoken to anyone yet, and no one has made a concrete offer to Sporting. I know there's a lot of talk in the press, but right now my main objective is to get the team to the final and help them win. That's what I have to focus on.'

And he does. Another fantastic performance on the wing against Argentina, whom many consider to be the favourites to go all the way. But Portugal beat Mascherano's men 3-0. Next they face Japan in Fréjus, but they are in for a nasty surprise. Having thought that the most difficult match was behind them, Rui Caçador's men relax and suffer an unexpected defeat, 1-0 thanks to a goal from Mogi. 'We didn't play the way we did in the other two matches,' comments Ronaldo, convinced that the team depends on him. 'We weren't up to scratch, we didn't assert ourselves and we missed a lot of chances. Now we have to beat Turkey if we want to make it to the final.' Goals from Nuno Viveiros and Danny make mincemeat of Raşit Çetiner's Turkish team and earn them their place in the Tournament final.

'A McVictory over spaghetti,' reads the headline in the Portuguese newspaper *Record* on Saturday 21 June, the day of the final. The coach had decided that the way to relieve the tension the night before was to take his twenty players out for a Big Mac. They had been begging to go and it's as good a way as any to relax – and escape the boring hotel food on offer. And so, the night before facing the Italians, they head down to McDonald's and queue patiently for their burgers.

It is not a match for the faint-hearted, a full 90 minutes of jam-packed action. And it's a painful 90 minutes for the Portuguese. In the 25th minute they are already down to ten men after a straight red card for Hugo Almeida and the Blues take control of possession. Just before the break, the scoreboard is level at 0-0, and the teams are level again after Bovo is sent off for a foul on Pedro Ribeiro. By the second half it is clear that the Italians are more rested – they have had an extra 24 hours' break since their last match against Poland.

The Blues are in control, and in the 67th minute Francesco Ruopolo goes on the counterattack and puts Italy in front. It's going to be hard for Portugal to come back from that against such a strong defence, and it looks like the game is all but over.

But they're wrong. Just over ten minutes before the final whistle: enter two substitutes who will turn the game around. João Paiva comes onto the pitch and scores with his first touch. Five minutes later Danny steals the ball from his opponent and puts them in the lead. Paiva makes it 3-1 in injury time and the celebrations begin. The winners' photo shows a Ronaldo with a curly blonde fringe, skinny and shirtless – yet to develop the muscles that he has today. He is beaming joyfully, arms raised. In his left hand he is holding a blue shirt – his victory bounty.

'It was a difficult game against an extremely good team who created a lot of problems for us,' says Cristiano. 'We knew beforehand that the Italians were a very strong team. We played well and we've put on some great performances throughout the whole tournament.' The Portuguese press praises the Under 20 squad and hails this generation as being up there with that of Figo and Rui Costa.

The team receives a hero's welcome on their return to Lisbon, with fans turning out in force to clap and cheer them at the Portela airport. Cristiano Ronaldo is not there as he hasn't travelled back with the team. He has stayed in France with his mother and one of his sisters for a holiday – a few days in the south followed by a trip to Paris. It's a well-deserved break before the Sporting preseason begins. On 6 August, after a friendly against Manchester United, his life will take an unexpected turn.

Chapter 7

Number 7

'I wanted number 28 but I couldn't go against the boss.'

The night before the match the deal is already done. At a meeting at the Quinta da Marinha Hotel, Sporting have reached an agreement with Manchester United which will see Cristiano become a Red Devil for 15 million Euros – just over £12 million. United coach Alex Ferguson, Sporting financial director Simões Almeida and Cristiano's agent Jorge Mendes have tied up all the loose ends; all that remains is for the player himself to sign the contract.

Cristiano already knows that his future is tied up with United, but the news is not made public until 12 August – and not before an entire week of denials from one party or another. No one wants to ruin Sporting's party. On 6 August 2003 the Alvalade XXI, the Lions' new stadium, is being inaugurated. It has been designed by architect Tomás Taveira with a view to being used during UEFA Euro 2004, which Portugal is hosting.

The inaugural match is played against Man United, who already have an agreement with the Lisbon club. The youth academy at Alcochete has become like a surrogate academy for United – they have first option on any promising Green and White youngsters and Sporting must inform them of any outside interest.

It's a stunning spectacle, opening with the inauguration of the new venue and topped off by the match and Cristiano's performance. The ceremony begins at 8.45pm with curtains rising to reveal a stage where national singer-songwriter Dulce Pontes sings her famous 'Amor a Portugal' ('Love of Portugal'); hundreds of people form the shape of the club's shield on the pitch; and finally the players make their way onto the field. The atmosphere is electric and there is not an empty seat in the house.

Dressed in his green and white striped number 28 shirt, white shorts and green and white striped socks, Cristiano Ronaldo is keen to show Manchester United what he is capable of. In fact, he is so focused that this will be the best match he has ever played with the Lions. He is off to a flying start and makes the United defenders suffer on the wing. He tests United goalkeeper Fabien Barthez's limits, with shots from afar and a one-on-one which the French goalie wins. In the 25th minute he serves up the ball for Luís Filipe to score the first goal. But above all, he amazes everyone with his dribbling, speed, bicycle kicks, change of pace and ability to evade his opponents.

During halftime Sir Alex is already thinking he needs to sign him, telling the club's former chief executive Peter Kenyon: 'We can't leave here without that kid.' Defender Phil Neville recalls the same discussion in the dressing room: 'We were all saying to the boss: "We've got to sign him."'

Ferguson says nothing. He has no intention of announcing to his players that the deal is all but done. He's a sly fox. He wants the kid to be accepted in the dressing room from day one, and what better way to do that than to allow them to think that they had something to do with bringing him over from Sporting. On the plane back to London, veteran

United players Rio Ferdinand, Paul Scholes and Roy Keane point out the young Portuguese player's attributes and ask if United can sign him. Sir Alex can only feel silently smug. At the end of the match (won by Sporting 3-1), and after having consulted Jorge Mendes, he has spoken directly to Cristiano, showered him with praise and invited him to Manchester.

Ronaldo is convinced that he will go there to sign the contract, have a medical, visit Old Trafford and take a look around the facilities and then return to Lisbon for a year on loan to Sporting. But Ferguson has other plans. Once he has arrived and has signed the contract (two million Euros a year – more than 150,000 Euros a month compared to the 2,000 he was making at Sporting), Ferguson sits down with Jorge Mendes.

'I didn't understand any of the English,' Cristiano tells Portuguese newspaper *Público* years later. 'Mendes explained to me that Ferguson wanted me to stay in Manchester. I was shocked and nervous.' He doesn't know what to do – he hasn't even brought his belongings. He'll start his training out in Carrington and he can go back later and get his things.

He is formally presented at Old Trafford on 13 August, alongside 24-year-old Brazilian José Kléberson, who has come from Atlético Paranaense. Ronaldo arrives in a virtually see-through white shirt and faded jeans, with highlights in his hair. The commentators do not exactly warm to him. They are unimpressed by his look, his age, and above all the price that United have shelled out for him. Ronaldo is the most expensive teenager in the history of the British game, and £12 million seems like far too high a price for an eighteen-year-old kid who only has one season, 25 matches and three goals with the first team on his CV.

But Ferguson has just sold Beckham to Real Madrid for £25 million and Juan Sebastián Verón to Chelsea for £15 million. He has also just lost out on signing Ronaldinho (the Brazilian has gone to Barcelona). He is convinced that he has made an excellent signing. He believes Cristiano will bring more to the table than Beckham and will be the piece of the puzzle that United has been missing for years. Portuguese footballing legend and 1965 Ballon d'Or winner Eusébio agrees: 'Ronaldo is not just a footballer, he is waiting to be an icon. He would enhance any team, any league, anywhere. I really believe he is that good.'

Ferguson and his band of scouts didn't just discover Ronaldo at the match at the Alvalade, they have been following him since he was fifteen years old. 'It was Carlos Queiroz who brought Cristiano Ronaldo's potential to our attention,' explains Ferguson, acknowledging his former assistant manager's role in the story. 'He was following the Portuguese youth teams and he realised immediately that he was a valuable player. He told us we had to sign him.'

And although the agreement has only just been signed, United have been courting the Lisbon club for quite a while. Israeli businessman and football agent Pini Zahavi, who has been responsible for brokering a number of United's major deals, is present at Cristiano's performance against Moreirense at the Alvalade in October 2002. After the match, he meets with the club's directors to see if an agreement can be reached about the future of the young number 28. And he's not the only one. The deal has been accelerated in recent weeks because that match at the Alvalade has been a game-changer: the competition are closing in on the youngster.

According to the Portuguese press, the Sporting directors have received offers of more than ten million Euros from Parma and Juve. Italian newspaper *Tuttosport* even runs with the headline: 'Juve: Ronaldo is yours.' Dozens of clubs have started to take an interest, from Barça to Milan, from Real Madrid to Chelsea. Liverpool, initially one of the most active clubs in terms of expressing interest, eventually withdraws from the race. As Gérard Houllier will explain years later to *The Daily Mail*: 'We had a wage scale and we weren't paying the sort of salary he wanted. I thought it would cause problems in our dressing room.'

Manchester United beats off the competition to walk away with the prize. Given Sporting's weak economic position, the Portuguese team are more than happy to make an immediate profit from their newest youth academy star, just as they did six months earlier when they sold Ricardo Quaresma to Barcelona for six million Euros. The club directors know that Ronaldo could walk free at the end of the 2003-04 season, and they don't want to lose their investment in his development.

At the presentation of the new signing, Sir Alex Ferguson announces: 'Ronaldo is an extremely talented footballer, a two-footed attacker who can play anywhere up front: on the right, the left or through the middle. He is one of the most exciting young players I've ever seen.' Not bad for a 'Portuguese teenager', as the British press persist in describing him. The teenager himself sticks to the niceties: 'I am very happy to be signing for the best team in the world, and especially proud to be the first Portuguese player to join Manchester United. I look forward to helping the team achieve even more success in the years to come.'

After the statements, it's time for the photo on the Old Trafford pitch. A smiling Ferguson is in the centre wearing a dark suit, white shirt and red tie. His right arm is around Kléberson and his left is around Ronaldo, both of whom are wearing the team strip. Looking the most serious of the three, Cristiano is sporting the number 7, worn by all the United greats before him: George Best, Steve Coppel, Bryan Robson, Eric Cantona and David Beckham.

How is it possible that a new signing who is so young gets to wear a shirt that carries the weight of the club's history? Ronaldo will later recount what happened to *The Sun*. 'I asked whether the number 28 shirt, which I had at Sporting Lisbon, was available. Alex Ferguson said to me, "No no, yours is the number 7." "Ok boss!" I wasn't going to say to him, "No no, mine is the number 28."'

Here's how Sir Alex explains the motives behind his decision to the press: 'We have given Ronaldo this shirt because he is young and he is going to do great things. A number of great players in the club's history have worn this shirt. Ronaldo has great confidence in his abilities and he is going to be here for a while. The number 7 shirt is his.'

'The number 7 shirt is an honour and a responsibility,' replies Cristiano. 'I hope it brings me a lot of luck.' And to the Portuguese press he explains: 'Everyone in Manchester has been telling me about Best and Cantona … I'm proud to follow in their footsteps. But there's something that the Brits don't know – number 7 is also special to me because it's the number that Luís Figo wore at Sporting. I have wanted to be like him since I was a little kid and wear the number 7, just like my great friend Quaresma who is now wearing it at Barcelona. Both of us can now say that our dreams have come true.'

His dreams may have come true, but isn't it scary for an eighteen-year-old to wear a legendary shirt and play for United in such a competitive and high-pressured league? 'I'm not afraid, not at all,' replies Ronaldo. 'I know it will be difficult, but I will learn so much playing alongside some of the best players in the world.' Years later he will reaffirm that feeling, adding that after what he went through during his first year in Lisbon, he was no longer afraid of anything.

Ronaldo debuts at Old Trafford three days after his official presentation. It is the first matchday of the season and Man United are at home to Bolton. Cristiano is on the bench, but in the 60th minute Ferguson needs to shake up a game that is stuck at 1-0 and he sends him on as a substitute for Nicky Butt. The spectators stand to applaud the new signing, while the commentators remind viewers that he is 'one of the most expensive teenagers in the game'.

The 67,647 fans certainly aren't disappointed by his running and dribbling, and during the remaining 30 minutes the new number 7 demonstrates his potential on the wing. He creates two chances and provokes a penalty which van Nistelrooy fails to convert. He is crowned man of the match and gets to pop his first bottle of champagne. Roy Keane is the first to congratulate him, followed by his other teammates, and he receives a standing ovation from the crowd.

'It looks like the fans have a new hero. It was a marvellous debut, almost unbelievable,' comments Ferguson after the 4-0 win. It's a great debut, but let's not jump the gun. There is no rush, and there's no need to place pressure on the youngster. The experienced Ferguson is all too aware of this: 'We have to be careful with the boy. You must remember he's only eighteen – we are going to have to gauge when we use him.'

And he does – protecting him just as he has done Beckham, Giggs or Scholes before him. There is time for play and time for rest, and there are matches spent on the bench. The kid from Madeira has to adapt to his new life and, more importantly, to English football: the style, the rules, Man United's game and his team-mates, as well as the climate, the food and the language. And let's not forget the English press who follow him closely and offer plenty of criticism – about his manner, the way he dresses, his supposed girlfriend, his past, his family and what he does on the pitch.

One of the first strictly sport-related criticisms concerns diving. It comes after a league match against Charlton when Chris Perry tells the press: 'Once or twice when you go down it's legitimate. But Ronaldo went down five or six times in the game and he certainly was not caught for every single one.' Ferguson's response to the opposition defence is succinct: 'I have watched the video again and Cristiano would have needed the strength of Atlas not to go down.'

Despite the manager's reassurance, the accusations continue to fly all season and in the years that follow about diving, fouling, complaining to the referee and the crowd and pulling faces of exaggerated pain after a foul. What Cristiano finds difficult is adapting to the more physical English game, where defenders are allowed to do things they cannot do in Portugal, where strikers take plenty of knocks, where his cockiness and tricks with the ball make opponents edgy and where complaining is not tolerated.

On 21 September, Ronaldo gets a taste of just what can happen in the Premier League in a match against Arsenal which finishes 0-0 but results in a punch-up. He comes up against Martin Keown and the FA fines him £4,000. He has got off lightly, because his opponent and two other Gunners players are suspended for three or four matches apiece.

On 1 October, the number 7 makes his Champions League debut against VfB Stuttgart. He is in the starting line-up and in the 67th minute he provokes a penalty which, this time, van Nistelrooy converts to help close the gap. It's 2-1 at the final whistle at the Gottlieb-Daimler-Stadion.

Just one month later on 1 November against Portsmouth at Old Trafford, he scores his first goal in the number 7 shirt from a free kick taken just outside the area. It's a powerful shot, the ball arcs over the defenders and strikers, deflects off the pitch and flies into the net. It's a moment of happiness and celebration, and a shot which the commentators claim reminds them of Beckham at his best. The boy from Madeira is off to a promising start, but by the end of the season he will have only scored four goals in 25 Premiership appearances.

It's Boxing Day 2003, Manchester United versus Everton, and the Red Devils are desperately in need of points to keep up with Arsenal. Cristiano puts on a stellar performance: he is keeping his opponents on their toes, he sparks the play that leads to Nicky Butt's goal, and he assists David Bellion in scoring the third. And all this in spite of continual fouling and scuffles on the wing with Wayne Rooney, who is on fire at the Theatre of Dreams. It's a duel between two promising young Premiership players which will give the viewers plenty to talk about. After Boxing Day, Ferguson gives his number 7 three weeks off to go back to Madeira. It's a reward and a way to relieve the pressure, although not everyone agrees with the manager's decision.

On 25 February 2004, Cristiano returns to Portugal once again, although this time it's not for a holiday. This time it's to play Porto in the final sixteen of the Champions League, and José Mourinho's team are definitely not rated as favourites. Ferguson is convinced that his team will be victorious at the Dragão stadium. But it's not to be, and at the final whistle it's 2-1 to Mourinho's men. What about Cristiano? He only plays fourteen minutes and he is powerless throughout. At the end of the match, Ferguson can only bemoan the role of Portuguese goalie Vítor Baía in the sending off of Roy Keane. And here begins Mourinho's long diatribe against the United manager. 'You would be sad if your team was clearly dominated by opponents who have been built on ten per cent of the budget,' he declares.

The Red Devils can only hope to even the score in the return leg at Old Trafford. Paul Scholes gets the scoreboard going with a header in the 31st minute, Porto struggle to get any chances, and Scholes has another goal disallowed offside. But Ferguson is confident and in the 74th minute he sends Ronaldo on for Darren Fletcher. Eight minutes later his game is over thanks to an ankle injury which forces him off the pitch. He can only watch from the bench as Francisco Costinha levels the score in the final minute to take Porto through to the quarter finals. José Mourinho celebrates coming one step closer to his first Champions League title.

On 15 May United play their final league match of the season against Aston Villa at Villa Park. Ronaldo scores his fourth league goal and receives his first red card since arriving in England. He had already been booked for playing up when he wasn't really hurt and, in the 80th minute, he kicks the ball unnecessarily out of anger. It's not a great end to his Premiership season.

Man United finish third on 79 points, four points behind Chelsea and fifteen behind Arsenal who take home the title. The final of the FA Cup is still to come, one last opportunity to win a title after being knocked out of all the others, including the Carling Cup. The match is against Millwall at the Millennium Stadium in Cardiff and this time Ronaldo shines. He heads a pass from Neville in the 44th minute to score the first goal, and he leads a United attack which goes on to win 3-0.

He is not man of the match – that honour is reserved for Ruud van Nistelrooy who has scored the other two goals.

But everyone is talking about him. As Gary Neville says: 'Ryan Giggs and Ruud van Nistelrooy produced some good moments for us, but Cristiano was particularly outstanding. I think Ronaldo can be one of the top footballers in the world.'

'Ronaldo was outstanding,' agrees Sir Alex. 'We need to look after him in the right way because he is going to be an outstanding footballer.' And it's not just his manager and team-mates who think so. The papers give him nine out of ten, the best in the team. The veterans compare his performance with that of Sir Stanley Matthews in the 1953 FA Cup final.

Cristiano Ronaldo finishes the end of his first season as a Red Devil on a high. He has scored eight goals in 39 appearances across all the various tournaments. And with more than 10,000 votes from the Man United fans, he is named the Sir Matt Busby Player of the Year. Commenting on the prize, Sir Alex Ferguson says: 'Ronaldo is a young player who made an immense impact last season. He fully deserves the Sir Matt Busby award. Sir Matt believed in giving young players a chance, and Ronaldo falls into that category.'

Now it's up to Cristiano to be just as convincing when he plays for Portugal.

Chapter 8

Greek tragedy

'It was a huge disappointment. I wanted to be the champion of Europe at nineteen.'

'Have faith' reads the headline on the front page of Portugal's daily sports paper *O Jogo – The Game* – accompanied by a picture of a weeping Cristiano Ronaldo, looking up to the heavens with his hands clasped as if in prayer. It is one of the few voices of hope in the Portuguese press on 13 June 2004. The other papers talk of 'a country on the verge of a nervous breakdown' and 'a country in tears'. Greece has beaten Portugal in the opening match of UEFA Euro 2004. No other host nation has ever been beaten in the opening match. And the Greeks have never won in the final stages of the tournament. How could this have happened?

'We went out there with an enormous amount of anticipation and the anxiety got the better of us. The atmosphere counted against us,' explains the captain, Luís Figo. 'We were overwhelmed by the pressure,' agrees fellow veteran Rui Costa, member of the 'golden generation' of Portuguese football which won two World Youth Championships in 1989 and 1991. 'We were very nervous,' adds Simão. 'We had never considered the possibility that we might lose.'

Without a doubt, the expectations of an entire country could well have placed undue pressure on the national team's European debut. But at the recent inauguration of Porto's new Dragão stadium, everyone present witnessed a Greek team that was extremely well organised, tidy at the back, disciplined, intent on destroying the opponent's game, and determined to take advantage of even the slightest chance, be it from a counterattack or a dead ball. It's a great example of the tight *Catenaccio* defensive style used by the Italians in the 1960s. In other words, it makes for a fairly boring match, with one team entrapping the other into a labyrinth from which it is impossible to escape.

This is what has happened to Figo's men. The Portuguese players have become trapped in the web woven by Otto Rehhagel, Greece's German manager. They have lost control of the match because veteran Lions such as Figo, Rui Costa and Couto are not on form. Neither are Costinha and Maniche and Brazilian manager Luiz Felipe Scolari is all too aware of it. At half time it is 1-0 to the Greeks after a long shot from Inter's Karagunis in the seventh minute – although not so powerful that Ricardo couldn't have stopped it.

During the break the manager sends Deco and Cristiano Ronaldo to warm up. In his green tracksuit, wearing number 17, highlighted Mohawk slicked back, two earrings glinting like headlights, Ronaldo takes off on a zigzagging run, kicks the ball around and returns to the dugout. He listens to Scolari's tactical instructions and then heads onto the pitch. It is obvious that he is incredibly excited.

Five minutes later, like an impetuous kid, he mows down Giourkas Seitaridis, the Greek bulldog guarding the left wing. Cristiano drags him from behind, regains his position, and in his inexperience he knocks him down. Italian referee Pierluigi Collina calls a penalty and Angelos Basinas makes it 2-0. The crowd is beginning to whistle at Rui Jorge and a very tired Figo, while the Greeks cheer every pass their players make.

Portugal's number 17 doubles his efforts on the left wing. He runs back and forth, dodging and feinting. He unsettles his opponents and keeps passing but there is no one there to receive his shots. In the 83rd minute he decides to try his luck and shoots: it's a forceful shot that just grazes Antonios Nikopolidis's right hand post. Cristiano looks up to the sky and clasps his hands in a silent prayer. Someone up there must hear his plea because ten minutes later he scores. It is his first goal in an official match with the national team, from a left-side corner taken by Figo. Ronaldo leaps into the air and swings his head at it, sending the ball flying in a perfect arc. Nikopolidis can only stand and watch.

It's a moment of great happiness for the nineteen-year-old boy who only made his debut with Portugal nine months earlier. On 14 August 2003 he received the call from his mother informing him of his first call up for the friendly against Kazakhstan. Shortly afterwards, his agent Jorge Mendes confirms the good news. 'I am happy and proud to be one of the chosen ones,' says Ronaldo. 'I am very grateful to the selectors. This is a very special moment in my life, all the good things have come at once – first Man United and now the national team. I want to play and I want to win.'

On 20 August 2003 in Chaves, Portugal, Ronaldo dons the red and green shirt for the first time. Luiz Felipe Scolari brings him on in the second half, replacing Luís Figo. He suddenly finds himself surrounded by the champions he has always looked up to as role models. His mentors Luís Figo and Rui Costa have told him to stay calm and play the way he always does. Above all, they tell him not to let his emotions get the better of him. The youngster follows their advice to the letter and the press later name him player of the match. Scolari congratulates him. Two months later in Lisbon on 11 October, he will be in the starting line-up for the first time against Albania. And gradually, he earns his way into the Euro 2004 squad.

But it's a European tournament that starts badly with an unexpected defeat. 'In such a short competition, you only have room for one mistake and we've already made ours,' says Scolari. 'Now the matches against Russia and Spain are life or death.' Luckily Portugal is on track in the other Group A matches. Scolari adjusts his strategy, throws political correctness out the window, and benches veterans Couto and Rui Costa. He calls on the Porto army – central defender Carvalho and playmaker Deco – as well as Cristiano Ronaldo.

Former Portugal and Benfica star Eusébio had implored the team to pick up their game. And they do as he asks. They dominate the next two games, securing a 2-0 victory over Russia, with goals from Maniche and Rui Costa, and a 1-0 win against Spain thanks to a goal from Nuno Gomes. They have made it through to the next round, along with Greece.

Against Russia, Cristiano comes on for Figo in the 78th minute and eleven minutes later he crosses from the left to Rui Costa, who scores an easy goal. He starts against Spain and immediately unsettles the Red Fury's defence, taking Puyol and then Raúl Bravo apart one by one. He creates chances, he shoots and he makes great passes to his teammates. He does everything Scolari has asked of him.

In the quarter finals, it's time to face England once again. Four years earlier in Eindhoven, Portugal beat them 3-2 thanks to goals from Figo (from nearly 40 yards), João Pinto and Nuno Gomes. Aside from the historic rivalry, Portugal-England sets the scene for three very interesting duels. The first is Scolari against Sven-Göran Eriksson. In the last World Cup Scolari was managing Brazil when they sent England home after an incredible 42-yard free kick from Ronaldinho which caught David Seaman off his line. The second duel is Figo-Beckham. The performance of the two Real Madrid stars in this tournament has been reflective of their season with the Whites. Figo has pulled out all the stops just when Portugal needed him most, while Beckham has been useful on occasion but more often than not has just been a bystander.

The third duel is Ronaldo against Rooney, perhaps the most interesting one in terms of speculating about the future. While the European tournament has marked the career end of veterans like Italy's Vieri and Spain's Raúl, it has also been a showcase for youngsters like Milan Baroš, Schweinsteiger and Robben. Rooney and Ronaldo have lived up to everyone's expectations. In September, eighteen-year-old Rooney will be leaving Everton after signing a £25.6 million deal with Man United. He is in the starting line-up against Portugal, having already scored four goals – two against Switzerland and two against Croatia – making him the youngest goal-scorer in the history of the European tournament. And during some of England's trickier moments the number 9 has emerged as a team leader.

As for Ronaldo, the United number 7 may have started on the bench in the first two matches, but he earned his spot in the starting line-up against Spain and treated the fans to an incredible performance. He will form Portugal's main attack against England alongside Deco and Nuno Gomes, while Rooney will pair up with 2001 Ballon d'Or winner Michael Owen up front for England. And it's Owen who scores the first goal in the third minute, thanks to a terrible error from Costinha. Cristiano, by comparison, is off to a magnificent start. The Portuguese number 17 is on fire, commanding control of the left wing and generally causing a headache for England's number 3, Ashley Cole.

And what about Rooney? He almost scores the second goal from a free kick taken just outside the area by David Beckham. But his match only lasts 23 minutes after he gets stamped on by Jorge Andrade. At first it doesn't seem serious, but Rooney is visibly limping and three minutes later he has to be substituted by Darius Vassell. He has broken the fifth metatarsal on his right foot.

Unfortunately for Rooney and for the match, the duel with Cristiano will have to wait until the 2006 World Cup. Meanwhile, despite the Portuguese onslaught, England manage to hold out until the 83rd minute, when Hélder Postiga heads in a great pass from Simão to take the game into extra time. Both teams are tired, but Portugal seems to have the edge. For Cristiano it's as if the match is just getting started, and Phil Neville receives a yellow card for trying to stop him in his tracks. In the 115th minute Rui Costa thinks he has closed the deal with a fantastic shot into David James's net. But England regroup and five minutes later Frank Lampard makes it 2-2 to take the game to penalties.

Beckham sends the first sailing over the bar; Rui Costa follows suit. Now it's Cristiano's turn. He places the ball meticulously on the spot and, without any sign of nerves, sends a medium height shot flying into the net. Portuguese goalie Ricardo blocks Darius Vassell's attempt, and shortly afterwards takes his own shot to secure his team a place in the semi-finals.

Next up is Dick Advocaat's Holland – another team who are hanging on by the skin of their teeth. They made it into the final stages after an eleventh-hour qualifier and their first three group matches have been tough. In the quarters they beat Sweden on penalties. And when it comes to the game against the host nation Advocaat really wants to win. He wants it for the team but he also wants to show the fans that a tiny country can reach the pinnacle of the footballing world.

But Dutch central defender Wilfred Bouma is convinced that the biggest threat in the Portuguese team is Cristiano Ronaldo. And he is right – the game has barely started before the Red and Green number 17 misses by a whisker after a fantastic cross from Figo. Minutes later another Ronaldo shot loses momentum and Edwin van der Sar saves it comfortably. It's a corner to Portugal in the 26th minute, the first of the match. Luís Figo takes it, Cristiano gets free in the box, and – in a similar move to his goal against Greece – he goes up for the ball and heads it into the corner of the net in full view of the powerless van der Sar and Edgar Davids, who is covering the post. The boy from Madeira pulls off his shirt, waves it in the air and runs to celebrate his second goal with his team-mates in front of the Portuguese fans in the stands. Out comes Swedish referee Anders Frisk's yellow card.

In the 67th minute Ronaldo is substituted by Petit. The score is 2-1 to Portugal (after an incredible diagonal shot from Maniche from 27 yards, and an own goal by Jorge Andrade) and that's how it stays. Portugal have beaten the rusty Dutchmen and are through to their first final.

On Sunday 4 July at the Estadio da Luz in Lisbon they will face Greece. Interestingly, it is the first time in Euro history that the same two teams who played the inaugural match will also close the tournament. They meet again after just 23 days – a final that very few would have predicted at the start. Before the tournament began, Portugal was considered one of the favourites, but the odds on Greece winning were more like 80 to one. The Greeks' journey has not been an easy one. They came second in Group A after their win over Portugal, a draw with Spain and a defeat at the hands of the Russians. They beat current title-holders France in the quarter finals and defeated the Czech Republic in the semis.

Scolari's team watched the Czech match on TV and were shaking their heads at the outcome. 'Greece again?' they said to each other. 'We have to end it with the team who beat us at the beginning?!' But they are all convinced that history will be different this time around. They think they can win it and clinch the big title for Portugal. The entire country is rooting for them, willing them to succeed. The whole of Lisbon is out in the streets waving and cheering and an enormous tide of supporters follows the coach as it carries the team to the stadium. The atmosphere in the stadium itself is electric, and at 7.45pm that Sunday evening, the whole of Portugal comes to a standstill.

Before the match, Greece coach Otto Rehhagel declares: 'We have come all this way and we have brought enormous happiness to the people of Greece. We have nothing to lose. In the opening match Portugal underestimated us – this time they'll be on their guard. It's obvious that they are the favourites, they'll have the support of 50,000 spectators.' And let's not forget the fact that Portugal haven't lost in Lisbon for seventeen years, not in the Alvalade or in the Estadio da Luz. They are the host nation – something which was a deciding factor for Spain in '64, Italy in '68 and France in '84.

But the home ground and the host advantage are worthless as Portugal stumble and fall into the same traps as before. The host nation's story ends just as it began, with a defeat by the Greeks, 1-0 thanks to a header in the 57th minute from Angelos Charisteas. Greece has pulled off a

Maracanazo – a term coined after Uruguay's 1950 World Cup win over Brazil at the Estádio do Maracaña in Rio. They have ruined the party planned with the blood, sweat and tears of an entire nation.

And the host nation's story ends just as it began – with tears from Cristiano Ronaldo. Looking lost and alone in the centre of the pitch, he is oblivious to the consolatory words and gestures from his team-mates, crying at the sadness of it all. And crying over missed chances; like in the 59th minute, when Nikopolidis thwarted his chance; or in the 74th, when he had acres of space in front of goal but he sent his shot over the bar, the 'Ahhh!' from the crowd audible on the pitch. He is crying because he never could have imagined losing to Greece. Because 'we had a fantastic team and we have played a great tournament and we don't deserve to lose like this'. Because he's 'an ambitious person' and he wants to be 'the champion of Europe at nineteen years old'.

'But now I have to move on,' adds Cristiano. 'I have to look forward. There will be many other opportunities to win in Europe throughout my career, and make up for this huge disappointment.'

Chapter 9

Martunis: a special boy

'A brave, beautiful and healthy boy.'

That morning he was playing, running after a ball on the beach. He was wearing his favourite shirt, the Portuguese football team's red and green strip. Along came an enormous wave and carried him away. Far, very far, God knows where. It took him along with the houses, the palm trees, the boats, the animals, the cars, the tourists. It took him along with thousands of other children, men and women, as well as his family, who tried desperately to flee the tidal wave in their pick-up truck.

Martunis was adrift for nineteen days. He survived by eating whatever he could find and drinking seawater. His guardian angel appeared in the form of Ian Dovaston, a British journalist for Sky News. He was the one who found the seven-year-old boy wandering alone on a beach in Banda Aceh, in the northern region of the island of Sumatra, Indonesia. He was weak, dehydrated, disoriented and covered in insect bites – but safe.

Dovaston and his interpreter offer him water and biscuits and take him to Save the Children. There they clean him up and administer first aid. 'It's a miracle he survived,' say the volunteers. At the hospital where he is assessed the prognosis is very positive – the boy has no serious injuries or illness. He is reunited with his fisherman father Sarbini, and his grandmother. He discovers that his mother and two sisters have not survived the tsunami which occurred on 26 December 2004, claiming 230,000 lives across South East Asia.

When the Sky News report about the rescue of a little boy wearing the national team shirt reaches Portuguese televisions, it unleashes a wave of emotion and solidarity across the country. Martunis immediately captures the hearts of the people of Portugal as well as many others across the footballing world. Gilberto Madaíl of the Portuguese Football Federation arranges for the clubs in the league to send joint humanitarian aid to Indonesia. He gets in touch with the British reporter to find out what they can do for the boy and his family. Meanwhile, some of the stars of the national team decide to 'adopt' the boy.

'When we saw the footage, we decided we had to respond immediately; buying some land and helping them build a new home seemed like the best idea,' explains national coach Luiz Felipe Scolari. 'The important thing to emphasise in this story is the boy's fight and struggle to regain his life, his attempt to rebuild what was destroyed by the tsunami. Martunis is an example to athletes and indeed to all of us, of how it is possible to overcome difficulties. He is a symbol of overcoming personal challenges, the classic sporting spirit,' he adds.

'I was just absolutely amazed that a child of seven years old could survive after so many days,' comments a visibly emotional Cristiano Ronaldo. 'It's incredible. It gives us all the strength to believe that it is possible to succeed even in the most difficult circumstances. I, together with the coach, hope to bring him over to Manchester, and to Portugal, to see some matches at Old Trafford and the Estádio da Luz. We already have people working on this to help make it happen as soon as possible. I hope we can arrange it, because this boy is a symbol of bravery, and since he was wearing the national shirt I'm sure he would love to come.'

Cristiano's dream of bringing the boy over to a match is realised six months later. On 31 May 2005, Martunis arrives in Portugal accompanied by his father and the psychologist who has been working with him since his rescue. The Portuguese Football Federation has invited him to attend an Under 21s match in Rio Maior on the third day of his stay, and on the fourth day he will see the national team take on Slovakia. Martunis visits the hotel where the team are staying and joins the footballers during their meal. He also gets to meet his idol, Cristiano Ronaldo, in person. He already knows all about him because he is a Man United fan. Cristiano gives him a kiss and presents him with a red and green shirt with the number 1 and 'Martunis' written across the back.

The following day at the Benfica ground, the boy from Indonesia sits next to Rui Costa wearing a cap, scarf and the shirt. Portuguese Football Federation president Madaíl gives him a cheque for 40,000 Euros, money contributed by all the members of the national team. FIFA president Sepp Blatter shakes his hand and they sit down to enjoy Portugal beating Slovakia 2-0. The second goal comes on the stroke of half time, when Cristiano Ronaldo scores from a free kick taken just outside the area.

The number 17 tells Martunis that he will see him again very soon. He is true to his word. On 11 June he lands in Banda Aceh, where he visits the coast of Ulèë Lheuë, one of the areas worst affected by the tsunami. He is shocked by the level of ruin and destruction and moved by the courage of the locals and their attempts to rebuild as much of their lives as possible. He is also overwhelmed by the kindness and affection that he receives everywhere he goes. Martunis accompanies him during his visit, while crowds of people follow him by foot, on bicycles or on motorbikes. He can't even get off the tour bus to play a match with the children at the local school – the pitch is invaded by people who want to see the United number 7.

He chats to Martunis using gestures and with the help of an interpreter. He gives him his number 17 national shirt and a mobile phone, and he takes out his computer to show the boy photos and videogames. Together they visit OIKOS, a Portuguese NGO currently operating in Aceh. Martunis is excited about everything that has happened, about becoming the hero of his island and about his famous new friend. He is shy and he talks very little, but his eyes sparkle with happiness.

'He's a brave, beautiful and healthy boy,' says Cristiano afterwards. 'I believe that many adults would not even be able to deal with what he has gone through. We must respect him. His was an act of strength and maturity. He's a special kid.'

The two of them spend the Saturday together and the boy's father Sarbini says that Martunis was delighted to spend time with such a great footballer, who treated him like a younger brother. On the Sunday Ronaldo flies to Jakarta where he will meet with Indonesian vice-president Jusuf Kalla at a fundraising dinner. As well as the dinner there is an auction (including three of his shirts from Portugal and Man United, a pair of boots and a signed football) which raises one billion rupiahs, around £60,000, to help rebuild Aceh.

Three years after the tsunami and Cristiano's visit, Martunis is interviewed for a FIFA documentary. 'My favourite hobby is playing football,' he says. 'It's fun. My grandfather was a footballer. I want to be a footballer when I grow up.'

Chapter 10

The saddest day

'My father was number one in my life. He is always in my heart.'

It is 9pm in Moscow. Cristiano is in his room watching a film when Portuguese manager Luiz Felipe Scolari summons him to his room. It is Tuesday 6 September 2005. The following day Portugal will face Russia, a key moment in their quest to qualify for the 2006 World Cup. If they win and Slovakia concedes points, they will be one step closer to Germany.

Portuguese captain Luís Figo is in the manager's hotel suite. Cristiano thinks it's a little odd to be meeting like this, but he suspects nothing. He presumes it must be about some strategic issue, something the coach and the captain want to discuss with him. But they have called him in to inform him of the death of his father. Dinis Aveiro has passed away at a clinic in London after being hospitalised several months earlier.

In July, the father of Man United's number 7 had been urgently admitted to Funchal's Centro Hospitalario with serious liver and renal problems. The doctors reserve judgement on his prognosis. In an attempt to help save him, Ronaldo requests that he be transferred to England for a liver transplant. But despite improving briefly, Dinis later dies. His untimely death has been caused by alcohol and Cristiano is devastated. 'It was as if our world crumbled around us,' says his sister Katia.

Scolari and the national directors offer Ronaldo the option of leaving Moscow immediately to be with his family. But CR7 says no, he wants to stay with the team, and he asks Scolari to let him play. 'I wanted to play. That was all I knew how to do,' Cristiano will later explain. 'I wanted to show everyone that I was able to compartmentalise, that I was a consummate professional and that I took my work seriously. I wanted to play that match in honour of my father. I wanted to score a goal for him. I was testing myself and all the people who love me.'

'I hope that playing will be a way of dealing with his emotions,' says Portuguese Football Federation president Gilberto Madaíl. And when the press ask him how the player is doing, he replies: 'I have seen a 22-year-old man who is destroyed over the loss of his father. It's a complicated situation; although it was expected, no one thought it would happen so quickly. It is a very painful period of mourning.'

The final decision over whether to start Cristiano rests with Scolari, a man who is very close to him in a difficult time. He reminds Cristiano that family comes first and football second, he tells him to have strength, and he empathises with his pain, recalling the death of his own father. Eusébio consoles the squad's star player, recalling the day his mother died and telling him how he played a match the same day and scored three goals.

The team is on hand to support him and all the staff try their best to make him as comfortable as possible. But on the day of the match, despite the support of the press ('Portugal is with you' says *A Bola*), there is a strange atmosphere in the dressing room at the Lokomotiv Moscow. The sadness is palpable. Faces downcast, nobody speaks, nobody jokes, there is none of the sense of anticipation that is usually felt before a big match. Cristiano realises what is happening and with an enormous effort he starts to do tricks with the ball as he has done before all of Portugal's matches. He is trying to show that life and the game must go on. But later, lined up next to the team, listening to the national anthem, the number 17 cannot contain his emotion.

The game against Russia ends in a 0-0 draw and Ronaldo doesn't manage to score the goal that he wanted to dedicate to his father. He will do it at the World Cup in Germany instead, converting the final penalty against England to take Portugal through to the semi-finals. He will raise his hand to the sky and say, 'This is for you, Dad.' But on 7 September at the Lokomotiv stadium he is the best on the pitch. Team-mate and Barcelona player Deco later explains: 'I think that he felt comfortable with us. What we did that day was to not dwell on it too much. We knew that once he was on the pitch he would feel better. Football brings him joy. But I will never forget how he dealt with that kind of pain. It was admirable, especially when you consider how young he was and the pressure he was under.'

After the match Cristiano Ronaldo returns to Madeira. His father's funeral is held at the Santo António cemetery in Funchal. The news of Dinis Aveiro's death has shaken the close-knit community. According to friends and neighbours, Ronaldo's father was 'a humble man who got on well with everybody and never had bad words with anyone'. A simple man who had not changed despite his son's success. He maintained the same traditions and friendships that he had enjoyed before anyone knew his name.

Although Cristiano had bought him a beautiful home overlooking the ocean and was able to give him every possible luxury, he continued to rise at dawn to help the Santo

António newspaper vendor. It was a hobby he never gave up. He would spend the morning with friends at the bar or at CF Andorinha, the club which first nurtured his son's talent. In the afternoon he would catch two buses home.

Hundreds of people attend the funeral – friends, neighbours, relatives, representatives from various local institutions as well as those from the footballing world, among them Luiz Felipe Scolari, Sporting manager Paulo Bento, and the Andorinha directors. Cristiano Ronaldo is dressed in a black shirt and sunglasses. With his family and his agent Jorge Mendes close to him at all times, he manages to maintain his composure. He does not shed any tears, but his eyes suggest that he has done plenty of crying. The family request that no photographs be taken during the ceremony.

Sometime later, Cristiano will speak out regarding the way the press handled the death of his father, which was front-page news for the following four days. 'It really hurt me and my family. We needed peace and quiet, and it ended up becoming quite a commotion.'

Controversy aside, in the little Funchal graveyard Cristiano bids his final farewell to the man who has been instrumental in both his personal and professional development. 'My father always encouraged me,' says Ronaldo. 'He always told me to be ambitious and he was proud of my footballing achievements. I love him and I will always love him. He will always be with me. He will always be a role model to me. I like to think that wherever you are you will see what I am doing and what I have achieved.'

Dinis disliked the cameras and the spotlight. He preferred to stay in the background but his relationship with his son was always strong. Before the 'little bee' went over to the continent to play with Sporting Lisbon, the two of them were inseparable. They remained close even when he moved to Manchester. Dinis was often with him, visiting him, supporting him and encouraging him until his illness would no longer allow it. Time and time again Cristiano tried to convince his father to check in to a clinic to treat his alcoholism, but he was unable to save him. Dinis continued drinking and there was nothing even England's best hospitals could do for him.

His death marks the start of a difficult time for Man United's number 7.

Chapter 11

A trap

_____

'It was a false accusation.'

Scotland Yard will not reveal any names. They will only confirm that a man in his twenties presented himself at a London police station after a woman filed a report. But the British press think they know who is involved. 'Ronaldo rape arrest. Football pin-up Cristiano Ronaldo was arrested over a sensational rape allegation,' declares the front page of *The Sun*. The story, which hits the headlines on 20 October 2005, soon spreads around the world.

Here's the story. A French woman claims to have been sexually assaulted by Ronaldo in a suite at the Sanderson Hotel in London on 2 October. She tells the police that she and a female friend met United's number 7 at Movida, a trendy club near Oxford Circus.

Cristiano is in the capital because he has just played a Premier League match against Fulham that afternoon, where United win 3-2. From Movida, Ronaldo, a friend and the two girls go on to the Long Bar at the Sanderson in the West End. They talk and drink for two hours before going up to the suite. And it is here that the rape takes place, according to the girl. At 5am the two girls leave the hotel and go to the hospital. On the Monday, they both file reports at the West End Central police station. After being examined and questioned, the police begin to take their statements extremely seriously.

On 19 October, Cristiano Ronaldo arrives at the West Didsbury police station in Manchester, accompanied by Manchester United's lawyer, after receiving a summons from the police in connection with an investigation sparked by reports of a serious sexual assault at a central London hotel. Scotland Yard's Sapphire command, which deals primarily with the investigation of rape and sexual violence, also questions a 30-year-old man, who is later released. Ronaldo remains at the police station. They take his fingerprints and a saliva sample and he is subjected to questioning. He robustly denies any claims of sexual assault. Nearly nine hours after arriving at the police station he is released without charge.

The police consider the possibility of referring the case to the Crown Prosecution Service, in the event that they deem it necessary to prosecute the player. 'At the moment we have no comment,' says Phil Townsend, director of communications at Manchester United. The only one talking is assistant manager Carlos Queiroz, who, in a telephone interview with the public service broadcasting organisation *Radio e Televisão de Portugal*, denies that Cristiano has been arrested. He says that Ronaldo appeared at the police station voluntarily and that his presence there was jointly arranged by representatives from the police and Manchester United.

'He went there to make a statement as planned. Based on that statement, the authorities will reach fair and correct conclusions. Cristiano is perfectly calm, but obviously he is extremely annoyed to be implicated in these false allegations. There are always two sides to stories like this, but this accusation is pathetic.' And he takes the opportunity to criticise the sensationalism of the press and the fact that they use the term 'arrested' without any evidence. 'This news has drawn an excessive amount of attention; they like to create scandalous stories with no basis in fact, and all they do is harm people,' declares Queiroz. 'The people who should be arrested are the journalists who persist in ignoring the fact that their words can do an enormous amount of damage.'

Cristiano's agent Jorge Mendes also joins the conversation to defend his client. In a statement, he says that the accusation of rape made against Cristiano Ronaldo is 'the product of imagination and fantasy' and that it is 'totally and categorically repudiated. As the investigations will demonstrate, these charges are not based on any credible facts.'

The allegations against Cristiano Ronaldo follow a string of cases in which Premier League players have been implicated in supposed acts of sexual abuse. Leeds player Jody Morris was detained in 2003 over an alleged rape. His case was later dismissed. In September of the same year, seven players from Chelsea and Newcastle were accused of raping a young woman at the Grosvenor House Hotel in London. She had been dating another Chelsea footballer who was friends with the men in question. The case caused a scandal across England but it was also dismissed.

In 2004, Grimsby Town defender Terrell Forbes was implicated in the rape of a fifteen-year-old girl, along with four friends. All five men were acquitted. In Cartagena in Spain in 2004, three Leicester City players were accused of raping three women. They were also acquitted. The final case is that of Dutch Arsenal player Robin van Persie, who is detained in Rotterdam after being accused of rape. He is released without charge two weeks later.

There are numerous cases, but no one can believe that Ronaldo could be guilty. Why not? Because despite his demonstrative and provocative behaviour on the pitch, off the pitch the Portuguese player is known as 'the quiet one'.

But this title only serves to enhance the rumours and theories in the British press. Luckily, Cristiano receives plenty of support from the club, the fans, and the Portuguese Football Federation.

At the beginning of November there are new developments in the case. According to *The Sun*, Cristiano's cousin Nuno Aveiro is detained and questioned at the same police station where the Man United number 7 gave his statement. The woman who accused the footballer claims that on that night at the Sanderson Hotel, Nuno held her down to prevent her from moving while Cristiano raped her. Nuno Aveiro denies the accusation and he is released on bail. Meanwhile, the other woman has returned to France and retracted her statement.

On 25 November the case is closed. Cristiano Ronaldo will not be prosecuted for rape. 'The Metropolitan Police Service submitted a file to the Crown Prosecution Service following allegations of a serious sexual assault at a central London hotel on October 2,' says a Scotland Yard spokesperson. 'We have been informed today by the CPS that there is insufficient evidence to charge. As such, the two men arrested during the course of this investigation will face no further action in connection with this matter.'

Cristiano Ronaldo responds with another statement: 'I have always strongly maintained my innocence of any wrong-doing and I am glad that this matter is at an end so that I can concentrate on playing for Manchester United.'

CR7 had always told his closest friends that the accusations were false and that he had been the victim of a trap. It's a theory supported by the now-defunct *News of the World*, which maintains that the accusations were the work of a prostitute who specialised in ensnaring the rich and famous.

All's well that ends well, but as the player himself points out: 'All the newspapers splashed the accusations against me across their front pages, but when the truth came out they printed it somewhere very small on an inside page.'

And it's not just legal problems Cristiano has had to face lately. He received a red card during Man United's derby against Manchester City. He has been clashing with Ruud van Nistelrooy during training. And in the Champions League he sticks his finger up at the Benfica fans when he is substituted during the match in Lisbon. It seems he is at odds with the whole world at the moment.

'The rape was a false accusation. It doesn't count,' explains Cristiano a few months later in an interview with Portuguese journalist and writer Joel Neto. 'But it is obvious that as far as everything else is concerned my father's death has really affected me. I can see myself treating people unfairly. Sometimes I just feel like saying: "Let me at them, I'm not in the mood to be the good guy right now!" I never wanted to draw attention to myself. I knew it would happen anyway and that the most important thing was just to continue working hard. But it's been a difficult time in my life. And despite the fact that I know it's important to learn to deal with tough times, it's easier said than done. Especially when it comes to football. It's extremely difficult to play when you're not in the right frame of mind.'

Chapter 12

'Give Ron one in the eye'

*'The things that have been said regarding me and my team-mate
and friend Rooney are incredible.'*

He has seen footage of the 1966 World Cup, when Eusébio's
Portugal were knocked out in the semis by Bobby Charlton's
England, who then went on to become the champions.
But his first World Cup memory is of the United States tournament in 1994. 'I was nine years old and I watched the
final with my family in Madeira. Everyone wanted Brazil
to win. But the image of Roberto Baggio missing that
crucial penalty is etched in my memory forever.' Nor has
he forgotten the 2002 World Cup when Portugal failed to
make it past the group stage after being beaten by South
Korea.

Four years on, Cristiano will not be watching the World
Cup on television. He is going to Germany to take part.
He is 21 years old and football fans from across the world
have included him on the shortlist of six candidates in
the running for the World Cup Best Young Player award,
along with Leo Messi and Luis Antonio Valencia. The
other three candidates, chosen by FIFA, are Cesc Fàbregas,
Swiss player Tranquillo Barnetta and the German Thomas
Podolski. Shortlisted players must have been born on or
after 1 January 1985, and the winner will be chosen based
on style, charisma, fair play and passion for the game.

Cristiano's third season at United has been a tough one, both on and off the pitch. He has lost a bet with Ferguson, having said he would score at least fifteen goals but only managing twelve. The boy from Madeira has improved significantly, but the fact remains that for the second year running, United have lagged behind José Mourinho's Chelsea. They were knocked out of the Champions League during the group stage after a defeat by Benfica, and by December they are out of Europe altogether.

The only trophy which has been added to the United display cabinet this year is the Carling Cup, after a 4-0 win over Wigan in the final. The third goal was scored by Ronaldo, who had in fact been awarded the 2005 FIFPro (International Federation of Professional Footballers) prize for best young footballer as chosen by the fans. Team-mate Wayne Rooney was awarded the official best young player prize. They don't know it yet, but the two United youngsters will be making headlines in Germany.

Portuguese coach Luiz Felipe Scolari has put his faith in United's number 7 and Portugal has put its faith in the team. So has Ronaldo. 'I think we have an excellent team, great players and a great coach,' he says. 'Personally, I hope to be better in the World Cup than I was in the European Championships.'

Group D seems relatively easy, with Angola, Mexico and Iran as opponents. The Portuguese team wins all three matches: 1-0 against its former colony Angola, 2-0 against Iran and 2-1 against Mexico. The second goal against Iran is a Cristiano penalty. With nine points, Portugal are through to the final sixteen after coming top of their group. It is the first time since the 1966 England World Cup that the Red and Greens have made it past the group phase.

On 25 June 2006, Portugal face the Netherlands in Nuremberg in a rematch of the Euro 2004 semi-final. Felipe Scolari will later describe it as a historic victory, while captain Luís Figo says it is the result of 'team unity, strength of character, and the support of the entire nation'. Unfortunately the match remains memorable for its second half, which consists mainly of scuffles, bookings and bad behaviour. Dutch players Gio van Bronckhorst and Boulahrouz are sent off, while Portugal lose Deco and Costinha, who will miss the quarter-finals. In total, referee Valentin Ivanov issues a FIFA record of 20 cards, sixteen yellow along with the four reds. Portugal are through thanks to a goal from Maniche in the 22nd minute, confirming the midfielder's goal-scoring talents.

An angry and tearful Ronaldo has to cede his spot to Simão in the 33rd minute after a vicious tackle by Boulahrouz means he can barely move his leg. He is doubtful for the quarter-final against England until the very last minute. He doesn't want to miss it – it's his chance to go head-to-head with some of his Man United team-mates and he is anticipating a probable duel on the wing with Gary Neville.

The teams are announced at the Arena AufSchalke in Gelsenkirchen at 5pm on 1 July. Ronaldo has recovered and will be playing, wearing number 17. In the final sixteen, England clawed their way to a 1-0 victory over Ecuador. The Three Lions' Swedish coach Sven-Göran Eriksson is apprehensive about the opponents and their coach. Luiz Felipe Scolari was the cause of England's downfall in the 2002 Korea/Japan World Cup when he was in the dugout with Brazil. After moving to Portugal he knocked England out in Euro 2004.

The game gets underway. In the stands 45,000 England fans are drowning out the 5,000 Portuguese. 'Stand up, for the Englanders,' they are chanting. But England are a weakened and frustrated team. Team leaders Lampard, Gerrard and Rooney don't look like they have the situation under control. Meanwhile Portugal have taken control of the ball in their own half, but beyond that they are trapped. They don't know how to get things moving, how to open up the game. They are missing Deco, and it's clear that neither Pauleta nor Postiga are going to get on the scoreboard. The strikers are striking out.

Cristiano is demonstrating his full potential, attempting to get things moving on the wing. He is slowly but surely unravelling the opposition defence on the far left and Gerrard and Lampard have no choice but to give Gary Neville a helping hand. But when the number 17 cuts into the middle, he loses his spark and momentum.

To make matters worse, there is an incident in the 62nd minute which will still be the subject of heated debate many months later. Ricardo Carvalho has kept Wayne Rooney on a tight leash, not allowing him to escape and denying him any room for manoeuvre. Frustrated, the England youngster goes deeper into the spider's web of Portuguese defenders and tries to make a break for it between Carvalho and Petit. After a bit of a struggle, Carvalho ends up on the ground and Rooney inadvertently tramples him, catching his studs in a rather painful area. The foul kick-starts a scuffle between the English and Portuguese players. Cristiano is the first on the scene, rushing over to reason with the referee. Rooney gives him a shove and appears to say something like: 'You stay out of it.' Owen Hargreaves tries to keep the two apart, while Maniche tries to calm everyone down.

The incident occurred directly under referee Horacio Elizondo's nose and the Portuguese are calling for Rooney's expulsion. The referee hesitates, then finally pulls out the red card. The England number 9, Cristiano's Man United team-mate, is heading for the dressing room. The British fans are furious at what they see as an unfair ruling. They start shouting 'cheat, cheat, cheat!' at Carvalho, who is now being carried off on a stretcher. Over the coming months, the British press continue to analyse the exchange between Cristiano and Rooney. But before we get into that, let's finish the match.

Eriksson decides to replace Joe Cole with Peter Crouch and England manage to hold it together despite being a man down. They stay deep and send down long passes for their tall team-mate, who has to hang onto the ball until reinforcements arrive. Meanwhile, Scolari moves Simão over to the left and sends Cristiano into the centre of the attack. But he seems out of place there, so the coach moves him back again.

The England players survive the Portuguese onslaught and the 90 minutes finish 0-0. Portugal have failed to take advantage of the extra man, thanks to some dangerous counterattacking from England. Extra time is more or less an assault on Robinson's goal, but the Portuguese have neither a clear plan nor imagination. England are still hanging in there and it's on to penalties.

Sporting Lisbon goalie Ricardo, the hero of Euro 2004 for blocking two England penalties, looks focused and calm on his goal-line. He seems completely detached from all the tension that has been building on the pitch. Up steps Frank Lampard to take the first shot for England. Ricardo blocks it. After the second from Hargreaves just escapes his outstretched fingers, he manages to stop the third from Gerrard. Next up for England is Jamie Carragher. After walking away from the spot, he does a quick half turn and shoots, but without waiting for the referee's whistle.

Elizondo sends him back to do it again. This time, Ricardo waits until the last second, then dives and blocks the ball, sending it spinning to the side.

It's 2-1 to Portugal and now it falls to Cristiano to see his country through to the semi-finals. The camera zooms in close to show him pursing his lips and grimacing – he looks nervous. He jumps up and down a little to flatten the penalty spot, kisses the ball, and places it carefully. After a long hesitation, he takes his run-up, pauses briefly, and shoots.

Goaaaaaaal! Ronaldo tips his head back and shouts to the heavens, while the fans and the team go wild. He points to the sky, dedicating the goal to his father. 'I was full of confidence and I shoot strong [sic],' he says afterwards. England are on their way home, just as they were in 2004. On that occasion it was David Beckham who missed. This time round he is out injured.

At the FIFA World Cup Stadium in Munich on 5 July, Portugal face Zinedine Zidane's France, who have surprised everyone by knocking out World Cup favourites, Ronaldinho's Brazil. Portugal are off to a good start, making mincemeat of the French, thanks to some excellent play from Figo, Cristiano Ronaldo and Deco. But in the 33rd minute Thierry Henry gets into the box and Ricardo Carvalho goes to tackle him. Carvalho stumbles and falls and his outstretched leg trips up Henry. Uruguayan referee Jorge Larrionda calls a penalty, provoking anger and disbelief in Scolari's camp. But there is nothing they can do.

Captain Zidane steps up to the mark. The France number 10 takes a short run up and shoots towards the post, too far out of Ricardo's reach. It's 1-0, and it will stay that way until the final whistle as Patrick Vieira and Claude Makélélé ensure their defence is not broken again. Portugal get the ball, they try their best to push forwards, Figo and Cristiano charge up the wing, but every attempt is blocked by the French and their Maginot Line. The only real scare for Fabien Barthez is a direct free kick from Cristiano which flies straight towards his gloves. The French goalie tries to hold onto it, but it deflects, giving Figo the chance for a header. He misses by a whisker.

The match ends with Cristiano crying as he did after the Euro 2004 final, and with Zidane consoling his ex-Real team-mate Luís Figo, who has played his final match for Portugal. Once again, the French have swiped a final out from under Portugal's nose. When they did it in Euro 2000, it was thanks to a goal from Henry and a Zidane penalty in extra time.

France are headed for the final against Italy in Berlin – the final of Zidane's headbutt and a fourth World Cup win for Italy. On 8 July, Portugal are defeated 3-1 by Germany in the race for third place at the Gottlieb-Daimler-Stadion in Stuttgart. The World Cup is over for Scolari's men.

Now let's go back to the 62nd minute of the Portugal-England match, seeing as how all hell has broken loose. The English fans and commentators are convinced that Ronaldo has convinced Horacio Elizondo to pull a red card on Roo, and they hold him ultimately responsible for England's defeat. They believe that, knowing his United team-mate's character, he did everything he could to make him snap.

But Cristiano doesn't care what they think. 'I am not a referee and I don't have the power to send off a player. I had nothing to do with the fact that the referee showed the red card,' he insists. Elizondo is equally disinterested, telling *The Times*: 'People can say what they want [about Ronaldo] but this had absolutely no influence. In general I don't pay much attention to that sort of thing because

I don't care about the pressure on my shoulders during a match. For me it was violent play, a clear red card.'

Ricardo's statement to the press does little to help: 'When someone loses there always has to be a scapegoat. I don't think Ronaldo influenced the ref. He was right there to see the action for himself.' Neither does Rooney's own statement: 'I bear no ill feeling to Cristiano but am disappointed he chose to get involved.'

The British tabloids discuss the matter in great detail, each offering completely different versions. *The Sun* writes that Rooney threatened to rip his team-mate a new one when they both got back to Manchester. It also claims that United will be showing Cristiano the door after his 'shameful' World Cup behaviour. The claim is unfounded, but apparently Cristiano hasn't taken it well. Sir Alex has tried to call him but has his old number, or so the story goes.

Everyone who is anyone weighs in on the debate. Former England striker Alan Shearer suggests that when Cristiano rocks up at training at Man United, Rooney should 'stick him one'. 'How could he do that to a team-mate?' asks Liverpool captain Steven Gerrard. 'It's unbelievable. If one of my team-mates did the same, I'd never speak to them again.' Meanwhile, Tottenham manager Martin Jol maintains that 'the biggest disgrace of all was Cristiano Ronaldo because he tried to influence the referee. What about sporting values?'

The message from the English fans is harsh: they have no intention of forgiving the United number 7. 'I don't want to see Ronaldo back at Man United', 'He is a disgrace to the sport' and 'You don't betray a friend like that' are just a few of the comments posted online.

Ronaldo immediately hits back, explaining that there are no issues between him and Rooney. 'At the end we texted each other and between us everything's been cleared.

He wished me the best of luck in the World Cup,' says the Portuguese. 'He told me that we had a great team and that if we continued to play like this, we would go far. He wasn't angry with me and, moreover, he told me to completely ignore what the English press has said, that all they wanted was to create confusion, but we are already used to that.' He adds: 'The things that have been said regarding me and my team-mate and friend Rooney are incredible.'

But the saga doesn't end there, not even when Ronaldo promises to call his team-mate and clear everything up. What is getting under the skin of the fans, the media and everyone else, is the image captured on camera at the moment that Rooney was sent off – Ronaldo winking in the direction of the Portugal dugout, as if to say, 'mission accomplished, we've had him sent off'. Try as he might to explain that his wink at Scolari was to show that he had understood what position he should move into on the pitch, no one wants to hear it.

The media take the perceived offence to heart and launch a campaign against Ronaldo. On 3 June, the front cover of *The Sun* shows a picture of Ronaldo's head on a dartboard, his winking eye positioned over the bullseye. 'Give Ron one in the eye,' suggests the headline. The article reads as follows: 'Here's every England fan's chance to get revenge on the world's biggest winker. Our human dartboard shows Portuguese nancy boy Cristiano Ronaldo. The Manchester United midfielder is caught in the act of winking to his team-mates after helping to get England and United star Wayne Rooney sent off. We've made Ronaldo's wink the bullseye. So put it up in your office – and give the sly señor one in the eye.' No comment.

The drama refuses to subside, continuing through July and August. Alex Ferguson and United chief executive David

Gill fly to Vale Do Lobo in the Algarve to talk to Cristiano. He says that he doesn't want to return to England, he wants to go to Spain, to either Barça or Real. He doesn't feel that the club has supported him throughout this ordeal. He explains his concerns to the coach: he is afraid of the press and the possible reactions from opposition fans if he returns to play on English soil.

Sir Alex tells him that Man United knows how to handle these kinds of situations. They dealt with people burning Beckham's photo outside London pubs after the English captain was sent off in the 1998 World Cup for kicking Argentine midfielder Simeone. He tells Cristiano that the English fans' bark is worse than their bite. They will boo him from the stands, but that will be it. They tell him that they have arranged a new house for him inside the club grounds, completely protected from outsiders. Eventually, they persuade him to come home and face the music.

In Macclesfield, where United are doing their preseason training, Cristiano and Wayne Rooney make their peace with each other. The coach has requested that they spend 45 minutes talking face to face, in order to hear each other out. The Portuguese striker avoids all the media, entering and leaving through a side door.

He later breaks his silence in an interview with *FourFourTwo* magazine. 'We were on opposite sides at the World Cup,' he says. 'There's no problem. There are no personal differences. It's all in the past. It's not an issue, it's gone and life goes on.' Or does it?

Chapter 13

Champagne

'The pressure only makes me stronger.'

Faced with a tough situation there are only two options: drown in your misery and never recover, or fight it with all your strength. Cristiano Ronaldo prefers the latter. In the face of accusations from the tabloids, threats, letters which arrive containing white powder (fake anthrax, a popular choice of threat at the time), the Man United number 7 pushes aside all thought of fleeing from his troubles. He returns to England and focuses on demonstrating not only his footballing talent, but the strength of character he developed during those difficult years in Lisbon.

'I managed to show that the pressure only makes me stronger,' writes Cristiano in his autobiography *Moments*. 'I tested myself and I came out victorious. Right from the beginning of the season I tried my best to relax and I put up an icy barrier during the matches where everyone was booing me continuously. I ignored them and they became an additional reason to stay motivated.'

One such occasion is 23 August 2006, the second match-day of the Premier League. United are away to Charlton at The Valley. When Ronaldo comes onto the pitch, it is as if a collective desire for vengeance radiates down from the stands. The entire crowd whistles, boos and hurls insults. But just before the half-time whistle, the United number 7 gets hold of the ball, dodges round one player and sends the ball smashing into the crossbar. The crowd falls silent, suddenly afraid of him, afraid of the possibility of him burying their team.

At the end of the match (3-0 to United) Ferguson takes Cristiano aside. 'You have found the correct response,' he tells him. 'You can silence them with your talents. You should never be afraid to show them what you can do. Show them your courage.'

Ronaldo will do just that throughout the rest of the season. The Germany World Cup and the continuous criticism he has had to bear have made him grow up quickly. He looks a bit different than he did a few months earlier – more serious, more determined, less of the arrogant little kid. He works hard, exerting himself more than anyone in training. He improves on both a physical and a tactical level. He is more thoughtful on the pitch and he gets on better with his team-mates. He has taken to heart all the advice given by Ferguson and Carlos Queiroz – the Portuguese coach who, after a lacklustre season at Real Madrid, has returned to Manchester. Now Cristiano knows when to dribble, when he's done enough running on the wing, when to pass and when to shoot. He is better at interpreting the game and being more measured with his efforts. He is starting to see results, at an individual level as much as at team level.

On 22 April 2007, Cristiano Ronaldo is named the Professional Footballers' Association Player of the Year, beating shortlisted team-mates Ryan Giggs and Paul Scholes, as well as opponents Steven Gerrard, Didier Drogba and Cesc Fàbregas. Ronaldo is the seventh United player to win the award, after Mark Hughes, Gary Pallister, Eric Cantona, Roy Keane, Teddy Sheringham and Ruud van Nistelrooy. But Cristiano also takes home the PFA Young Player of the Year, becoming the first in 30 years to win both – the last was Aston Villa's Andy Gray in 1977. He is also included in the PFA 2007 Premier League Team of the Year.

It's the first time he has won individual recognition. He knew that his season at Man United had been a good one, but in all honesty he had not believed he would win any trophies against such tough competition. The news comes as a big surprise and at the presentation ceremony in a London hotel he is nervous and excited. He is accompanied by Jorge Mendes, Man United icon Bobby Charlton and Sir Alex. The Scottish coach is charged with announcing the winner and runners-up. First he announces Paul Scholes in third place and Didier Drogba in second. Then, with a big smile on his face, he says: 'In first place … the winner is … Cristiano.'

In a black suit, white shirt and bow tie, Ronaldo gets up from his table, hugs Mendes and his brother-in-law Zé, and goes up on stage. He takes the trophy from Ferguson and watches the video clip in which the organisers explain why he has won. Then it's his chance to respond to the presenter's questions, but not before he thanks his fellow PFA members who have voted for him, 'because the players know the qualities of the players'. Here come the questions:

'What does this trophy mean to you?'

'It is amazing and a big honour for me to win trophies like this in the English Premier League. I am very proud. I am very happy for this. Thank you everyone, thank you to my family, thank you to my team, thank you to my manager.'

'What is it about English football that you love so much?'

'Well, this is why I sign five years more,' replies Ronaldo, who nine days earlier on 13 April extended his United contract for a further five seasons. Concerned about possible interest from Real Madrid and Inter, the club's directors have decided to lock in their Portuguese star. 'I love this football. I'm enjoying it. I think this is the best football in the world. I'm enjoying playing here.'

The presenter asks him about wearing the number 7 at United and then moves on to interview Sir Alex, who has no problem showering praise on his player: 'At this moment in time I think he is the best player in the world and his season has been incredible.'

Cristiano has the final word: 'I want to keep working hard and getting better because these trophies have now given me more motivation.' After the party a private plane is on hand to take Ronaldo and the United contingent straight back to Manchester. They have a match at Old Trafford two days later on 24 April – the first leg of the Champions League semi-final against AC Milan.

Ronaldo scores the first goal of the match in the sixth minute. Thanks to a fired-up Kaká, Carlo Ancelotti's men manage to pull it back to 1-2, but two goals from Wayne Rooney seal a 3-2 victory for the Red Devils. The return leg is on 2 May at the San Siro and it's a whitewash. The final score is 3-0 to the *Rossoneri* and a humiliated Man United team must bid farewell to their Champions League dreams.

Now it's time to focus on the Premier League. With only three matches remaining, United have a five-point lead over José Mourinho's Chelsea, who have just been knocked out of the other Champions League semi-final at the hands of Rafa Benítez's Liverpool. On Saturday 5 May, Ferguson's men face the first hurdle in their race for the title: the Man City derby. The Blues do not have any great objectives as far as the league is concerned. But nothing would give the fans more pleasure than upsetting their eternal rivals after their European setback.

But that wouldn't happen – Ronaldo and Van der Sar wouldn't allow it. And while it's a relatively quiet match for Rooney and Giggs, Cristiano lights up the Etihad Stadium. Michael Ball makes life difficult for him, but Ronaldo's efforts pay off in the 33rd minute when the left-back fouls him in the box. CR7 steps up to convert the penalty, making it 0-1 to United. Thanks to Van der Saar, the score-line remains unchanged at the final whistle. In the last moments of the match, the Dutch goalie blocks a penalty from Man City striker Darius Vassell, sealing the win for United. Ronaldo's penalty takes his tally to seventeen Premier League goals, third top scorer in the league after Chelsea's Drogba (twenty) and Benni McCarthy of Blackburn Rovers (eighteen). Above all, his goal has kept United in the running for their sixteenth league title – his first big trophy.

He wins it on a Sunday afternoon from an armchair in front of the TV. Second-in-the-league Chelsea are playing Arsenal at the Emirates Stadium. If they lose or draw, United will be champions. Things are off to a good start. The Gunners have scored a penalty and Chelsea's Dutch defender Khalid Boulahrouz has been sent off. Cristiano, Zé and his cousin Nuno are ecstatic. But the match is not over yet and Michael Essien equalises for the Blues.

The final twenty minutes are heart-stopping. Ronaldo has all his fingers crossed and has bitten down all his nails. He doesn't want to wait another week to be crowned champion. And he doesn't have to, as Chelsea draw 1-1. Man United are the champions and Ronaldo pops the champagne. He calls his mother and his friends, he receives dozens of congratulatory messages, and he races into town to celebrate with his team-mates. The party goes on into the early hours of the morning and continues the next day in the dressing room. But the most emotional celebrations are yet to come.

On Wednesday 9 May at Stamford Bridge, the Chelsea players form a walkway of honour for their opponents. United have regained the English crown after four years of drought, ending the reign of the Blues, who won in 2005 and 2006. Above all, they have won it with some impressive figures: best attack in the league (83 goals), second best defence after Chelsea (only 26 goals conceded), only four defeats – and they have held the top spot since day one.

Ferguson's gamble on an attacking game has paid off, even against Chelsea, who have asserted their dominance with a faultless formation and a cast-iron defence. Winning his ninth league title, Sir Alex has managed to teach even Mourinho a lesson. The Special One will not hesitate to exact his revenge: on 19 May Chelsea will beat United in the FA Cup final, 1-0 thanks to a Drogba goal. But on that Sunday, 13 May, the final day of the Premier League, United have the chance to celebrate in front of the fans at Old Trafford.

Enveloped in a Portuguese flag, Ronaldo gets to lift the trophy and take it round the pitch with his mother, his brother Hugo, Zé, Nuno and Rogelio. They end up soaked to the skin by rain and champagne, before gathering for a family photo in the centre of the pitch. A smiling Ronaldo is pictured, thumbs up, surrounded by his loved ones.

Chapter 14

A great season

'I thought it was going to be the worst day of my life. But despite my mistake, my team-mates still believed we could win. In the end it was the happiest day of my life.'

It's 21 May 2008. The two English superpowers, Chelsea and Manchester United, are meeting in the final of the Champions League at the Luzhniki Stadium in Moscow, after a nail-biting finish on the final matchday of the Premier League. In the 26th minute, Paul Scholes went past the Blues' defence, Wes Brown crossed and Cristiano Ronaldo put a phenomenal header past Petr Čech to make it 1-0.

At 23 years of age and after five seasons with the Red Devils, the boy from Madeira has become a visionary. And that's not all. He has retained the playing style he had as a kid: the run-ins from the touchline, the tricks, the games, the backheels, the 'sombrero' chips. He has also expanded his repertoire: he shoots with both feet, from free kicks, from headers ... he is a better team player. This Champions League final at a former Olympic stadium could be the perfect chance to cement his champion status.

'In order to be the best in the world I have to win titles like the Premier League and the Champions League,' he says before the match, all too aware of the opportunity at stake. 'I'm a winner, and this season I'm dreaming of a double. Why not?'

It seems as if his dreams are on track. Cristiano is on fire on the wing and has already opened the scoring. But a few seconds before half-time, a long shot from Essien deflects off two United players and Frank Lampard doesn't waste an opportunity. With a little bit of luck, a double deflection and a slip from Van der Sar, the score is level once again. The equaliser has given Chelsea a confidence boost and now Makélélé, Lampard, Ballack, Cole and Essien are on the attack. Cristiano cannot get free and the chances are coming thick and fast from the camp of Avram Grant, the Israeli coach who has taken over from José Mourinho. Thanks to Drogba and Lampard, the final is transformed into a heroic and agonising match. After 120 minutes nothing has changed and the game goes to penalties in the pouring rain.

Carlos Tévez is first up and he makes it 1-0 to United. Next it's Michael Ballack: 1-1. Both Michael Carrick and Juliano Belletti convert theirs to take it to 2-2.

The third penalty falls to Man United's number 7. Ten days earlier on 11 May, Cristiano scored from the penalty spot, punishing Wigan and winning their 17th league title in the process. Earlier in the season he missed one in the Champions League semi-final against Barça at the Nou Camp. But the English TV commentators haven't forgotten the one he converted in Gelsenkirchen in the summer of 2006 which knocked England out of the Germany World Cup.

The Portuguese has scored 42 goals in a single season. He is the crowd favourite and everyone is focusing intently on what he's about to do. It's the best player in the world against the best goalkeeper in the world, say the pundits. Ronaldo kisses the ball and places it carefully on the penalty spot. He puts his hands on his hips as always, lowers his head, takes a deep breath and waits for the referee's whistle. He takes his run up, opting for the Brazilian-style 'paradinha', the little stop intended to confuse the goalie. But Čech anticipates the move and still manages to block the shot. 'Saved!' screams the commentator into the microphone.

Cristiano buries his face in his hands and slowly walks away, devastated, while Čech steps aside for Van der Sar. Many great players have missed penalties at crucial moments – including Roberto Baggio, Raúl, Michel Platini and Zico to name but a few. But this is little comfort to the boy from Madeira.

'After I missed I thought we were going to lose,' says CR7. 'I thought it was going to be the worst day of my life. But despite my mistake, my team-mates still believed we could win.' And they do, thanks to Hargreaves, Nani and Giggs who all score, and Van der Sar who saves the final shot from Nicolas Anelka.

Chelsea captain John Terry has the chance to secure the win but he slips on the waterlogged pitch and misses, gifting United the victory. The Blues' centre-back ends the game with tears of frustration, while Cristiano is finally able to cry tears of happiness. His team-mates rush towards the goal like madmen, where Van der Sar is already celebrating. Cristiano is on the edge of the box, crying with his face pressed into the grass. He wants to be alone to savour the most beautiful moment in his footballing career so far. 'In the end it was the happiest day of my life,' he says later. 'Penalties are a lottery, but we deserved to win because over the course of the 120 minutes we were better.'

Fifty years after the Munich air disaster on 6 February 1958, which led to the death of 23 of the 44 passengers on their way back from United's European Cup quarter-final triumph, and 40 years after the team's first European title win – led by George Best in 1968 – Manchester United are crowned the kings of continental football for the third time.

United have a solid defence and the brilliance of Cristiano Ronaldo to thank for the win. The Reds' number 7 has undoubtedly been the star of the tournament, and with eight decisive goals he is the top goal-scorer and player of the tournament.

The first goal was scored on 19 September 2007 at the Alvalade against his former team, Sporting Lisbon, in the Group F opening match. It is the first time he has come up against his old team-mates since he left in 2003. After a pass from Wes Brown on the right wing, he heads the ball into the net, but doesn't celebrate the goal out of respect for the Sporting fans, who gave him a standing ovation as his name was announced before kick-off. The game finishes 0-1.

Next, the Portuguese winger manages three goals against Dynamo Kyiv: two goals in Ukraine, one of which is a penalty, and the final goal of the 4-0 win at Old Trafford, sending Man United into the final sixteen. On 27 November Ferguson praises Cristiano after he scores from a direct free kick in the final minute against Sporting, claiming the victory for United. 'It was a marvellous goal by Cristiano Ronaldo,' the United manager tells the press. 'Ronaldo always wants to do well against his old club. He owes a lot to Sporting, he respects that and has great admiration for the club. Cristiano was only eighteen when he started playing European football. Now he's maturing – he does what we expect him to do.'

And Ronaldo shows his gratitude by taking United into the quarter-finals, overwhelming Olympique Lyonnais goalkeeper Grégory Coupet in the return leg of the final sixteen match on 5 March 2008. A low left-footed shot after recovering the rebound from a miscued shot by Anderson, and the game is all but over.

In the quarters United are up against Francesco Totti and coach Luciano Spalletti's Roma once again. In the group phase they managed a victory against the Italians at home and a draw away. The quarter-final home leg at the Stadio Olimpico has 'defeat' written all over it. But Cristiano sets off on a run, leaps over Cassetti and heads a cross from Paul Scholes into the net. It is his 36th goal of the season. In the second half Rooney will seal the victory, taking the final score to 0-2. The return leg is a mere formality, topped off with a goal by Tévez. Ronaldo remains firmly on the bench: Lionel Messi is waiting for him at the Nou Camp in the semis.

Naturally the Barça defenders are worried about facing Cristiano. As Gianluca Zambrotta explains: 'You have to try and predict what Cristiano Ronaldo is going to do. He has similar talents to Messi and his team-mates look to him to try and create good chances. It is not easy to mark him because he approaches the box from different angles, he dominates a lot of the play and gets very involved. You have to be extremely focused because he is very quick on his feet and he likes to do tricks with the ball. There's no way to stop him in a one-on-one unless you have back-up from the fullbacks or a central midfielder. It's better if he just never gets possession of the ball.'

And naturally, Messi strikes fear in the hearts of the United defence. His speed is a particular concern, but most of all they dread going up against the little Argentine one-on-one. They have been focusing on how best to stop him before he has a chance to slip away on one of his incredible runs. Both teams may be unbeaten when they meet at the semi-final on 23 April, but they have had very different journeys. United have destroyed everyone in their path, while Barça have made it to the Champions League after two particularly bleak seasons with no silverware.

The match at the Nou Camp is a significant outing for Ronaldo, playing in front of 96,000 spectators. His first touches provoke a foul, a corner and a penalty. It has barely been two minutes since referee Massimo Busacca got the match underway and already CR7 is placing the ball on the penalty spot after his attempt to head in a corner was blocked by Gabriel Milito's hand-ball. It's Cristiano against Víctor Valdés. The Portuguese takes a deep breath and focuses on the opposition goalie. He chips and misses. It's over the bar. Ronaldo has missed out on the opportunity to get one in the bag early on.

But he is still a tour de force for United. Ferguson has put him in charge of the attack and he is on fire ... just as long as rival Lionel Messi is on the pitch. The Argentine has been unwell but is attempting to play for as long as he can to try and help his team's chances. He lasts for half an hour before finally relinquishing his spot to Bojan. And his exit extinguishes Ronaldo's energy. Without the two stars, the two most dangerous players on planet football, the game becomes boring and predictable. Barça dominate but can't seal the deal, while United turn defensive. The game ends 0-0.

The return leg at the Theatre of Dreams will decide whether Cristiano or Messi will get to go to their first Champions League final. It's Cristiano – thanks to Paul Scholes – who pulls off an incredible shot from outside of area in the fourteenth minute. The solitary goal is enough to send United through to the final.

A smiling Cristiano fulfils one of his lifelong dreams as he lifts the double-handled trophy under a rainy Moscow sky. For CR7 it's the perfect end to a season which has seen him racking up the goals, clinching titles and earning star status.

He has scored a total of 42 goals this season. He is the top Premier League scorer with 31, beating Adebayor and Fernando Torres who have managed 24 apiece. On 12 January 2008 he scored a hat-trick for United against Newcastle. On 19 March, Alex Ferguson awarded him the coveted captain's armband before the Bolton game, where he went on to score two goals. He will score another two on 15 November against Stoke City, taking him to more than 100 goals with Manchester United.

His 2007-08 season achievements include the Charity Shield trophy, his second consecutive PFA Players' Player of the Year award, the Premier League title (United finish with 87 points, two above Chelsea and four above Arsenal) and, of course, the Champions League.

'No one could legitimately dispute that he has developed into the world's most devastating attacker,' writes *The Guardian*. And no one disagrees.

Chapter 15

Ballon d'Or

'This Ballon d'Or is just the first step towards
something even greater.'

With 446 points out of a possible 480, Cristiano Ronaldo is the only player out of the 30 nominees to feature on every single one of the 96 jurors' ballot papers. He has beaten Lionel Messi by a landslide, with the Barcelona star amassing a mere 281 points. The Argentine has had a great season, but Barça have not won any significant titles. His only major triumph has been with Argentina's *Albiceleste* national team, who were crowned world champions at the 2008 Beijing Olympic Games. Fernando Torres is third with 179 points, thanks to a great first season with Liverpool, a tally of 24 goals, and his role as the protagonist in Spain's Euro 2008 victory over Germany in Vienna.

The international press have hailed Cristiano as the best in his class. From Beijing to LA, from Johannesburg to Reykjavík, the journalists called upon to vote by *France Football* – the French sports magazine which has been awarding the Ballon d'Or since 1956 – are unanimous in their praise of his talents.

Despite not shining in Europe, despite the ongoing soap opera surrounding his possible move to Madrid, rumours about his personal life and his arrogance and provocation on the pitch, he has been crowned the winner. All that matter are his ability to put on a stunning performance, his enormous talent, the goals that earned him the Premier League Golden Boot, and the Premier and Champions League titles he won with Manchester United.

At 23 years of age, and after coming second in 2007 behind Kaká and ahead of Leo Messi, fourteenth in 2006, twentieth in 2005 and twelfth in 2004, Cristiano has become the fifth youngest footballer to take home the trophy, after the other Ronaldo who was 21 when he won in 1997, George Best (1968) and Michael Owen (2001), who were both 22, and Ukrainian Oleg Blokhin (1975) who was 23. He is the third Portuguese to win the title after Eusébio (1965) and Figo (2000).

He receives a personal congratulatory message from the Portuguese president, Aníbal Cavaco Silva, who emphasises how this honour 'has helped promote Portugal's sporting reputation internationally and contributes to the country's appreciation of sport, which is significant encouragement for many of our nation's young sportsmen and women'.

Ronaldo is the fourth United player to win the Ballon d'Or after Denis Law in 1964, Bobby Charlton in 1966 and the aforementioned Best in 1968. He is also the first Premier League player to win since Owen.

On 2 December 2008, *France Football* announces the winner of the 53rd Ballon d'Or on its website and publishes a special edition dedicated to Cristiano. Everyone has already predicted the win, everyone is betting on the Portuguese, from Zidane ('He's the favourite, he won the league and the Champions League and he's the top scorer') to Kaká ('He deserves it, he's been the crucial element in United's victories'), from 2006 winner Fabio Cannavaro ('It's obvious he'll win it') to Ibrahimović ('I would give it to him, although he didn't do so well in Europe'), and finally Fernando Torres ('He's a goal-scoring machine').

Even Cristiano himself is convinced that 2008 will be his year, admitting that he fancies his chances a few days before the winner is announced. 'I think I have done more to deserve it than anyone, I'm feeling confident,' he tells Italian paper *Gazzetto dello Sport*. 'If you look at the past season, I think I did better than I have done any other season.' Regarding his competition, he admits that 'there are two or three others who deserve to win. But if you evaluate what each of them has achieved over the course of the entire season, I still think I have done more than anyone else. What else should I have to do to get the Ballon d'Or besides winning the Premier and Champions League?'

The newspaper responds to his rhetorical question by reminding him of Euro 2008, warning Cristiano against getting his hopes up … despite the fact that he played through an ankle injury in order not to let down his country and coach Luiz Felipe Scolari. ('It was like being stabbed with a knife, I never want to feel pain like that again, it was torturous, both physically and psychologically.')

After Torres, shortlisted players from Spain's winning Euro 2008 team include Iker Casillas in fourth place, Xavi Hernández in fifth, David Villa seventh and Marcos Senna eleventh, while Cesc Fàbregas is joint nineteenth and Sergio Ramos joint 21st. But in the end, the Austria-Switzerland tournament, which saw Portugal beaten 3-2 in the quarter-finals by Germany, is not what swings the votes from the 96 journalists. As juror Michel Dubois from Belgian daily newspaper *La Dernière Heure* writes: 'Although Ronaldo wasn't up to scratch in the Euro 2008 quarter-final, everything else he has done has been incredible.' And speaking of votes, 77 of the 96 jurors nominate him as their first choice.

Ronaldo is only notified of his achievement at the last minute, the day before the announcement, or at least that is *France Football*'s justification as to why, unlike in previous years, there is no picture of the winner holding the Ballon d'Or to accompany the online statement. The number 7 will have to wait until Sunday 7 December to lift the trophy when he goes to Paris with his family.

The trophy is presented to him live on television by Denis Chaumier, editorial director of *France Football*, during *Telefoot*, a programme on French national channel TF1 all about the 2008 Ballon d'Or winner. An excited Cristiano is wearing a dark suit and tie and a grey and white shirt, with his hair slicked back. He apologises for the late arrival of his plane and the Paris traffic, then takes a look at the trophy which he has been desperate to hold since he found out about his victory. He lifts it, commenting on how fantastic it is and adding that he is very happy.

'As everyone knows, winning the Ballon d'Or is something I have dreamt about since I was a little kid, which is why this is a very emotional and wonderful moment for me. I would like to take this opportunity to dedicate this trophy to my family, who are here with me,' he explains, turning and gesturing towards his loved ones. 'I dedicate it to my mother, my father, my sisters Elma and Katia, my brother Hugo, my closest friends Rodrigo and Zé, my agent Jorge Mendes ... this is hard, there are too many people to mention ... but I'm really happy.'

And he will be even more choked up after hearing the compliments from Patrice Evra, Kaká, Nicolas Anelka, Karim Benzema, Samuel Eto'o, Pedro Miguel Pauleta, Luís Figo, Francisco Alonso, Luiz Felipe Scolari, Alex Ferguson, his sister Elma Aveiro, his godfather Fernão Sousa and his mother Dolores – who is beaming into the camera as she concludes the pre-recorded tributes to the 2008 Ballon d'Or. 'I'm so proud of you. You're the best son in the world. Kisses,' she says. Live in the studio, the camera zooms in to show the champion's mother crying in the audience. But the compliments are not over yet.

The programme's host brings up the 7 on his shirt, a number considered special at Old Trafford. 'Best, Robson, Eric Cantona, David Beckham, and now you have taken on this highly-prized number. It's certainly the number of the aristocracy at United.' Alex Ferguson appears as if by magic on the French stage to offer his opinion. 'Cristiano deserves it and the club is thrilled with this latest success. Manchester United has been waiting for this moment for 40 years,' he says, adding that Ronaldo is exceptional and has matured so fast, to a point that even he couldn't have imagined five years ago. 'He is only 23 and has his whole career ahead of him,' he adds.

'One of Ronaldo's lesser known virtues is his courage and bravery,' Ferguson said of his star player a few weeks earlier. 'Courage in football, as in life, manifests itself in different ways. But the courage to move forward, no matter how many times he is going to be kicked, identifies Ronaldo. Very few players have that level of courage. Some believe the greatest courage in football is the courage to win the ball. The other kind of courage – and it's a moral courage – is the courage to keep the ball. That's what Ronaldo has. All the great players had it.'

After such a showering of praise, Cristiano concedes that he is extremely happy at Man United and that the club feels like home. 'I'm ambitious. I have a strong personality and I want to follow in the footsteps of other great players, winning both individual and team trophies,' he concludes.

On 21 December 2008 there is another team trophy to lift as Cristiano Ronaldo & Co. triumph in the FIFA World Club Cup at the Yokohama stadium in Japan. Man United have beaten South American Copa Libertadores champions LDU Quito 1-0 in the final, thanks to a goal from Wayne Rooney in the 72nd minute.

And on 12 January 2009 Ronaldo cements his status as best footballer in the world when he wins the FIFA World Player of the Year award – the votes from the managers and captains of 155 national teams reaffirming *France Football*'s Ballon d'Or choice. The presentation gala at the Zurich Opera House opens with footage of the five finalists in action. Images of the top footballers doing tricks with the ball flash across the screen: 2007 winner Kaká, Leo Messi, Cristiano, Fernando Torres and Xavi Hernández.

The honour of presenting the trophy to the winner falls to Pelé. He goes up on stage, tripping slightly on the step, and picks up the envelope with the winner's name inside. Speaking into the microphone, he admits that he is more excited than the candidates in the seats of honour. He opens the envelope and takes a look at the name, but before revealing it to the audience he says that he has a little story to tell. 'Last year I presented the trophy to Kaká. Afterwards I shook Cristiano's hand and I told him in Portuguese: "Next year I'll be giving it to you."' He lifts the card and softly announces: 'Cristiano Ronaldo.'

The number 7 smiles, gets up, buttons his dark jacket and heads towards the stage. He hugs 'O Rei' Pelé and lifts the 2008 trophy. Another film clip of his best moments plays in the background, and then it is time for him to speak. He moves away from the table where Pelé's envelope is lying, takes the microphone, and folds his arms waiting patiently for a question from the hosts. 'The audience is all yours,' they tell him.

'This is a very special moment in my life, very exciting,' he says in Portuguese. 'First of all I have to thank my mother, my father, my family and friends, Jorge … I don't have to name everyone, they know who they are. I would also like to dedicate this to my team-mates. Without them I would not have been able to win this trophy' – he looks down at the trophy, beaming. 'I am very happy, today is one of the happiest days of my life. I hope I get to come back here again one day. Thank you. Thank you very much.'

The audience bursts into applause. Presenter Sylvie Van der Vaart, wife of former Real and current Tottenham player Rafael, announces: 'Cristiano Ronaldo is the FIFA World Player of 2008. He has won with 935 votes. Messi received 678, Torres 203, Kaká 183 and Xavi 155.' As Sylvie says, he is 'the best footballer in the world'.

Chapter 16

Rome

'I want to win so I can make history.'

'It is the dream final,' says Ryan Giggs. 'United and Barcelona are two massive clubs, with massive histories, who play football the right way and who have so many great individuals.' The Welshman knows a thing or two about the Champions League, having won two finals with Man United – one against Bayern Munich, and one against Chelsea just the previous year. The Rome final against Barcelona on 27 May 2009 is the most hotly anticipated match in European football, the best possible line-up with two teams that will undoubtedly put on the best show on the continent.

The final pits the La Liga title-holders and 2006 European champions against the Premier League kings and current European champions. It also brings managers Sir Alex Ferguson and Pep Guardiola face to face. The former, born in 1941, boasts an exceptional list of achievements and infinite experience. The latter, born in 1971, is this season's success story.

It is also a contest between two teams bursting with talented footballers. Starting for Barcelona are Valdés, Puyol, Touré, Piqué, Sylvinho, Busquets, Iniesta, Xavi, Messi, Henry and Eto'o, while Man United boasts Van der Sar, O'Shea, Ferdinand, Vidić, Evra, Anderson, Carrick, Giggs, Park, Rooney and Cristiano Ronaldo.

What's more, it's the match the press are selling as the big duel between Cristiano Ronaldo and Leo Messi. But CR7 dismisses the hype. 'Messi is a great player, but tomorrow it's about Barcelona and Manchester United,' he says the night before the match. Leo agrees, saying that to focus on an individual duel 'would be disrespectful to two great teams – the two teams who are currently playing the best football. Two teams who have many other players who can be decisive.'

But Cristiano versus Messi dominates the discussion. Even Sir Alex Ferguson weighs in on it, although he can't decide: 'They're both fantastic players who can create and score goals, both of them. When great players get to that level, it's all about the small details. One of them could have an off-night on the night. Other than that, what can you say about such good players?' The press maintain that in Rome, CR7 and the Flea will be playing for the 2009 Ballon d'Or.

'Whoever wins may well have a better chance,' concedes Ronaldo, 'but that's not important. What I really want is to win the Champions League.' It would be United's second consecutive win and, to use Cristiano's words, they would 'go down in history'. Since the Champions League was created, no team has won two years running.

Cristiano is coming off a better-than-average season. He has played in 53 games and scored 26 goals, including eighteen in the Premier League and four in the Champions League. Before coming to Rome, Manchester United retained their spot as kings of England with a four-point lead over Liverpool in the league, and on 1 March they beat Spurs in the League Cup Final at Wembley. The only title that slipped through their fingers was the FA Cup, from which they were knocked out on penalties by Everton in the semi-final.

It hasn't been as strong a season for Cristiano as the previous one, but he is the current Ballon d'Or holder and he wants to show that he can still take on Messi, who has scored eight Champions League goals, 23 in La Liga and has been decisive in the Spanish title race and Barça's Copa del Rey triumph.

Kick off at the Stadio Olimpico is at 20.46.

First minute: Yaya Touré takes down Anderson. First free kick of the match. It's more than 35 yards from Barça's goal. Five steps back as usual, Cristiano Ronaldo balances on his left foot … then shoots. The ball spins through the air and deflects off the chest of Víctor Valdés, who fails to control it. Piqué desperately blocks Park's rebound shot at the post. CR7 buries his head in his hands.

Man United put the pressure on, pushing forward into their opponents' half and Barça are struggling to find their feet. Ronaldo is exceptional – the driving force behind United's game.

Seventh minute: Cristiano shoots from almost 40 yards, but it's just wide.

Eighth minute: after a good back-and-forth between Anderson and Evra, Ronaldo takes a left-footed shoot which is just wide of Barça's right post.

It seems as if United have Barça on the back foot. But looks can be deceiving. In the tenth minute Eto'o gets past Vidić in the box and his shot is too good for Van der Sar. It's 1-0 to Barça.

Thirteenth minute: a dud pass by Messi puts Man United on the counterattack. Cristiano receives a long pass and storms towards the goal. Gerard Piqué tries to body block him, earning himself a yellow card.

Eighteenth minute: Pep Guardiola is playing Messi as a false nine in an attempt to disrupt United's defensive line. 'It surprised us and made it extremely difficult for us,' Ferguson will say later. The Flea takes off from the right hand side of the pitch, heads towards the centre and takes a left-footed shot from 33 yards, which just skims over the bar.

Twentieth minute: Cristiano is on the back foot. He has got one past Touré with a bicycle kick but when it comes to the finish he is out of position – the angle is too awkward. He has to make do with a pass to Wayne Rooney.

22nd minute: United corner. Giggs aims it towards the far post. Cristiano goes up for the header, but he puts it just over the bar. It is the sixth shot in 22 minutes from the number 7. He seems ready and willing to win the game alone if necessary.

36th minute: Touré blocks a run from Cristiano.

41st minute: this time it's Valdés who blocks a run, coming off his line and powering towards the Portuguese like a steam train.

42nd minute: Sir Alex switches Rooney and Ronaldo. The Portuguese is now on the right wing, Rooney is in the centre, and Giggs goes up the left hand side. But it doesn't make a difference: Barça are still in control.

44th minute: great run by Messi from inside his own half, dodging past numerous United players. His shot almost from the halfway line looks worrying for Van der Sar.

46th minute: Cristiano moves up front with Carlos Tévez, who has just come onto the pitch.

55th minute: great pass from Rooney. Ronaldo misses by a whisker. Barcelona are still in control. Xavi's free kick is dangerously close but deflects off United's right goal post.

59th minute: another offside for Ronaldo after a cross from Michael Carrick on the left wing.

65th minute: Cristiano spoils a United counterattack, messing up a diagonal pass into the centre.

68th minute: Carrick's pass to CR7 is too long. The number 7 is getting desperate.

70th minute: Xavi recovers the ball after a deflection from the United defence. He heads for the box, looks up and unleashes a spinning cross, smooth and precise. With his back to the defenders, Messi ascends to the Roman heavens, leaping high into the air and heading the ball towards the post, just as the goalie dives the wrong way. At 1.69 metres, the smallest player on the pitch has jumped the highest. It's 2-0.

72nd minute: Víctor Valdés gets a hand to a jaw-dropping shot from Ronaldo, a failed attempt to close the gap.

73rd minute: referee Massimo Busacca lets Cristiano's frustrated foul on Carles Puyol slide.

78th minute: Cristiano is becoming more irritable. He's tired and bored. He argues with Rooney and receives a yellow card for swinging his arm at Puyol when he had no way of reaching the ball. It's a pointless foul.

After three minutes of injury time, the final whistle goes and Barça have won their third Champions League title. The *Blaugrana* fans celebrate. Leo Messi is the first to hug Guardiola.

Cristiano Ronaldo has missed out on the history-making win he wanted so badly. When he goes up to collect his medal from UEFA president Michel Platini, the hissing and booing is audible – the Barça fans already see him as a symbol of Real Madrid, who have been actively pursuing him. Later in his suit, and still hurting, he will say: 'It wasn't a match between Messi and me, but his team was better than us, and he was too because he scored.'

Leo Messi hugs and kisses the trophy adoringly, takes it on a lap around the pitch and celebrates with his teammates, friends and family. 'I feel like the happiest man in the world,' he says.

Sometime later Cristiano will explain: 'I was very fragile that night. I was on the verge of crying on the pitch in front of millions of TV viewers. I hate losing, especially in a final like that.'

It's his last final in a Man United shirt.

Chapter 17

£80 million

'I realise it's got people talking, but it makes me feel proud to be the most expensive player in footballing history.'

'Manchester United have received a world-record, unconditional offer of £80 million for Cristiano Ronaldo from Real Madrid. At Cristiano's request, who has again expressed his desire to leave, and after discussion with the player's representatives, United have agreed to give Real Madrid permission to talk to the player. Matters are expected to be concluded by June 30. The club will not comment until further notice.'

At 9.30am on 11 June 2009, Man United effectively accept Real Madrid's offer of £80 million with this statement released on the official club website.

Shortly afterwards, Real releases an official statement confirming that it has 'made an offer to Manchester United to acquire the player Cristiano Ronaldo' and that the club 'hopes to reach an agreement with the player in the next few days'.

Cristiano Ronaldo hears the news at 2am while on holiday in Los Angeles when Jorge Mendes calls him to update him on what is happening. One of the first things CR7 does is call his mother Dolores to tell her the good news. Shortly afterwards he makes his first statement. 'I have had my time at Man United. Now I can look forward to Real Madrid and a new stage in my career. This deal is historic. £80 million is quite a sum of money.'

It certainly is a large sum of money, the most that has ever been paid for a footballer. Cristiano is now at the top of an illustrious list (in an approximate figure of Euros for comparison purposes):

1. Cristiano Ronaldo: Manchester United to Real Madrid (2009) – 94 million Euros
2. Zinedine Zidane: Juventus to Real Madrid (2001) – 75 million Euros
3. Kaká: Milan to Real Madrid (2000) – 63 million Euros
4. Luís Figo: Barcelona to Real Madrid (2000) – 61 million Euros
5. Hernán Crespo: Parma to Lazio (2000) – 56 million Euros
6. Gaizka Mendieta: Valencia to Lazio (2001) – 48 million Euros
7. Rio Ferdinand: Leeds to Manchester United (2002) – 47 million Euros
8. Andriy Shevchenko: Milan to Chelsea (2006) – 46 million Euros
9. Juan Sebastián Verón: Lazio to Manchester United (2001) – 46 million Euros
10. Ronaldo Nazário da Lima: Inter Milan to Real Madrid (2002) – 45 million Euros

On top of the £80 million transfer fee, Cristiano will receive an annual net salary of 9.5 million Euros, while his agent Jorge Mendes will receive a ten million Euro commission. Every aspect of the deal is record-breaking and is enough to fill the front pages of the international press, not to mention provoke a wave of reactions and comments – some critical, others merely astonished.

Gordon Brown tells the BBC: 'He's one of the most brilliant players in the world. I think people will be sad that he's lost to the game in England. At the same time, I know Sir Alex Ferguson well, and I know he'll have plans that will be rebuilding and renewing his team. And I would expect that Manchester United and English football will emerge not weaker, but emerge in a new way and probably stronger in the long run.'

While the prime minister is keen to focus on the sporting aspect, minister for sport and tourism Gerry Sutcliffe celebrates United's exceptional business deal and comments on the politics of transfers with Madrid and the future of the industry. 'We saw Madrid spend £59 million on Kaká from AC Milan just recently and that's why we've written to the Premier League and to the Football Association – and we are concerned about the sustainability of the game. They are big businesses now and this type of money is around but we've got to make sure that there's a link and … sustainability for this because we don't want to see clubs go to the wall.'

'These transfers are a serious challenge to the idea of fair play and the concept of financial balance in our competitions,' declares UEFA president Michel Platini, who considers Real Madrid's offer excessive and 'very puzzling at a time when football faces some of its worst ever financial challenges'.

By contrast, FIFA president Sepp Blatter praises such deals: 'This is an example of a fantastic investment – there may be a global financial crisis, but football is still on the rise.' Manchester City manager Mark Hughes is of a similar opinion, saying that it 'stimulates the market'. He adds: 'There is a lot of money out there now and the amount needed in order to attract the best players in the world is enormous.' Regarding his rivals' recent deal he says:

'Manchester United should celebrate having signed a great deal. Sir Alex Ferguson makes key decisions very quickly. He has made what he thinks is the right decision for the club and we have to respect that.'

Adriano Galliani, on the board at AC Milan (which sold Kaká to Real), is convinced that 'Cristiano's signing is yet another example of the fact that, thanks to its financial strength, Spanish football has become the best in Europe'. In Spain, Barça vice-president and director of marketing Jaume Ferrer insists that 'there is no player in the world worth 94 million Euros', explaining that the figure is 'not in line with the current market. When you pay such high prices it allows other clubs to demand enormous figures. It can cause a sharp inflation in the market.'

Spain's sport secretary of state Jaime Lissavetzky washes his hands of the whole affair: 'The astronomical prices paid for some of these players is a private matter for the clubs: it has no bearing on public coffers,' he explains.

Only one man can end this debate: Real Madrid president Florentino Pérez, the man responsible for shaking up the market by signing 2007 Ballon d'Or winner Kaká and 2008 Ballon d'Or winner Cristiano. A few days later he signs French striker Karim Benzema for 35 million Euros, and offers the final word on the subject: 'The signings which seem the most expensive are in fact the cheapest.'

What does he mean by that? According to the club's directors, Ronaldo and Kaká – along with Messi – are in fact the players that generate the most income.

'Cristiano is an unbelievable footballer. We paid what we did because it's worth it – we'll make it all back, with interest. It's an investment in a club which is in the business of putting on a great performance,' explains Real Madrid general manager Jorge Valdano. 'Having Cristiano Ronaldo or Kaká brings a global market to our doorstep. And in a time of crisis, that guarantees us economic potential that we wouldn't otherwise have.'

Everyone is in agreement: having CR7 and the other millionaire footballers is a way of convincing companies that investing in Real Madrid will remain profitable. Real will use them to help renegotiate higher advertising contracts with Coca-Cola, Audi, Adidas, Telefónica and the Mahou-San Miguel Group, as well as selling VIP blocks at the Bernabéu. The club's directors are convinced that the 94 million Euros spent on Ronaldo, funded largely by the banks (Caja Madrid and Banco Santander, which retain audiovisual contracts and rights as collateral), is a worthwhile investment which will lead to a sold out Bernabéu, summer tours, TV rights (700 million Euros over the next five years), merchandising and increased sponsorship (currently only online betting company Bwin has signed up to spend 30 million Euros over the next three years to put its logo on the white shirt).

It's an investment which they plan to recoup over the next six years to the tune of fifteen million Euros a year. And that's even with a worst-case-scenario calculation of just two per cent growth in each area of activity. The addition of David Beckham into Florentino's fold in 2003 saw a 137 per cent growth in merchandising. If things continue in this vein, the club could increase its annual income from 400 to 500 million Euros.

It is worth remembering that according to research by Deloitte, Real Madrid has the highest income of any club in the world, with a turnover of 366 million Euros in 2008. And let's not forget that during his first presidential stint (2000-2006), Florentino Pérez managed to increase gross income from 100 to 300 million Euros thanks to stellar signings like Zidane, Figo, Beckham, Owen and the original Ronaldo. Pérez the Powerful has returned for a second term as a hero and national saviour, and he's ready to reapply his winning philosophy. He's convinced that there is no better course of action during a time of financial crisis than signing stars like Cristiano who will attract a following.

And let's not forget that in signing Ronaldo, the current president has succeeded where his predecessor and enemy Ramón Calderón did not, despite promising Ronaldo as part of a failed re-election bid. The single cash payment of £80 million is nothing more than the fulfilment of one of the clauses of a contract signed by the two clubs in 2008, when they agreed that United were obliged to sell Cristiano after 1 July 2009 if Real's offer was still on the table. It was a way to free the Portuguese player from his contract and enable him to sign a new one. From the very moment Florentino declared Cristiano a priority, he reaped the rewards from the previous directorate's efforts and closed the deal on Operation CR7.

It's a soap opera that had begun a number of years earlier, gaining traction in the summer of 2006. By the start of 2007 the situation had reached boiling point. Let's review what happened during that critical time.

4 January 2007: Real want to secure Cristiano during the January transfer window. A statement is made to the Spanish press: Ramón Calderón, sports director Peđa Mijatović and coach Fabio Capello are united in their efforts to sign the new Ronaldo. The Man United bosses do not want to lose their star player, who will turn 22 in February and is valued at 70 million Euros. But Real are not put off by the Red Devils' position – they make it known that they're willing to shell out 40 million.

27 January 2007: Alex Ferguson responds: 'We sell players we want to sell and there is absolutely no way Cristiano Ronaldo is leaving.'

29 January 2007: Ronaldo weighs in: 'I know that Real Madrid are interested but I can't comment on the issue. I have talked it over with Alex Ferguson and Carlos Queiroz and they have forbidden me from talking to Real Madrid.'

16 February 2007: Ferguson assures everyone that he is confident United will retain Ronaldo.

19 February 2007: Inter president Massimo Moratti declares his interest in the player.

8 March 2007: Ronaldo speaks out: 'Everyone knows I love Spain. I would love to play there someday. But right now I'm happy at Man United. If I stay another two, three, four, five years, I'll be happy. It's a great club.'

13 April 2007: CR7 signs a new contract with Manchester United for a further five seasons.

11 January 2008: United chief executive David Gill declares: 'There's no chance of us selling him. Absolutely no way, whatever the money.'

22 January 2008: Ronaldo's mother Dolores says she would 'die happy' if her son were to sign for Real Madrid. She is photographed wearing the Whites' team shirt.

23 January 208: Peđa Mijatović says he fears it is 'an impossible deal'.

2 April 2008: Bernd Schuster, Real's new coach, says: 'It's best to stay realistic in times like these. Cristiano Ronaldo is currently the best player in the world. But I can't see Manchester United selling him.'

15 April 2008: 'We want Cristiano to become an iconic part of Madrid,' says Mijatović.

16 May 2008: Ronaldo reiterates: 'I have said thousands of times that it's my dream to play in Spain. Sometimes dreams don't come true, but I'll keep dreaming. I am happy at Man United but no one knows what the future holds.'

23 May 2008: Ferguson lambasts what he sees as Real Madrid's lack of ethic and compares them to Franco's dictatorship.

25 May 2008: Spanish daily sports newspaper *Marca* reveals Real Madrid's offer of 9.5 million Euros a year to Cristiano and 80 million Euros to Man United.

27 May 2008: United bosses threaten to lodge a complaint with FIFA over Real Madrid's 'completely unacceptable' behaviour towards Ronaldo.

9 June 2008: United reports Real Madrid to FIFA.

19 June 2008: Real Madrid representatives say they hope Ronaldo will make the first move towards allowing them to commence negotiations with Man United.

19 June 2008: after Portugal's defeat by Germany in UEFA Euro 2008, Ronaldo admits to the press that 'there is a strong possibility [of signing for Real]; the train [to Madrid] only comes once in a lifetime and everyone, including those at Man United, knows what I want and what my family and I have been dreaming about.'

20 June 2008: United reaffirm their position that Ronaldo is not for sale. 'Ronaldo has continually been linked with a move to Spanish side Real Madrid this summer,' reads the latest statement. 'The club has moved to reiterate its stance on the matter: United are not listening to offers.'

4 July 2008: Real Madrid's latest figure of 85 million Euros is their 'final offer'.

5 July 2008: according to the Spanish press, United demand 100 million Euros to let Cristiano go.

9 July 2008: FIFA president Sepp Blatter confirms that United should relinquish Ronaldo and compares the signing of players to 'slavery'. Cristiano will later borrow this term.

17 July 2008: Santander approves a credit of more than 100 million Euros so that Real can sign Ronaldo. It is only a matter of days.

18 July 2008: Ferguson reassures everyone that Ronaldo will be staying at United.

5 August 2008: Real Madrid sign Rafael van der Vaart, suggesting that they have backed down in their attempt to sign Ronaldo.

6 August 2008: 'I can confirm that I will be playing at Manchester United next season,' Ronaldo tells Portuguese newspaper *Público*. 'Alex Ferguson has heard my views and I have heard his. Staying in England is the best thing for me. And before anyone says that I'll be unhappy if I stay, I want to clarify something: whoever says or writes that is wrong. I will play with all my heart. I will give 100 per cent to Manchester United, I will honour the red shirt the way I always have. It's true that I've created some of the hype by publicly expressing my desire to go to Madrid. And for a while I was hoping that United would give me the green light to go – I'd be lying to you and myself if I said otherwise. So I've been inadvertently responsible for the conflict between the two clubs.'

7 August 2008: *Marca* reveals the key to CR7's future at Madrid: 'An agreement has been reached between the player and the English club to go to Madrid on 1 July 2009.'

18 December 2008: Real director Pedro Trapote says that the club has already signed Ronaldo but cannot officially announce it for contractual reasons.

2 January 2009: 'I want to stay here. I feel at home here. I feel very happy here.' A positive start to the new year for Cristiano. But there is no shortage of criticism in the media. 'What people are saying now [about a deal being struck with Madrid] is not true. Whoever says that is a liar. There's always speculation, not just about me but about the future of players all around the world.'

16 January 2009: Ramón Calderón resigns after three days of corruption accusations on the front pages of the Spanish press.

17 February 2009: acting president Vicente Boluda reiterates the club's position that Ronaldo will become a Real Madrid player. He informs the presidential candidates that the deal is practically done and that he will finish up the negotiations.

18 April 2009: Ronaldo expresses his desire to win trophies with Man United.

27 May 2009: Man United lose to Barcelona in the Champions League final.

29 May 2009: in his first interview as newly elected club president, Florentino Pérez says it would be great if Cristiano came to Real. He describes him as the ideal signing.

11 June 2009: Man United confirm that they have accepted an offer of 94 million Euros (£80 million) for Ronaldo from Real Madrid.

26 June 2009: 'Real Madrid Football Club and Manchester United have signed a definitive agreement for the transfer of the footballer Cristiano Ronaldo on 1 July,' reads the statement on the Whites' website. 'The player will be signed to Real Madrid for the next six seasons and will be presented at the Santiago Bernabéu stadium on 6 July.'

Chapter 18

Hysteria at the Bernabéu

'Is there a match tonight?'

'A very good evening and welcome to the Santiago Bernabéu Stadium. Thank you for joining us! Those of you who are here tonight represent the very best of the Real spirit – the passion of the fans, shareholders and followers from all over the world. You are an essential part of what continues to make this club so respected and admired.'

Real Madrid president Florentino Pérez is presiding as grand master of ceremonies. He climbs the steps to the temporary stage at the south end of the stadium, accompanied by 'the blond arrow' Alfredo Di Stéfano, the club's honorary president. The crowd cheers as they come onto the stage. It is 9pm. Pérez waves to the crowd and motions to Alfredo to take a seat. In his regulation jacket and blue tie, he positions himself behind the lectern and microphones to get proceedings underway for the third presentation since his second term in office began.

Tonight is all about the 'Florenteam', the group of players who have re-conquered the world, stealing the crown from their eternal rivals Barcelona. They are a machine, ready to put on spectacular performances, win titles and make money. At least, that's what everyone hopes. And expectations are high with regard to the newcomer being

(right) Just the beginning: Cristiano at Sporting Lisbon. (VI Images)

(below) During the World Cup quarterfinal between England and Portugal, July 2006, Ronaldo and Petit (left) plead with referee Horacio Elizondo after team-mate Ricardo Carvalho (bottom) tangled with England's Wayne Rooney. Rooney was issued a red card. (AP Photo/Paulo Duarte)

(left) Holding the 2008 PFA Players Player of the Year award with Manchester United manager Sir Alex Ferguson. (PA Wire)

(below) July 6, 2009 – Being presented to the Real Madrid fans at the Santiago Bernabéu Stadium following his record £80 million signing to the club. Behind are club president Florentino Pérez (left) and honorary president Alfredo Di Stéfano (right). (AP Photo/Paul White)

(right) Real Madrid coach Jose Mourinho watches Ronaldo during a training session. (AP Photo/Paul White)

(below) Messi and Ronaldo vie for the ball during a 2011 Champions League semi-final between Barcelona and Real Madrid at the Nou Camp. (AP Photo/Andres Kudacki)

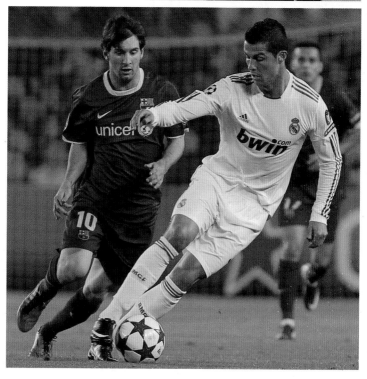

(above) Ronaldo holds aloft the Champions League trophy in Lisbon, May 2014.
(Jean Catuffe/Getty Images)

(below) He shows his third Ballon d'Or trophy to the crowd at the Bernabéu in January 2015
(Javier Soriano/AFP/Getty Images)

presented tonight: Cristiano Ronaldo, the most expensive player in footballing history.

It is 6 July 2009, a beautiful warm summer's evening, as it can be in Madrid at this time of year. Many of the fans queued all day outside the stadium to be here tonight. The gates opened at 7pm and closed an hour later – and five thousand people missed out on getting a seat inside the stadium. They will watch CR7's presentation on a screen which has been set up at the last minute in tower B. Inside the ground, only one block undergoing some maintenance work is empty. The rest is packed with 80,000 people, significantly outdoing the the 40,000 who went to the San Siro to see Ronaldinho's arrival at AC Milan from Barça, or the 50,000 who invaded the Bernabéu on 30 June to welcome the Brazilian Ricardo Izecson Dos Santos Leite – Kaká to his friends – who bade farewell to Milan's red and black shirt to join Real for the modest sum of 65 million Euros. And Ronaldo's fans even outnumber the previous record set on 5 July 1984: the 65,000 Napoli fans who waited for hours in the blazing sun outside the San Paolo stadium to witness the arrival of Diego Armando Maradona.

This is certainly a first in footballing history. The following day he will be front page news everywhere from Portugal ('Madrid at his feet ... Insanity for Ronaldo at the Bernabéu ... Cristiano was presented amidst the delirium of 80,000 fans' *Record*) to England ('Cristiano was presented as Real Madrid's new player amidst hysteria at the Bernabéu' *Daily Telegraph*), from France ('Eighty thousand for C. Ronaldo ... He will wear the number "9" shirt at his new club' *L'Équipe*) to Italy ('Ronaldo beats Kaká with 80,000 fans at the Bernabéu' *La Gazzetta dello Sport*), and even Brazil ('Portuguese phenomenon ... Cristiano Ronaldo's presentation at Real Madrid breaks the record established by Kaká' *Globoesporte*).

Florentino knows this is something special and he makes the most of it: 'What is happening here tonight sets a new precedent. The incredible turnout at our stadium is a testament to the Real Madrid spirit. Thank you for coming to witness this unique moment, the culmination of all our hopes and dreams. Thank you to everyone from Portugal who has joined us here to welcome one of your own into our home. It is an honour for us that you are with us tonight. It is also an honour for us to welcome one of the best players of all time – here with us tonight is a player who is a symbol of exceptional Portuguese and European football. Please welcome the legendary Eusébio.'

The 1965 Ballon d'Or winner, known as the Black Panther, comes onto the stage in a beige suit. He waves to the crowd, who are chanting his name, then hugs Alfredo and Florentino. 'Thank you very much,' he says into the microphone.

More applause, and then Florentino continues. 'Many of you are very young, but you should know that thanks to the incredible relationships that football can create, we have here on stage two lifelong friends, who are also two of the best players the sport has ever seen: Eusébio and our honorary president Alfredo Di Stéfano.

'There are few players in the world who catch the eye of the legends who have gone before them. Tonight, together with these two stars, we are going to welcome one such player. Tonight, Real Madrid is delighted to introduce someone who is capable of igniting the hopes and dreams of millions of fans around the world. The moment has arrived, please welcome to his new home: Cristiano Ronaldo!'

The £80 million superstar emerges from the dressing room tunnel wearing the white shirt with Ronaldo and the number 9 on the back. The legendary club shirt number became available after the departure of Javier Saviola to Benfica. It was worn by Di Stéfano during his time at Madrid from 1953 to 1964, as well as Carlos Santillana, the Mexican Hugo Sánchez, the Chilean Iván Zamorano, Fernando Morientes and the Brazilian Ronaldo Luís Nazário de Lima. Inheriting the tradition from a distinguished ancestry of strikers, Cristiano cannot stop smiling as he makes his way down the green walkway, applauding the crowds who are screaming his name.

It is now 9.17pm, but CR7's D-Day began as early as 10am in Lisbon when a private plane arrived to take him and twelve of his family and friends to Madrid. They landed at the Torrejón de Ardoz base twenty minutes late, at 12.50pm. Tanned after three months' holiday, hair trimmed short with the usual spikes on top, diamond stud in his ear, wearing jeans, a red leather jacket and a white T-shirt sporting the logo of his Nike sponsors, Cristiano disembarks from the plane and already has to stop and sign his first autograph and pose for his first picture on Spanish soil.

Two security guards accompany him to the official car, a white Audi with tinted windows. He sits between Jorge Mendes, his friend and manager, who has represented him for more than eight years, and his friend and brother-in-law Zé. The official Real Madrid Television camera stays focused on him every second of the way. He seems calm, smiling and joking about Jorge's Spanish, and he even has a little snooze as the car heads up the motorway. From a distance, they can see the four concrete and glass towers where the old Sports City of Real Madrid Pavilion used to stand.

First stop is the Sanitas de la Moraleja clinic for a medical. It's just a formality, as Ronaldo has already had a thorough examination in Portugal ten days earlier. The clinic has been besieged by a wave of cameras, microphones and fans. An eighteen-year-old girl is frantically waving a placard which reads 'I love you Cristiano'.

The security guards make a passage for him to get through, before handing him over to clinic staff and the Real Madrid medics. Cristiano pauses in front of the entrance for a family photo. Inside, staff and patients are waiting on the stairs to welcome him, forming what looks like a human amphitheatre. Everyone wants to catch a glimpse of Florentino's star signing.

The cameras follow him everywhere, while he has blood and urine tests, an ECG, an echocardiogram, an MRI, a chest x-ray and examinations of his feet and joints. Lying on a bed with blue electrodes attached to his body, he gives a thumbs-up, smiles, and poses for photos with his muscular brown chest on display. He is wearing a white chain with a crucifix around his neck, a diamond ring on his left hand, and an enormous watch on his wrist. He passes his half-hour of tests with flying colours.

'The player is in perfectly good health,' confirms Real Madrid's chief of medical staff, Dr Carlos Díez. 'He has exceptional heart and lung capacity. We have re-evaluated everything we covered in Portugal and also done some more specific tests. Now we will be able to tailor his future check-ups to help improve his performance.' After getting the all-clear, it's time to go, but not before signing more autographs, posing for more photos, and a momentary mishap concerning a group of boys who have broken through the security cordon and surrounded Cristiano's car. He waves at them through the windows.

Next stop is the Santiago Bernabéu stadium. On the way, the car stops at a red light, and two girls appear out of nowhere. 'You're the greatest!' they yell, trying to take a picture of him. Cristiano rolls down the window. 'Take it, take the photo,' he tells them. Overjoyed, they take a quick snap and shake the hand of their idol. 'We'll see you at the presentation,' they promise. Others try their luck while the car is still moving, in the middle of the Paseo de la Castellana, the avenue which runs along the west side of the stadium. 'Can we take a picture?' they shout. He opens the window again and waves with a 'Ciao'.

Finally the white Audi enters the bowels of the stadium, and Cristiano goes up in the lift to the club's offices. It's a day of never-ending presentations. First they show him all the Spanish sports papers – he is on every front cover. Then he signs the first shirt with his name on. In less than an hour, thousands have already been sold in the club shop. The supergalactic marketing machine is already in motion.

Real Madrid general manager Jorge Valdano guides him through the plans for the day, explaining the format of the presentation and pointing out the details through the enormous glass windows which overlook the pitch. Below them, the staff are putting the finishing touches to the stage. At 2pm, the press follow Cristiano to the restaurant at Gate 57, where he meets with Di Stéfano, Eusébio and other club veterans, including Zoco, Santamaría, Pachín and Amancio. Cristiano and Valdano sit at a reserved table with Jorge Mendes, Zé and the club's historic stars. After taking the final photos and footage, the doors close and the press finally leave the new player in peace.

But it's only a matter of hours. At 7pm they are back on his tail. After a quick nap at the Mirasierra Suites, Cristiano is ready to continue his intense first day as a Real player.

He has changed out of his sporting attire into a beige suit and white open-necked shirt. The fans waiting in the hotel lobby give him a rock-star's welcome. He shakes hands and signs autographs before getting into the car to go to the stadium. As they approach the Bernabéu, he is amazed to see the long queues of fans patiently waiting for their tickets to the main event.

Once inside the stadium, he has an appointment with Real Madrid TV: makeup, spotlights and a stage draped with Spanish and Real flags. Here come the questions.

'I suppose this is an incredibly important day in your professional career?'

'Of course, today is the day I am presented to the club, it's a very memorable day for me … I am very happy.'

'In 24 hours' time you will have achieved one of your greatest dreams,' continues the interviewer.

'Absolutely, I have said many times that it was my dream to play at Real. Thank God my dream of playing here has come true. I want to win many titles here, and I am confident that I will do so.'

After a quarter of an hour in Spanish and a quarter of an hour in English (the two languages of the club's TV channel), it's time to go. The president is expecting him.

Florentino takes him into the royal box. From behind the glass, they watch as the stands begin to fill up. 'Is there a match tonight, president?' quips Cristiano. Florentino smiles. He is delighted to have the most expensive player in his new sticker album.

In the boardroom, they celebrate the signing of the contract which officially ties Cristiano to Real. Seated around the oval table with Pérez and Cristiano are Alfredo, Eusébio and the other club directors. Four folders and four signatures from the president and the player to seal the agreement. The deal is done. Everyone in the room applauds and the moment is immortalised in yet more photos. Florentino gives Cristiano the pen he used to sign the contract, a model of the Bernabéu and a new watch.

It's time to get kitted up. In the changing room, between Kaká's number 8 and Sneijder's number 10, Cristiano takes off his suit. Getting ready is something of a ritual, like a bullfighter before going into the ring. Shorts, socks, boots – right first, then left – and finally, the shirt bearing his name. He smoothes it out and looks in the mirror to make sure everything is in order. 'White suits you!' says Florentino.

Now it's time for a photo shoot for his Real ID card and publicity material. He is photographed with shirts with his name in Chinese, Japanese and Arabic. They throw him a ball and he does tricks, then he poses with a scarf like the perfect model. After the publicity stunts, it's nearly time to go on stage. He's getting a bit impatient, so he warms up as if he were about to start a match. He can hear the stadium loudspeakers, the music, the official club song. They ask if he is nervous. 'No, not now,' he replies. But the waiting seems infinite and the camera shows otherwise. He sits down, takes off his shoes, puts them back on, stands up, adjusts his unruly hair … until finally he hears Florentino saying: 'Please welcome, Cristiano Ronaldo!'

The moment has arrived. He walks down the tunnel to the pitch, climbs the steps leading up to the green walkway they have constructed, and makes his way towards the directors, the VIPs, the press, the video cameras and the photographers. He hugs Florentino, Eusébio and Di Stéfano … he turns on the spot, applauding and smiling. '*Sí, sí, sí … Cristiano ya está aquí,*' chant the 80,000-strong crowd, in a rhyme celebrating his arrival. The president addresses him: 'My dear Cristiano, from today onwards these are your fans. The same fans who, throughout history, have helped Real reach the height of the footballing world.' Images of Cristiano's best moments flash across the gigantic screen, playing in his Man United shirt, smiling, lifting the Champions League trophy, kissing the Ballon d'Or.

'They will demand 110 per cent from you, but in return you will give them your utmost,' continues Florentino. 'Your professionalism, your full dedication to this sport, your undeniable talents have helped you realise one of your greatest dreams. We are absolutely delighted that you have made the decision to play at Real Madrid. Welcome to your Real Madrid.'

The presentation has finished. Now it's Cristiano's turn. Hands on hips, with the nine European cups in a row behind him, he has to wait in front of the microphone for the roar of the fans shouting 'Ronaldo, Ronaldo' to die down. The Portuguese is very emotional. He can hardly speak. 'Good evening … I am very happy to be here … '

He has to stop. The screaming is overwhelming. The cameras pan over the numerous Portuguese flags in the crowd. 'Today I have fulfilled a dream I have had since I was a kid, to play for Real Madrid … ' He pauses again. 'I had no idea that so many people would come out just to see me. This is incredible. Thank you.'

Then, taking the advice of a journalist who interviewed him before the presentation, he decides to surprise the crowds. 'Now I'm going to count to three and everyone say with me: "Come on Madrid!" One, two, three, come on Madrid!' The whole of the Bernabéu shouts in unison. With those few words, the entire fan base is putty in his hands.

Next, he delights them by playing tricks with the ball, kicking and heading and generally entertaining them. He signs the ball for a young boy who will undoubtedly be the envy of the 80,000 fans. He gives a shirt to another boy, who immediately puts it on. The fans shout for him to kiss the club crest. He poses with it, before making his way down the green walkway to greet his public. He goes over to the stands, shakes hands, signs footballs, kisses a reporter and waves to the crowds.

After the lap of honour, he goes back up on stage once more to wait for a photo with the directors. Johann Strauss Senior's Radetzky March is playing in the background. Suddenly, more than a thousand fans take the security guards by surprise, jumping over the fences and storming the walkway to try to hug their idol. The situation starts to get a bit out of hand – he is completely surrounded. With the help of the Real Madrid security staff, he gets off the pitch as fast as he can.

But the coming-out party is not over yet. The world's press are anxiously awaiting him in the conference room to hear his responses to the first questions on Spanish soil. The press conference table is flanked by a human wall of photographers and cameramen. At 10.17pm Cristiano arrives in the same outfit he wore to sign the contract, accompanied by Valdano and Antonio Galeano, the club's director of communications. Before anyone can get a word in, they have to wait a long time for all the flashes to subside. Cristiano smiles, sits down and waits for Galeano's introduction, before bracing himself for the infinite series of questions that follows.

*In the final of the Champions League, you complained about
playing as a striker. In his first statements as Real manager,
Manuel Pellegrini has confirmed that he would like you to play up
front. Will that be a problem for you?*
'I have never said that I didn't like playing up front. What I
said was that I didn't feel as comfortable there in that match
because I hadn't been playing in that position. If I have the
choice, I prefer to play on the wing, but it's not a problem
if I have to play up front. It's just a question of getting used
to it.'

*If you had to sum up everything that has happened at your
presentation today in a single word, what would it be?*
'Incredible.'

*What was going through your mind when you came onto the pitch
and saw more than 80,000 people in the stands?*
'It was a fantastic feeling, I really enjoyed it. I had never
imagined that the stadium would be so full. It was a dream
come true to come out and see it like that … it was amazing.
I was also thinking a lot about my family, my father and my
mother.'

*Are you aware of the fact that you have won people over when
you have been pictured at your most emotional, your most fragile,
despite the fact that you are known for being someone with a lot of
self-confidence?*
'I feel that people have a lot of love for me. I know that I
will be under even more pressure here than I was at Man
United, but I am still confident. I want to do everything I
can to show I am capable of giving 100 per cent, right from
the outset.'

Is there any message you would like to share with your former Man United team-mates and your former coach, Sir Alex Ferguson?

'I would like to thank everyone at the club. I spent six years there, and I have left behind some very good friends and some incredible relationships. I think they understand and respect my decision, they knew it was a goal, a dream of mine to play in Madrid. That's life. I have a new life now, a new club, and I'm going to give it 100 per cent.'

What was it like meeting Di Stéfano, one of Real Madrid's most legendary players?

'That was a very special moment for me because he is one of the club's most renowned players. It was like meeting Bobby Charlton when I arrived at United. He wished me lots of luck. This whole day has been one of the most incredible days of my life.'

When you dreamt as a child about playing for Real Madrid, did you ever imagine that the club would make such a huge economic investment in you?

'The club that wants the best players has to pay for them. Real Madrid is making the right choices and I want to help demonstrate that that's the case.'

When you entered your new dressing room, did you think about what you've been through to get here?

'Yes, because I have always dreamt of playing here, throughout my life. After everything I achieved at Man United I wanted a change, and this club is the greatest in my eyes. So of course you feel something special when you put that shirt on for the first time, when you go out to meet the fans ... '

Here's the picture of you in front of nine European Cups. Do you dream about breaking the curse of the final sixteen that seems to have been haunting Real Madrid the last few years?

'I don't play alone. Yes, I was alone at tonight's presentation, but during a match I will have ten team-mates, as well as everyone in the dugout. We have a great team and a great coach, all we have to do is approach things calmly, work hard and, of course, focus on winning the Champions League.'

You scored 25 goals with United last season. How many do you think you'll score in your first season at Real?

'What I want to do is adapt as quickly as I can because then the goals come naturally. I'm not going to set any targets, I want to score as many goals and give as many assists as possible.'

Did you see all the Portuguese flags in the stands?

'There were Portuguese flags and Madeiran flags and it made me feel very proud to see them outside my own country.'

Would you have played for Real Madrid under the old management?

'I don't know. That's not really a question I can answer.'

Your new coach is Manuel Pellegrini, what do you know about him?

'I have heard great things about him and if he is here it's because he deserves to be here. I have played against [Pellegrini's former team] Villarreal a number of times and they made things very tricky for us, so that's the best test. It will be a pleasure to work with him and work hard to win many titles together.'

Are you prepared for the level of pressure you will be under at Real? I'm sure you are aware that Madrid is a city with plenty of nightlife …
'I work hard to be successful and after that there is time for other things. I haven't got to where I am today on the philosophy of only working hard and doing nothing else. There is time for everything – for work and enjoyment. But above all for work, and winning individual prizes as well as titles with the club.'

What do you think of Franck Ribéry, who could become your team-mate at Real Madrid?
'He is a great player, but it's not up to me to talk about whether a player will transfer or not. My job is to play here and do well, nothing more.'

Ramón Calderón spent two years trying to sign you and failed. Has Florentino been the deciding factor in bringing you here?
'I have heard a wide variety of claims made by the press. They take a shot in the dark – sometimes they're right, sometimes they're wrong. The president made an offer and we signed, that's it. I'm here and I'm very happy.'

Are you sad to leave behind the number 7 and take up the number 9, the same number that Ronaldo wore?
'I wanted to wear number 7, but I know that 9 is a special number at this club. I'm concerned about playing well, not about the number. I'm the one that's playing, not the number on my back.'

Have you had a chance to speak to your friends here, Heinze, Pepe, Di Salvo … ?
'Everyone has welcomed me, they were all happy for me because they're very old friends. I hope they stay here

because it would help me adapt, although I don't think it will be a problem for me. I speak a little Spanish and I know that I will make plenty of new friends.'

Is there any Real Madrid player in particular with whom you've always dreamt of playing?
'The dream has always been just to play for Real Madrid – there are great players every year. It's a privilege to be here and to play with those who are here and those who may join in the future. We have a very strong team and we are going to work hard to win titles. Pellegrini is going to find it difficult to choose which is his favourite trophy … '

Do you feel that you have arrived at Real after a difficult year?
'No, because my last year at United was a good one. We won the league and the cup and I think it was the right decision for me to stay there.'

Barcelona have just won the triple. Do you think Real are ready to win all the titles?
'You have to aim high. We will try our best to win all three, although I would be happy with La Liga and the Champions League. We have to play like an organised team, with a good spirit and a strong formation. Once we have ticked all those boxes there's still room to dream. If we work hard then of course we could win all the titles.'

Do you carry any resentment towards Barça over that Champions League final that you lost?
'Revenge is not a word that exists in my vocabulary. Of course I want to play against Barcelona and beat them. It will be fantastic to be a part of it – two big teams, great entertainment for the fans.'

You have traded the Premier League for La Liga after six seasons …

'La Liga is very different. In the Premier League the play is much quicker, but both are very competitive. In Spain, even the smaller teams always try their best to play great football. I am really looking forward to taking part in La Liga.'

And the referees?

'In England they are very good. In Spain they are excellent.'

You have never played at the Bernabéu, how did it feel to go out there for the first time?

'I have never felt anything like it. It was a great first impression. What I really want is to keep working hard and proving to the whole world that it has been worth all the effort.'

You and Kaká are very different people with very different lifestyles. What kind of relationship do you think you'll have with him?

'We'll get on fine, of course we will. We will be great friends and if you were to ask him I'm sure he would say the same.'

Are you concerned about pressure from the tabloids and the paparazzi?

'It's not a problem. When I'm in training I stay very low-key, I prefer to focus on the football. I'm planning to do the same here, to look after myself so that I can stay in good shape for training and matches.'

What do you think of Karim Benzema, another one of your new team-mates?

'He is a very good player, a great signing. Everyone has high hopes for him because he has done so well in Lyon. He is also new here so we can learn the ropes together.'

What would you say to a kid who dreams of becoming a footballer regarding choosing Real Madrid over Barcelona?
'Real is very special to me. Barcelona is a great club, but Real is special. In terms of what I would say to a kid, I would tell them to follow their dreams, whichever club that may be.'

Which opponent are you most looking forward to competing against in Spain?
'I want to play all of them. Of course all footballers love the big matches. The derbies, the *Clásico* against Barcelona ... But I want to play them all and I want to win them all.'

What's more important: putting on a great show for the fans or winning matches?
'Winning. Getting points is the most important thing. If we manage to entertain everyone, so much the better. But we are here to win points.'

What do you think of the race for this year's individual titles – the Ballon d'Or, the FIFA World Player?
'I'm not thinking about it. I'm only focusing on having a good season. Individual prizes are important, but they're not the most important thing.'

Would you like to keep taking free kicks?
'That's up to the coach, but yes, I would like to.'

Finally, at 11.05pm, it's time for the last question.

Who is the best in the world: you, Messi or Kaká?
'Real Madrid is the best.' Everyone laughs.

'Thank you everyone, good night.' The director of communications brings the new number 9's first press conference to a close. The presentation of the most expensive player in footballing history is over, but the Real Madrid TV cameras still follow him down the corridors. 'It has been an incredible day,' says Cristiano. 'I have really enjoyed it. Thank you so much everyone.' He waves, and then he's gone.

Chapter 19

Sir Alex and Cristiano

'Ferguson has always been like a second father to me.'

'Cristiano has been a marvellous player for Manchester United,' says Sir Alex Ferguson. 'His contribution has been a major factor in the club's success in that time and his talent, his ability to entertain and his infectious personality have enthralled fans the world over.' The Man United manager has nothing but praise for CR7 upon his departure from the club, wishing him the best in the next stage of his professional career at Real Madrid.

Contrary to what everyone says about Ferguson not taking it well when stars leave the club, Cristiano's farewell has been very positive. Sir Alex's parting words are proof of that, and Ronaldo reaffirms it during his first outing with the press at the Bernabéu. 'I have no problem speaking openly about my relationship with him. It always was and always will be very good. I spoke to him about it and everything is fine. Life has to go on … '

Life goes on, but Ferguson has not forgotten his star player. 'We knew we could never replace Ronaldo,' he explains at the start of the 2009–10 season. 'No matter what anyone says about the lad, for me he is the best footballer in the world. When you've had someone who is the best at what he does, it is no good trying to find someone to do the same job. And when you know you can't replace someone or something, you look for a different way.' He adds: 'We will miss Ronaldo's goals, that is obvious. But Berbatov will do well this year and Wayne Rooney and Michael Owen are both capable of getting twenty goals.'

The manager knows that Cristiano is a huge loss for the club, that it won't be the same without the Portuguese number 7, but he has to defend his team. That's his job, just as it's his job to rise to the challenge of rebuilding a team that has lost a key player. He did it when Paul Ince went to Inter Milan and Mark Hughes left for Chelsea in 1995, when Eric Cantona hung up his boots in 1997, and when Beckham went to Madrid in 2003.

In any case, it's completely normal to miss a player who has just left, especially one whom you have helped develop from talented youngster into world-class superstar. But even after some time, Sir Alex has not forgotten about Ronaldo. In March 2010, when things don't seem to be going as well for Cristiano as he had hoped, his former manager tells the *Daily Express*: 'Cristiano knows the value of Manchester United. That's the thing. What the players have got here is protection. They come to training every day and there is nobody here to disturb them. I don't think Real Madrid is an easy club to play for. There is a circus attached to it. There are often loads of fans and an intensive media always filming them.'

He almost seems to open the door for Ronaldo to return. 'You would like to think that one day he will come back, but you never know,' he admits. 'I don't think he will stay at Real Madrid for life or anything like that. There will be other challenges and he is that type of player who welcomes them … I have a good bond with him. He is a good guy. I like Cristiano.'

And he reiterates his feelings just before the first leg of the 2011 Champions League semi-final between Real and

Barça, the duel between Cristiano and Leo. 'I had Ronaldo here as a player and I think he is the best player in the world,' Ferguson tells the club's official website. 'He can play with both feet, he has fantastic skill, strength and bravery, and he's a great header of the ball. But Messi is an absolutely fantastic player also. It's difficult to choose between the two, it's the toss of a coin.

'It depends on how you view your player. The fact that I had Ronaldo here so long, I know him well. I saw how he dedicated himself in training sessions to becoming the best player in the world and so that would weigh heavily on my view of him as a player and as a person. But you look at the boy Messi and you know that he's a serious player. He loves playing football. He's as brave as a lion because he will always take the ball in any situation. They are different types of player but there's no doubt both provide a fantastic end product.'

Messi or Cristiano? They ask him again after the final of the 2011 Copa del Rey, which Real win thanks to a Cristiano header. Ferguson says he will always choose Ronaldo over Messi despite them both being great players. 'I've got loyalties towards Ronaldo and I know the qualities he's got,' he explains.

Why does the surly Scotsman have such a loyalty towards the Portuguese? Because he took a gamble in 2003. Thanks to some great advice from Carlos Queiroz, his right hand man at the time, he was able to anticipate the advances of all the other clubs that were interested in the boy from Madeira. On top of that, Ronaldo always showed him that he is one of those players who never settles, he wants to get better every day. He is a footballer who never rests on his laurels – even after a title or a trophy win, he always wants more, he always wants to win more. And he demonstrated that to him consistently over six years.

Working hard means immersing oneself in a team, being the first to arrive at training and the last to leave. As Ferguson often revealed, when the others were hitting the showers Cristiano was still on the pitch practising free kicks, shots, penalties, or in the gym building up his fitness, gaining weight (he went from 75 to 85 kilos during his time there), strengthening his muscles, and above all, learning how football is played at the top.

Ferguson bet on him symbolically on day one when he gave him the number 7 shirt. And, as he explained at a managerial conference, he gradually taught his new player how to channel his self-confidence for the benefit of the team. And he succeeded: with goals, titles and trophies. For Ferguson, Cristiano is a special player, particularly when it comes to making decisions. 'He never feels afraid or pressured. He does what he thinks is best.'

Ferguson knows that Ronaldo is capable of captivating a crowd, of bringing that magic that the English admire onto the football pitch. United veteran Denis Law agrees. The 1956 Ballon d'Or says Ronaldo really knows how to get the fans going, while club legend and 1966 Ballon d'Or winner Bobby Charlton says he 'dazzled' the Old Trafford crowd from day one.

But the relationship between the manager and United's number 7 was not always a bed of roses. As with every relationship, there have been good times and more testing ones. The 2008 Ballon d'Or was a happy occasion, particularly after Sir Alex and the whole town had been waiting 40 years to see a United player honoured with the coveted trophy. And the Champions League win in 2009 was the culmination of an incredible season – Cristiano's way of showing Ferguson that everything he had taught him had paid off in the way of goals and statistics.

As for the difficult moments, they started when Ferguson benched Ronaldo right at the beginning – part of his way of easing the kid into his new surroundings, ensuring he wasn't under too much pressure and was able to adapt and progress. But the player's anger at being benched or not starting a game was unprecedented. The Rooney World Cup incident in July 2006 was also a testing time, but with the support of the directors, the experienced manager succeeded in convincing him to come back to the club.

And in June 2008 when Cristiano declared that he wanted to play for Real Madrid, the British media talked openly about the rift between the coach and his star player and maintained that Cristiano had said Ferguson would not be welcome in the Portuguese camp at Euro 2008. But none of these conflicts have changed Sir Alex's opinion. Even as he bade farewell to Cristiano, he said he was convinced that his number 7's best years were still ahead of him.

But what does Ronaldo think of his former coach? 'He has always been like a second father to me,' the Real player tells Sky Sports, explaining that it has been that way since he arrived at Man United at the age of eighteen. And it's not just a question of having respect for one of the greatest football coaches in the world. He really does feel the same affection towards Ferguson as a son does for his father – a much deeper bond than simply that of coach and player.

'Sometimes he used to talk to me about things that had nothing to do with football, and I would always listen because his words made me a better person,' he has explained. In terms of football, 'he has been a key influence throughout my career. He has encouraged me to develop and improve. I learned from him every day and he has helped me become who I am today.'

Cristiano recalls how the United coach always supported him, encouraged him and taught him to deal with his problems. He motivated him in innumerable ways, such as betting on how many goals he would score each season. 'I have good memories from Manchester and when I watch the games I miss it a lot because it's part of me left in England,' he tells Sky Sports. 'Just because I play in Madrid I'm not going to miss speaking with the old guys, so when I have an opportunity I speak with Sir Alex Ferguson. It was important for me when I played there, when my life was there, so it is good to speak with him because I'll never forget who really helped me.'

Chapter 20

Zero titles

'The truth is I feel sad and frustrated at not having won a single title in my first season at Real Madrid.'

The alarm clock goes off early. It's Friday 10 July and Cristiano has an appointment at 8.30am sharp at Real Madrid's training facilities in the Valdebebas complex, around fifteen kilometres north of the city. Before he can start the first training session of the season, there is the obligatory blood test followed by breakfast, then he has to meet the tailors to be measured up for his official Hugo Boss team suit. A pin here, an adjustment there, and then he's ready for his photo. It's a first-day-of-school moment of nerves and smiles.

Once the measuring and posing is over, it's time for the 29-strong squad to head out onto the pitch. A few members are missing, including Florentino's other star signing Kaká, who has been playing in the Confederations Cup.

Green grass, white goalposts, swallows flying low, empty stands, and seats painted to spell out 'Real Madrid'. In the distance they can see the ever-expanding residential neighbourhoods and the stadium's four towers of glass and steel gleaming in the sun.

In the press box on the second floor of the training complex, an army of cameras and microphones is impatiently awaiting the most expensive player in the world's appearance on the pitch. Captain Raúl is the first to emerge at 9.30am, followed by the others in dribs and drabs. Finally, Cristiano appears in a white T-shirt and black trousers. The cameras flash wildly.

The players gather in a circle in the centre of the pitch for the first team talk from Manuel Pellegrini and his colleagues. After a five minute warm-up, they start their stretching exercises and ball technique. Cristiano teams up with Brazilian winger Marcelo, Argentine defender Gabriel Heinze, and the Brazilian defender Pepe, who now has Portuguese nationality. Cristiano knows Heinze from his stint in Man United between 2004 and 2007, and his 1998-99 season at Sporting when Ronaldo was just a ball-boy for the first team. After fifteen minutes the blinds of the press box are drawn, obscuring the rest of the training session from the media.

On 13 July, after three days of training at Valdebebas, the team flies to Dublin. After four years, the Whites are swapping the town of Irdning in the foothills of the Austrian Alps for Maynooth, a small town in Ireland's County Kildare, 22 kilometres from the capital. The base for preseason training is the Carton House Hotel, an eighteenth century former stately home belonging to the Dukes of Leinster, which has played host to royalty including Queen Victoria, Prince Rainier of Monaco and Grace Kelly.

Ronaldo is the centre of attention. The fans try to catch glimpses of him on the golf course and the press try their best to corner him. At first he is accompanied by hotel security wherever he goes, but he is not comfortable having to be so cloak-and-dagger, so the Real management decide to remove the bodyguards.

In these first few days and weeks of the preseason, Cristiano surprises his team-mates. Spanish defender Michel

Salgado reveals that 'Ronaldo goes at warp speed', and comments that 'he is taking the team to another level, offering height, speed and movement'. The Argentine Ezequiel Garay, another new addition to the white camp, says he loves watching him train, while Raúl sings his praises, affirming that Cristiano is 'a down-to-earth, hardworking kid'.

New coach Pellegrini has plenty to say: 'I have had a chance to see Cristiano play the way I knew he could. The public persona he has built for himself is one thing – as a player he is something else altogether. He is completely down-to-earth and unassuming, with no superstar pretensions. He is always the first to arrive at training. He has integrated himself into the team very quickly and bonded with his team-mates.'

Cristiano is staying in room 223 and in the dining room he tends to sit with Raúl, Heinze, Guti, Salgado and Benzema. They enjoy lengthy discussions and debates over their meals – and not just about football. In his first Irish press conference, the Portuguese admits that 'I had no idea it would be so great. It's a fantastic group and I'm delighted that all the players were so welcoming when I arrived. I wasn't expecting such a reception. I had been reading the papers and they weren't saying very nice things. But I'm here now, and I'm very happy. Whoever was saying that there was a bad atmosphere in the Real Madrid dressing room was wrong.'

The first friendly is on 20 July against Shamrock Rovers and the Tallaght Stadium is packed. Everyone wants to see Real Madrid take on the Hoops, Ireland's most successful team, who have fifteen league titles and 24 cups to their name and came second in the league last season. Cristiano is starting on the right wing. Before the match, Rovers goalie Barry Murphy warns that no Real player, not even Ronaldo, will get one past him. He ultimately manages to deny Cristiano, although it's fair to say that during the 45 minutes he is on the pitch the Portuguese creates the best chances for the Whites, showing off his full repertoire of bicycle kicks, tackles and runs. It's a great debut which ends in a 1-0 victory for Real, thanks to a Benzema goal.

It's a long preseason: eight matches between the Peace Cup, a Stateside tour and the Santiago Bernabéu trophy. Cristiano plays a total of 603 minutes and scores three goals (just two shy of Raúl and Benzema's totals). Spanish sports paper *Marca* writes that Cristiano still has not found his feet at Madrid, that the Portuguese star is suffering from 'Zidane syndrome' – anxiety and pressure due to an enormous amount of expectation and failure to adapt.

But once the season begins everything changes, and his performances and his goal-scoring average improve significantly. On 29 August, the first matchday of La Liga, he scores his first goal in an official match against Deportivo de La Coruña at the Bernabéu – a penalty that puts Real in the lead. He celebrates by looking towards the stands and leaping into the air, fist raised.

After five games, his tally is up to seven. In one against Villarreal, he sets off on a slalom from the halfway line and dodges past three opponents, before taking on goalkeeper Diego López, who is powerless to block his shot. He scores two against Zürich in his Champions League debut, both from free kicks, with the ball travelling at more than 100 kilometres per hour. It's a fantastic start, the best of his career, and one of the most stellar debuts in Real Madrid history.

There is just one thing that bothers Cristiano in those opening weeks: being substituted. Pellegrini has already done it once, and on 26 September in the 79th minute against Tenerife at the Bernabéu, he decides to bench him for a second time. This is the first match in which Cristiano has not scored and he marches angrily to the dugout, sits down without shaking the manager's hand, and kicks away a ball that is lying near him on the ground. It's unclear if this is a sign of frustration towards Pellegrini.

The coach plays down the incident: 'It's not important. No one likes being substituted. I don't think it's an issue.' The Chilean coach had already decided that he should rotate the team in order to rest his top players, especially given the number of games Real have to play this season. But Cristiano doesn't like the swapping around. As Jorge Valdano points out: 'Ronaldo is a very ambitious player. He is genuinely anxious to ensure he manages to score and bring something great to every game.' In other words, he wants to be the star and he wants to be on the pitch as much as possible.

Three days later on 30 September, it's not a substitution but bad luck which will prevent him from staying on in the second Champions League match. He scores two goals against Olympique de Marseille, but bad-tempered defender Souleymane Diawara later takes him down in the box, stamping on his right ankle. Ronaldo cries out in pain from the ground, tries to get up, realises he is limping, and leaves Kaká to take the penalty. Despite his injury he goes on to score a third, but in the 66th minute he is substituted by Gonzalo Higuaín and he watches the rest of the match with a bag of ice on his ankle.

The doctors say he has severe bruising and a slight sprain – he'll be out for two or three weeks. He doesn't play in the match against Sevilla, the Whites' first La Liga defeat of the season, but he does fly to Lisbon to join his national team squad, who are in training for World Cup 2010 qualifiers against Hungary and Malta. Even though he is not

100 per cent fit, he says he feels fine, making every effort to be available to his team – something which is extremely important to him. But on 10 October against Hungary, he only lasts 27 minutes on the pitch, suffering a relapse in the process.

'I have probably lost Cristiano Ronaldo for the match against Malta,' admits coach Carlos Queiroz. 'I have spoken to the medics and it's not looking good.' The Portuguese Football Federation allows him to leave the squad and go back to the original clinic to have his injury re-evaluated. The Real medics say it's a grade I to II sprain of the lateral ligament with inflammation and swelling of the ankle.

The injury keeps him off the pitch for three or four weeks, during which time his club loses to Atlético Madrid in La Liga and Milan in the Champions League. 'I am very sad about my injury relapse,' Ronaldo tells Portuguese daily sports paper *O Jogo* (*The Game*). 'I'm not the club saviour, but I just wanted to be able to help my Real Madrid team-mates.'

But he will be unable to help them for 55 days. And a lot will happen in those two long months: the advent of Pepe the wizard, the *Alcorconazo* in the Copa del Rey, a journey to Amsterdam and a dispute between Real Madrid and the Portuguese Federation. Let's start at the beginning.

In the middle of September, Florentino Pérez receives a letter addressed to him at Real Madrid which reads: 'I am not an *antimadridista*. I have nothing against this great club. I am a professional and I am paid very well to put my powers to good use. I have been contracted to see to it that Cristiano Ronaldo suffers an injury. It doesn't necessarily have to be a very serious injury, just enough that he spends more time off the pitch than on.'

The club writes the letter off as the work of a madman, 'just like any of the other nutters that Real Madrid has to deal with on a daily basis'. Those close to the player also pay very little attention to the incident, but a few days later Ronaldo has his relapse while playing with Portugal. And the ominous spectre of 'Pepe the wizard', the author of the letter, starts to cause some concerns. Not least because the 57-year-old from Malaga, who claims to have been paid 30,000 Euros to ensure Ronaldo comes to harm, is becoming increasingly threatening in each interview that he gives.

In October, the Spanish wizard tells Portuguese paper *Correio da Manhã* that after the current injury, Ronaldo will suffer another blow 'causing him to be out for two or three months. After that, another injury will prevent him playing football ever again.' Who on earth is paying this guy to harm the footballer? 'It's a young woman who wants revenge against Cristiano,' claims the shaman. 'She is not Portuguese, she doesn't speak Spanish, but she is from a powerful family. She had a fling with Ronaldo and helped him make some high society contacts. But then he rejected her.'

He also claims that he knows that Cristiano's mother has hired Fernando Nogueira, a Portuguese magician from Fafe who uses white magic. The absurd war of voodoo and black magic against white magic is on. Cristiano, who has been trying to recover, now has the added worry of a curse which has seemingly been placed on him. Fans start to light candles on his behalf, asking the Virgin Mary to watch over Real Madrid and ward off the evil eye from the Portuguese.

Next up on the list of Real's woes is the match against AD Alcorcón in the 2009-10 Copa del Rey. Alcorcón is a commuter town of 168,000 inhabitants, around fifteen kilometres from the centre of Madrid. Its football team was founded in 1971 and plays in the third division. On

26 October, Real goes out to play against them at the Municipal de Santo Domingo stadium in the first leg of the final 32 round. There is no comparison between the two clubs – Alcorcón's highest paid player earns 6,000 Euros a year and works part time as a pizza chef, while Ronaldo can hope to pocket thirteen million Euros this season.

Cristiano is not in the starting line-up. Nor are Casillas, Sergio Ramos, Xabi Alonso or Kaká. Nonetheless, Pellegrini's team seems more than adequate for the match in question: Dudek, Arbeloa, Albiol, Metzelder, Drenthe, Granero, Guti, Diarra, van der Vaart, Raúl and Benzema. But disaster strikes when Alcorcón blast the visitors with a whopping 4-0 defeat.

'Humiliation', 'Historic defeat', 'The thrashing of the century', read the headlines in the following day's papers. And the front page of *Marca* carries a photo of Pellegrini with the simple words 'Go home!' It has barely been four months since he was hired and the coach's position in the dugout is already on shaky ground. He says he will stand strong and refuses to resign, but rumour has it the search is already on for his replacement. It seems unlikely that he will make it past Christmas.

The manager had already been heavily criticised for the team's performance in the two defeats by Sevilla and Milan. Now he is being hung out to dry. He has two matches to redeem himself: in La Liga against Getafe, and at the San Siro in the return leg against Milan. After a victory over the neighbours and a draw at Milan, Pellegrini can breathe easily once again.

On 4 November, after the doctors have confirmed that the physio on his ankle has not had the desired results, Cristiano flies to Amsterdam for a consultation with specialist trauma and orthopaedic surgeon Cornelis van Dijk. The

Dutchman is already familiar with Cristiano's ankle problems, having operated on it on 8 July 2008 after Portugal were eliminated from Euro 2008. On that occasion he was unable to play for four months, and he was even unable to train with Man United for a full two months.

The initial rumours that Cristiano will again be out for two or three months are prompted by fear. The sinister predictions of Pepe the wizard are on everyone's minds. In the end it's not as bad as it seems. He will be back on the pitch at the Bernabéu after just twenty days. But not before a row erupts between the club and the Portuguese Federation – and not before Real crash out of the Copa del Rey.

Carlos Queiroz calls him up for the 2010 World Cup qualifier against Bosnia. Pellegrini tries to be diplomatic: 'Of course he wants to be there and it's understandable that the selectors want him in the team. But there is a medical issue to consider as well. I think it's a bad idea, both for Portugal and for the player. Cristiano is in the course of undergoing medical treatment.' The Real staff, who have never fully understood why Ronaldo was allowed to play against Hungary in the first place, send a letter outlining their concerns, signed by Cristiano, Jorge Valdano, club medics and Professor van Dijk. It's going to be a struggle to keep the number 9 from going to Lisbon.

In the end, the club wins and Cristiano stays put to continue his recuperation. But on 10 November he is still not ready to play in the return leg against Alcorcón. Without him, the team manages a single goal – nowhere near enough to counteract the defeat in the first leg. Real Madrid are out of the Copa del Rey. The first trophy has slipped through their fingers.

On 25 November, Cristiano Ronaldo comes on to replace Raúl in the 70th minute against Zürich at the Bernabéu.

The crowd cheers him on like a hero returning home after an epic journey. The Portuguese's healed ankle is seen by the fans as enough of a reason to celebrate. In twenty minutes, Cristiano entertains them with a few tricks, a *rabona* which doesn't quite come off, and a good shot which Swiss goalkeeper Johnny Leoni blocks with difficulty. He's back on form.

He has missed a total of ten Real Madrid matches: six in La Liga, two in the Champions League, and the two Copa del Rey matches against Alcorcón. It is calculated that his timeout has cost the club 1.7 million Euros. But Copa del Rey and the *Alcorconazo* aside, at this stage in the season there is still everything to play for. Real are top of La Liga with a one-point lead over Barcelona and they have made it through to the final sixteen in the Champions League. And the *Clásico* against Barça is just four days away.

It is raining at the Nou Camp. Cristiano runs out onto the pitch, hair slicked back. He looks to be in good shape. The crowd starts up a chant which was invented nine years earlier when Luís Figo betrayed the *Blaugrana* to join the Whites. 'That Portuguese, what a son-of-a-bitch!' The Spanish rhyme is to be the theme throughout the evening. The number 9 ignores the insults and braces himself for the game ahead.

In the first half, Real are powerful, fast, efficient and lethal on the counterattack. For quite a while they seem to have the match under their control thanks to Kaká, who is an effective second striker, and Cristiano, who is in his favourite position. After half an hour, Ronaldo is the one who is helping push the Real attack forward. Manuel Pellegrini rushes out of the dugout screaming 'Go on! Keep going!' The number 9 obeys his orders, running into a space between Henry and Abidal.

Marcelo passes to Kaká, who takes on Alves and Puyol and gets past them both. He sees a space up front and passes to Cristiano who is all alone – Piqué has forgotten all about him. Now it's just Cristiano against Valdés, who comes out of his goal in an attempt to block his shot. A one-on-one could be lethal. Cristiano shoots with the inside of his right foot, aiming for the far post, but due to his recent injury it's an awkward shot, ending up more central than he intended. The Barça goalie stops it without any problem. A collective sigh of relief is heard around the Nou Camp.

For the fourth time, Ronaldo has failed to score against the eternal rivals. In the 66 minutes he is on the pitch before being substituted by Benzema, he proves that he is on good form, he doesn't seem to be getting tired and he faces up to his opponents without any difficulty. But by the second half, the Catalans are gradually closing in around him, giving him less room to move. Barça are taking control. Alves passes to new signing Ibrahimović (45 million Euros plus Samuel Eto'o to Inter) who shoots at Casillas, taking the score to 1-0.

Barça overtake Real to regain the La Liga top spot with a two-point lead. But it's not over yet and the race for the title will be an exciting fight to the bitter end.

On 6 December there is more bad news in store for Cristiano as Messi is awarded the *France Football* Ballon d'Or title. It's a real whitewash: 473 points to Ronaldo's 233. And the Argentine is crowned king once again on 21 December at the Zurich Opera House during the FIFA World Player of the Year gala, racking up a score of 1,073 – more than three times that of Ronaldo, who managed 352. Nobody can get near the Flea, particularly after Barça's incredible year, during which they have won six titles: La Liga, the Champions League, the Copa del Rey, the Spanish Super

Cup, the UEFA Super Cup and the World Club Cup. In January the *Blaugrana* fall from grace, eliminated by Sevilla in the Copa del Rey. But they are still very much in control as far as La Liga is concerned, extending their lead over Real to five points.

Cristiano, meanwhile, makes the headlines on 25 January for all the wrong reasons. Real are playing Málaga at the Bernabéu and the Portuguese is dominating the match. After three league games without scoring, he nets two spectacular goals which seal the result. Unfortunately, he also manages to get tangled up and elbow Patrick Mtiliga, who has been pulling on his shirt. Direct red card.

It's his second of the season, after the one he received against Almería when he aimed a kick at Juanma Ortiz. He apologised later that evening: 'It was in the heat of the moment, I was in competitive mode. I apologise to everyone concerned.' He received a one-match ban, missing the duel against Valencia at Mestalla.

This elbow against Mtiliga, on the other hand, doesn't seem worthy of a sending off. First, he sinks to his knees on the pitch. Then he tries to show the crowd and the referee how his opponent had been grabbing his shirt. And when Málaga's Toribio tells him to 'come and see what you've done to my team-mate', he responds: 'What are you talking about? You didn't see how he was grabbing me.' In the end he is heading back to the dressing room, shaking his head.

'I'm barely allowed to move. I touch the opponent and it's a red,' he later complains to the press. 'That wasn't a red. You can interpret it however you want, but anyone who knows anything about football knows that that wasn't an expulsion because I had no intention of harming my opponent.' Referee Pérez Lasa responds: 'I felt it was a red because he hit the opponent in the face with his arm and drew blood – he ended up having to be substituted.' But Cristiano is not convinced, he thinks there is some kind of conspiracy against him. 'I feel like this only happens to me because of who I am,' he insists.

After he heads down to the Málaga dressing room, he apologises to the defender and is alarmed to see that Mtiliga's nose is in fact broken. Nonetheless, he will not be swayed regarding his convictions surrounding the red card. The dispute is perfect fodder for the tabloids, which waste no time in naming them the hero and villain, the goody and the baddy. *El País* leads with: 'Cristiano, out of control. Real Madrid staff admit it is difficult to put the brakes on the Portuguese's strong personality.'

Valter Di Salvo who was his fitness coach at Man United explains: 'His career at Real will always be like this – oscillating between moments of glory and more difficult times. It will continue like that until such time as he can sit down and relax, away from all the tension in his life. He spends all his time trying to be the best because that's what people expect of him. It's difficult to keep someone under control who spends their whole life under such pressure. And he does. In England he was in the tabloids once a fortnight and here he's under constant pressure to keep up with Benzema and Kaká.'

Jorge Valdano defends his star player: 'It's part of his personality. He goes out onto the pitch in a state of overexcitement. That's what enables him to turn a game around.'

But not everyone agrees. There are many people in the Real camp who are concerned about his ego, not to mention the fact that after just twelve La Liga matches he has already received half the number of red cards that he saw in five years with Manchester United.

Between all the back and forth, the disputes and the goals, the final sixteen of the Champions League rolls around on 16 February. It's a crucial moment in the season, because Real Madrid haven't made it past this point in the tournament for five years. In addition, the Champions League final will be played at the Bernabéu on 22 May. It would be the ideal setting for the club's tenth title win.

Their opponents are Karim Benzema's former team, Olympique Lyonnais. The first leg is at the Gerland stadium, where the Whites have never scored but have been defeated 2-0 and 3-0. This time everything feels different, thanks to the 'super team' that Florentino has created. But it turns out to be a bad evening all round. Real don't seem to be playing the way they usually do and they are unable to pull off the same kind of performance which seemed so easy in La Liga. They have no idea how to corner Claude Puel's team, who have the home advantage, play a very physical game, and are very good at closing all the gaps.

In the first half, the Whites only manage a single shot and it goes wide. They are powerless in the face of Jean Makoun's goal, a bullet into the left corner of the net that nobody, not even Casillas, sees coming. Only in the final fifteen minutes do Pellegrini's men have any decent chances, mounting an attack on Hugo Lloris's goal. The Frenchman saves a shot from Cristiano with an impressive dive across to the opposite post, comes out of his goal to take on the Portuguese head-to-head, and ultimately succeeds in keeping a clean sheet.

No one doubts Real's ability to turn it around at the Bernabéu, but they have certainly managed to get themselves into a bit of a mess. Before the return leg, Cristiano speaks out: 'We are going to do everything we can from the first minute until the final whistle goes. We have to show Lyon that we are in charge at the Bernabéu.'

For the first half, at least, they do seem to be in control. They are on devastating form and look impossible to tame. Cristiano is tearing across the pitch like a whirlwind – no amount of reinforcements can stop him. In fact, the entire attack is doing a great job of blasting through the Lyon defence. Guti notices that Ronaldo has managed to find space between Révellière and Cris and is attempting to push forward as much as possible while still staying onside. He passes to the Portuguese, who shoots with his left foot. The ball goes between Lloris's legs.

It's only the sixth minute, but the goal signals the first of dozens of Real chances. At first it seems as if Lyon will probably be heading home, but time after time the goals are just out of reach. In the end, the reality is brutal, a harsh reminder to the Florenteam that money and Ballon d'Or prizes have no bearing on the game at hand. In the 75th minute, Miralem Pjanić equalises, knocking Real out of the Champions League for the sixth consecutive year. It's a failure, a disaster ... although no one in the club will admit it at the time.

The following day's papers take no prisoners. 'Catastrophe' bemoans *As*, while *Marca* calls for Pellegrini to go with a categorical 'Out' as its headline. Elsewhere, *El País* writes: 'Football cannot be bought. Lyon brings Florentino Pérez's extravagant project to a new low.'

Now all that remains for the Florenteam is La Liga, and the race against Barça is going to be tough. It all comes down to the 31st matchday of the season when the rivals meet at the Bernabéu. After the match, Cristiano passes briefly through the press area, offering one thought: 'When a team wins it is because they are the best. We have to accept the criticism we have received. Today Barcelona were better than we were, from the moment they scored the first goal.'

It's Lionel Messi who scores that opening goal, 40 seconds after being fouled by Sergio Ramos, who has managed to kick him in the face during a little scuffle on the left wing. The Argentine brushes it off, gets Maxwell to take the free kick as quickly as possible, receives the ball, passes to Xavi who passes it back to him in the box, and shoots. It's a big psychological blow to the Whites.

Little Messi's performance has been the complete opposite of Ronaldo's – almost invisible up until the moment he scored. He has been lost in the middle of the pitch, seemingly absent from the play. Cristiano, on the other hand, has done well to get himself noticed, receiving countless long passes, heading, controlling the ball well, keeping the play going, running for the ball, dictating the flow, going up against defenders one-on-one, taking on Piqué, and generally pushing things forward. He is a constant presence, energetic, determined, and keen to show off his abilities with every touch of the ball. But it's not working for him the way it usually does, and despite all his efforts, his contribution is not enough to turn the derby around.

The second goal from Pedro seals the game. Messi and Pep Guardiola have beaten Ronaldo and Pellegrini. Barça are back in the lead with a three-point advantage over their rivals, 80 to 77.

But Real aren't ready to give up just yet. On the 35th matchday, they make history when they rack up 29 league wins in a single season. And it's all thanks to Cristiano, who has been holding the team together throughout La Liga, coming to the rescue time and again and encouraging his team-mates. He is reminiscent of the late Juanito, instigating comebacks in the final moments of a match, like the one against Osasuna on 2 May. He responds to two consecutive hat-tricks by Messi (against Valencia and Zaragoza) with a hat-trick of his own against Mallorca. He single-handedly keeps up the pressure on Barça, who have just been knocked out of the Champions League by Mourinho's Inter Milan.

By the penultimate matchday, there is just one point separating the two Spanish giants. Barça and Real have moved so far ahead that third place Valencia trail the leaders by a staggering 28 points.

It's Sunday 16 May, the final matchday of the season and the finish line is in sight. Barcelona smash Valladolid 4-0, while Real can only manage a draw away to Málaga at the Rosaleda. The *Blaugrana* are home and dry, celebrating their twentieth La Liga title and a record 99 points to Real's 96. The entire championship has been an incredible duel between the nation's two greatest teams.

Despite two months out due to injury, Cristiano Ronaldo has scored 33 goals: 26 in La Liga compared with Messi's 34, and seven in the Champions League compared with Messi's eight. As a team Real have actually beaten Barça by four goals, with a total tally of 102. Cristiano has dazzled the fans at the Bernabéu and managed to convince his team-mates that he is something special. Anyone who had preconceived ideas about him being a diva or a narcissist has discovered a down-to-earth, affectionate and generous player, who speaks his mind and above all who is a born competitor.

Casillas sums up the feeling in the dressing room: 'Cristiano has a winning mentality. You always know he will give that little bit extra in a match. He has a knack of destabilising the opponent. He is always mentally focused.' In short, he has provided a much needed dose of adrenaline to a tired team. Manuel Pellegrini is particularly impressed.

'I have encouraged the team to play for him,' he says, although it's not strictly true.

Cristiano has reassured the club directors, who were worried about the possibility of him going out partying, getting into scandals with girls and appearing on the covers of the tabloids every week. In actual fact, he has been out very little and has proven himself a consummate professional who puts his club duties first. When he has a day off or a holiday that's another matter. Ultimately, Cristiano has divided public opinion down the middle, resulting in the 'anti-Cristianos' and the staunch loyalists, each ready to defend their corner.

Most importantly for the club, the most expensive player in footballing history has proven extremely profitable thanks to his global image, his goal-scoring abilities, and good marketing. He has completely overtaken Florentino's other two 'galactic' signings, Kaká and Benzema, neither of whom have managed to live up to what was expected of them. His balance sheet is definitely in the black.

But it's still not good enough as far as the man himself is concerned, admitting that he is never satisfied with his achievements. 'I feel sad and frustrated at not having won a single title,' he says, summing up his first season in an interview with *Público*. 'We are all a little bit to blame. But I'm not surprised that the finger has been pointed at Pellegrini. Football is wonderful but it has its own rulebook. And one rule is that the coach is always the weakest member of the team. It has always been and will always be that way. There is not much more you can say.'

He explains that the new team has been 'a work in progress. There have been many new signings and you can't build a team overnight. We have some great players, that's undeniable, but our team is not fully formed, we're not completely integrated and polished like Barcelona.' On the subject of his rivals, he adds: 'Barcelona scored 99 points in La Liga. It's obvious that they won fair and square. Anyone who loves football will tell you that you have to admire a good performance. Barça play very attractive football, it's very well executed. As a football fan I would be lying if I said that I didn't enjoy watching them play. I like watching them, but I also love watching Real Madrid. We still don't have a perfect team, we're not as polished as they are, but we will be. We just need time to win the titles and I'm sure that next season will be an entirely different story.'

But before we get carried away talking about next season, there's the South Africa World Cup to contend with first. What better way to draw a line under the frustrations of this season and move on to better things.

Chapter 21

Spain v Portugal

*'I think Spain have a good chance of winning the World Cup,
but I'm not afraid of them in the slightest.'*

Ronaldo's performance with Portugal in the qualifiers has
been null and void in terms of goals. It's been fifteen months
since he scored, but he's not too worried. And paraphrasing
what van Nistelrooy said to Higuaín to cheer him up at Real
Madrid, he maintains that 'Goals are like ketchup. Once
they start flowing they come in sudden bursts, all at once.'

At a press release in Magaliesberg – his first since arriving in South Africa on 13 June – a smiling and relaxed
Portugal captain indicates that the team are 'fine, prepared
and motivated. Everyone is doing great and I'm very happy
to be a part of this group.'

Addressing his own performance, he adds: 'I want to
play well, I want to be the best in the tournament. I'm not
saying I'll necessarily be the top goal-scorer or anything like
that, but I'm going to give it my all and try and be the best.
It's always my aim to be the best, but we'll see. I really want
to do well in this World Cup and I believe I can succeed. But
when I say that I want to play well, have a good tournament
and help my team win, that doesn't mean to say I have to
prove myself to anyone.'

Group G sees Portugal up against Brazil, North Korea
and the Ivory Coast – a tough ask. Cristiano believes it is

the most difficult group in the competition, adding that the Ivory Coast match is crucial. 'It's extremely important to hit the ground running in the World Cup.'

If Portugal get through the group stages they could face Spain's Red Fury. 'It would be great to face Spain,' says CR7 in reply to the obvious question from the Spanish press. 'It would mean that we've made it through the group stage, which is our main objective. After that we'll see what happens. Spain are one of the favourites, I think they have a good chance of winning the World Cup. They have a great team, but I'm not afraid of them in the slightest and if we face them we'll try to beat them. In the knockout stages anything is possible.'

Portugal make it through the group stages – unbeaten and the only team of the 32 World Cup finalists to have kept a completely clean sheet. It's a continuation of a great run of form: they have only conceded one goal in eleven matches (in a friendly against Cameroon) and they remain undefeated in eighteen matches. Portuguese selector Carlos Queiroz, Sir Alex Ferguson's former right-hand man and ex-Real coach, has created an indestructible defence line-up. And goalkeeper Eduardo has been a pleasant surprise. It's been difficult to get past him.

Their score-line reads 0-0 against the Ivory Coast, 7-0 against North Korea and 0-0 against Brazil. With five points, Portugal have made it through to the final sixteen after coming second in the group to the Brazilian Canaries. On 29 June at the Green Point stadium in Cape Town they will face Spain, who have come top in Group H despite a defeat in their opening match against Ottmar Hitzfeld's Switzerland. It's the clash all the pundits predicted at the start of the tournament.

Portugal v Spain is a special match, not just because they are two great teams and not just because of the neighbourly rivalry – be it historic, cultural, social or sporting. It's a peninsula derby 'with the same intensity as Argentina-Brazil', explains Queiroz. The two national teams have never played each other in a World Cup. Of the 32 times they have played each other, Spain have won fifteen, Portugal five and twelve have been drawn. In Euro 2004, hosts Portugal knocked Spain out of the tournament with a 1-0 win on 20 June. Six years on, the Red Fury are ready to even the score.

And let's not forget the Cristiano factor. The number 7 has terrorised the Spanish defenders in La Liga, he has won entire games on his own, he's the leader of the Portuguese team and star of the World Cup along with Leo Messi. It's true that with Portugal he hasn't put on quite such a stellar performance, and he hasn't succeeded in showing the fans what he has shown the Spanish crowds during his first year at Real. But against North Korea in South Africa he has broken his scoring curse and netted six of Portugal's seven goals. One of them is a particular crowd-pleaser: as he tries to get past goalkeeper Ri Myong-Guk, the ball deflects off the Korean, spins over Cristiano's head and lands on the back of his neck. He manages to control it, heading it back into the air and then scoring. His two-year goal drought with the Red and Greens is over and he is awarded best player in the group phase. He is seen as the number one threat in the upcoming match against Spain.

Spanish coach Vicente del Bosque praises the Portuguese star, but he says: 'I don't think we are obsessing over Cristiano. The most important thing is to focus on Portugal as a team. They have shown themselves to be very adept, both in defence and up front. They have come to this World Cup on top form, ready to fight for it.' Cesc Fàbregas agrees, telling Spanish national daily newspaper *El País*: 'Portugal as a team are much more on form than Cristiano. They're powerful and extremely dangerous on the counterattack. They're a very competitive team and their defence is not to be messed with. Alves is the Porto captain, Carvalho has made a name for himself at Chelsea … '

Nonetheless, the obsession with Cristiano Ronaldo is alive and well. To the Spanish fans, Portugal *is* Ronaldo, despite all the statements to the contrary from the Red Fury camp. Besides, the fans are dying to see how he will fair against his own team-mates, Sergio Ramos and Iker Casillas, as well as against Barça defenders Piqué and Puyol, whom he has faced in some historic duels, both during his time at Man United and in the last season at Real Madrid. Everyone in the Spanish defence is afraid of him.

Álvaro Arbeloa has played against him during his time at Liverpool: 'There is no magic formula for putting the brakes on Cristiano. That's exactly why he's one of the best players in the world – most people try to stop him and fail. If he's near the box you have to stay on top of him and try to disrupt his shot at goal. If you give him space to run he'll put enormous pressure on you. His run is devastating.' As the rival captain, Casillas knows Cristiano's technique and shots by heart – and he is even more categorical than his team-mates: 'When a player like him is inspired, it's almost impossible to stop him.'

It's not just the opposition that recognise his talents. Bookmaker William Hill is offering 7/1 on him scoring against Spain – the best odds on any Portuguese player, despite the fact that they are not favourites to win – a price of 2.62 against 1.44 on Spain according to the bookies.

'They can still win without being the favourites,' says Francois Pienaar, South African rugby captain and 1995 world champion. The man who inspired Clint Eastwood's film *Invictus*, starring Matt Damon and Morgan Freeman, visits the Portuguese team the night before the match in an effort to psych up Cristiano & Co. Carlos Queiroz has invited him to chat to the players, explaining that 'he is a symbol of South Africa – the man who led a mixed race team for the first time. They were the underdogs but they became world champions. He represents the idea that anything is possible.'

The Iberian derby takes place against an impressive backdrop: Green Point stadium has thirteen stands and 62,955 spectators, not to mention a view of Table Mountain and two converging oceans. Almeida has been reintroduced as a centre forward, leaving Ronaldo free to command the wing. The Portuguese captain has finally won over Queiroz to claim his desired spot. After the clash with Brazil where he played in the number 9 position, Cristiano tried to stay diplomatic: 'The gaffer knows I don't like playing up front, it's not my preferred position. But the important thing is that we qualified,' he explained. 'If we had needed Cristiano to play in goal he would have played in goal,' responded the coach. Nonetheless, against Spain he lets him play where he feels most comfortable.

The Spanish selectors opt for the same line-up that beat Chile. Xabi Alonso has recovered and Del Bosque bets on Fernando Torres once again as a partner up front for David Villa. The national anthems play and Cristiano remains silent. It's a bad sign, almost a premonition of how his performance will pan out. It's a disaster. Four shots, two on target. In the sixteenth minute a long free kick lands safely into the hands of Casillas. In the 27th he repeats the move from 33 yards, the Spanish captain doesn't manage to stop it completely, but luckily it's out of the reach of the Portuguese strikers.

Other than that Cristiano makes two passes into the box, he is fouled once and makes two failed attempts at a run.

The only moment worth mentioning is when he crosses with a *rabona*, a speciality of his, where one leg crosses behind the other to kick the ball, avoiding having to turn. That's about it in terms of his performance. He starts on the right, later moves to the left wing and then plays in the centre in the number 9 position after Queiroz brings on Dany for Almeida. But no matter where he plays, he fails to make an impact. Capdevila, Sergio Ramos and Puyol all manage to block him, with a little help from Villa, Busquets and Xabi Alonso. 'They managed to make Ronaldo go virtually unnoticed. They rendered him powerless,' explains Del Bosque later. 'It's more of a compliment to them than it is a criticism of Cristiano.'

At the end of the first half, with the score-line still at 0-0, the number 7 is the first to head for the dressing room. He is not happy with how the team are playing: too reserved, too sensible, not decisive enough and far too trapped in their own half. He is not happy with how the first 45 minutes have played out.

In the second half, after David Villa's goal in the 67th minute, he is seen standing alone, hands on hips, looking over at the dugout, as if demanding an explanation, pleading for some help and advice in order to turn their fortunes around. But Carlos Queiroz doesn't have the answers. At the final whistle, Spain celebrates a win which will take them into the quarter-finals. Portuguese goalkeeper Eduardo, who has performed miracles but was powerless in the face of Villa's double shot, is sitting on the ground crying into his hands. Iker Casillas puts his arm around him.

Cristiano Ronaldo walks away from his defeated and broken team. He is booed by the Spanish fans, and even some of the Portuguese. The camera follows him closely as he heads for the dressing room, his face expressionless. Suddenly he turns and spits – it's unclear whether it's directed at the cameraman or the ground. Either way it's an ugly gesture and the Barcelona press pounce on it, criticising the Real player's behaviour. His pointed statement after the match also sparks plenty of anger: 'How do I explain Portugal's elimination? Ask Carlos Queiroz.' It is not a great example of how a captain should bow out of a World Cup.

The coach takes the opportunity to respond at the press conference: 'While I'm in charge of the national team, if the size of the shirt is too small for anybody they do not need to be here ... Nobody is above the national selection and never will be while I'm here.' But when asked if he perhaps should not have given the important captaincy role to Cristiano, he is annoyed: 'That question is out of order. [He] is our leader, our captain ... you must believe that we did it for the right reasons.'

Former Portugal captain and hero Luís Figo disagrees: 'Regardless of failure or elimination, a captain always has to defend his team. Even if he was the one who took the biggest hit in terms of his reputation. Above all, he should put on a brave face for the team throughout, even in the most difficult moments.'

Cristiano's new coach José Mourinho comes out in defence of his player via a statement made to the Portuguese press agency: 'With me, Cristiano will not have to shoulder all the responsibility. In my team, when we win, we are all winners. When we lose, I am the one who loses ... That's why Ronaldo can relax and enjoy his holiday. I will not allow anyone to put all the pressure on him. Players become stars because they are the best, but everyone needs the support of their team and Portugal lost because Spain was better.'

Respected Benfica coach Jorge Jesús also sides with Cristiano, maintaining that his statement was to be expected. 'He has what it takes,' he explains. 'And it's not just about whether the press value him; throughout Spain he is a revered and respected player. Here in Portugal, not so much … but that's just how the Portuguese are.'

A handful of advocates aside, Cristiano's behaviour is causing quite a stir and eventually Jorge Mendes's agency GestiFute releases a statement on the player's behalf. 'I am suffering and I have the right to suffer alone. When I said people should ask the coach [why Portugal were eliminated], it was because he was at the press conference and I didn't feel I was in the right frame of mind to explain things. As the captain I have always taken my responsibilities seriously and will continue to do so, but at that moment I would not have been able to string together more than three or four coherent sentences. I never thought that such a simple comment would provoke such a reaction. Don't go looking for phantoms – you won't find any.'

Unfortunately for Cristiano, his other World Cup phantoms are much more real than the polemic sparked by his comments to the press. The biggest thing haunting the most expensive player in the world – the national team captain, the universal superstar, who has scored a total of 159 goals during his time at Sporting, Man United and Real – is his woeful World Cup balance sheet. In Germany he was protected from criticism because he was only 21 and Portugal put on such a good performance anyway. But his contributions were one penalty against Iran and one against England.

In South Africa he has played the full length of each of the four matches and he has managed 21 shots on target (third after Messi and the Ghanaian Gyan), but he has only scored one goal. There has been no sign of the dazzling footballer, the competitor, the talented athlete, the player who never gives up and always wants to win. 'Did the formation limit Cristiano, or was he the one who was unable to give more?' asks Lisbon sports paper *Record*. It's a fair question. Perhaps the answer will emerge in Euro 2012.

Chapter 22

Fatherhood

*'Of course I change my son's nappies. It's not my favourite thing
in the world, but I do it.'*

'It is with great joy and emotion that I inform I have recently
become father to a baby boy. As agreed with the baby's
mother, who prefers to have her identity kept confidential,
my son will be under my exclusive guardianship. No further
information will be provided on this subject and I request
everyone to fully respect my right to privacy (and that of the
child) at least on issues as personal as these are.'

On 3 July 2010, Cristiano Ronaldo announces on
Facebook and Twitter that he has become a father. The
Real number 7 shocks the world with this statement, which
comes just a few days after Portugal's elimination from the
South Africa World Cup. It is a complete surprise because
no one even knew that Ronaldo was in any kind of long
term relationship, let alone expecting.

The last photos picturing the player with a woman were
taken in May, when the paparazzi snapped Ronaldo and
Irina Shayk on a luxury cruise near Corsica. But Irina didn't
look pregnant, and she doesn't seem particularly thrilled
about the arrival of CR7's new offspring. The day after
the news goes public around the world, the model writes
the following on Facebook and Twitter: 'Why have you
done this? You've had a baby with another woman without

telling me. You have broken my heart. Thanks for making me cry.'

But the message is a fake. The Russian's modelling agency releases a statement to put an end to speculation: 'Unfortunately certain individuals take it upon themselves to create fake profiles or post fake messages for some reason. Miss Shayk has currently suspended her Twitter account while rumours of this nature are circulating.'

It's not the statement that puts an end to speculation so much as the couple's show of affection, making it clear that the relationship is still intact. After Ronaldo goes public with the news of his son's arrival, he and Irina are seen in New York together. The footballer spends the trip shopping and relaxing, while his girlfriend enjoys the New York nightlife with a number of other models. They have been seen canoodling in the pool of their Manhattan hotel and dining together at an expensive restaurant. Photos and sources confirm that they are still very much an item and that there don't seem to be any secrets or misunderstandings between the two.

And what about the baby? He is in Marina de Vilamoura in the Algarve, being looked after by Ronaldo's mother, Dolores. His sister Katia, who is spending the summer there, reveals: 'Cristiano is very, very happy. What father wouldn't be?' Regarding the baby, she adds: 'He has dark eyes and brown hair like Cristiano and he is very well settled – he just eats and sleeps.'

Portuguese television channel RTP announces that he is called Cristiano Junior, and that at birth he measured 53 centimetres and weighed 4.3 kilograms. He was born on 17 June, two days after his father played with the national team against the Ivory Coast in South Africa. This is undoubtedly all useful information, but what really interests the

British tabloids, the celebrity magazines and the Portuguese media is the mystery surrounding the mother. Who is she? Why has she relinquished custody of the child? The conspiracy theories are flowing thick and fast.

Portuguese daily newspaper *Diário de Notícias* claims that the baby was conceived artificially the previous year in San Diego, with the help of an American surrogate – just around the time that the footballer was on holiday in California and was seen out celebrating his Real Madrid signing with Paris Hilton at a private party in Los Angeles. The paper claims, Dolores, Katia and Cristiano's other sister Elma came to the States to deal with the legal proceedings which would allow them to take the baby back to Portugal.

The tabloid *Correio da Manhã* says that Cristiano Ronaldo has paid to have a baby, while *The Sun* claims the player has shelled out no fewer than sixteen million Euros to buy the silence of the mother and ensure that she would give up her right to see the child. That's just one theory. Other Portuguese media think that Cristiano Junior is the product of a one-night stand and that the young mother wants nothing to do with the baby.

The soap opera doesn't end there. Six months later, the *Daily Mirror* announces that the identity of the woman who gave birth to the Real number 7's son has been discovered. According to the tabloid, she is a twenty-year-old student from London. It's a theory which Cristiano's ex-girlfriend Nereida Gallardo supports in a Spanish TV interview. The model from Mallorca says that the girl contacted her on Facebook months before the birth was announced, claiming that she was expecting Cristiano's child.

Months later, the press claim that the girl regrets having given up custody of the child and says she is ready to fight to get him back. Sources who claim to be close to the girl tell the media: 'She feels as if she has sold her soul. She is living like a millionaire, but she will never be able to tell her friends and family what happened and that makes her feel extremely lonely.'

But the plot is about to thicken once again. In an interview with *The Sun*, Katia Aveiro adds to the mystery. 'There is no woman calling. There is no mother here, there are no phone calls, nothing,' she says. 'The mother has died. The baby has no mother. The child is ours. I am not going to comment on how he came into the world, but I can guarantee you that he is my brother's son, my nephew, our flesh and blood. My mother is now his mother – she is the one who looks after him 24 hours a day.'

The first photos of little Cristiano, published exclusively in the Portuguese magazine *TV Mais*, show him in his grandmother's arms. The baby's face is deliberately pixelated, but it is possible to make out a child with dark skin tones and similar characteristics to his father. Grandma Dolores is taking care of him at Cristiano's home in Madrid. On 8 December, she takes him to the Bernabéu to watch his father play for the first time. Ronaldo has already dedicated various goals to his son. But this is a special occasion. In the 50th minute, after scoring Real's second goal of the night against Auxerre in the Champions League group match, he mimes sucking on a dummy and waves in the direction of his private box. The cameras catch a glimpse of the boy and at that moment Cristiano Junior steals the limelight from his father. All eyes in the stadium are on the baby.

Shortly afterwards, the Whites' number 7 breaks his silence over his recent fatherhood in an interview with Real Madrid TV. He admits that becoming a father has changed him: 'It's a different type of responsibility. I am still learning. It's a feeling I can't easily put into words. Waking up in the morning and seeing someone who is your own flesh and blood is amazing. This is a very special time in my life. You could say that I am feeling very content. I am always happier when things are going well – with my family, the club, my friends …'

He reveals that he has no problem taking on the role of hands-on father: 'Of course I change my son's nappies. It's not my favourite thing in the world, but I do it.' He talks about the future, the possibility of more children, marriage, and what he would like his son to do when he grows up: 'I would love for him to play football and be my successor, but let's wait and see. My son will be whoever he wants to be.' And he says that, although Cristiano Junior usually goes to sleep without any problem, on one occasion when his father was playing a match he cried all day, and they couldn't get him to calm down and go to sleep until he had seen his daddy score a goal.

Chapter 23

53 goals

*'Scoring 50 goals is no mean feat and I'm thrilled with such
a great personal achievement. But I'm not completely satisfied
because I wanted to win more titles.'*

He is not a centre forward. Mourinho has never thought
of him that way and he has almost never made him play in
that position. Yet he has managed to set some extraordinary records in Spanish footballing history – 53 goals across
three competitions in the 2010-11 season: La Liga, the Copa
del Rey and the Champions League. It is a figure which seals
his place as a shooting machine and top goal-scorer of all
the European leagues, winning him the European Golden
Shoe award. He has scored 28 with his right foot, eight with
his left and four with his head; six from outside the area,
eight from the penalty spot and four from direct free kicks.

On 21 May, the final matchday of the league, it only takes
him five minutes to get one past Esteban, the Almería goalkeeper. In the second half he scores his second, kick-starting
the celebrations at the Bernabéu. The fans chant his name,
while Cristiano raises his arms to the sky and looks towards
the VIP box where his family and friends are sitting. He has
just scored his 40th league goal in 34 matches.

'Some say it's 41, others say 40 … I let Pepe have one
of them,' jokes Cristiano after a match which finishes 8-1.
He is referring to a free kick which deflected off the White

defender's back and ended up in the net. It's a goal which some authorities attribute to him, others to Pepe. But these are minor details – no one else in Spanish football has come close to matching his achievements. Cristiano has smashed the records of Athletic Bilbao's Telmo Zarra, who scored 38 league goals in 30 matches in the 1950-51 season, and Real's own Hugo Sánchez, who scored 38 in 35 matches in the 1989-90 season. The Mexican scored at a rate of once every 80 minutes, Zarra once every 71.05 and Ronaldo once every 72.

'Cristiano has had a truly heroic season – he has been a generous player all year. Whoever scores 40 goals is generous to the team and a lethal weapon for winning matches,' declares Real Madrid general manager Jorge Valdano. 'I came here today to see him make footballing history. He is a tremendous player.' Even in Real's final four league matches, when Barça had already done enough to secure the title, CR7 scored a total of eleven goals. Four against Sevilla at the Sánchez Pizjuán (2-6), three against Getafe at the Bernabéu (4-0), two against Villarreal at El Madrigal and the two against Almería. A goal-scoring machine.

'Let's see who'll beat my record now,' jokes Ronaldo, who has already broken all of his own. In the 2007-08 season with Manchester United he scored a total of 42 goals, while during his first season at Real Madrid he racked up a decent 33.

Not only has Cristiano scored more goals than any individual, he has also scored more than some La Liga teams in the 2010-11 season. His 40 league goals beat Sporting de Gijón (35), Deportivo de La Coruña (31), Hércules (36) and Almería (36). Compared to other championships outside Spain, Ronaldo's stats are on another level. He has scored almost as many goals as the two top scorers of the

Premier League put together, Man United's Berbatov and Manchester City's Tévez, who scored 21 apiece.

'I'm delighted to have won the 'Pichichi' [award for the top European goal-scorer] and to have broken the Spanish record,' says Ronaldo. 'I want to thank those who have helped me, the coach for believing in me and my team-mates. I am generous because my team-mates are generous to me and football is a team sport. Winning the Pichichi and the Golden Shoe is wonderful, because they are the result of the collective efforts of my team-mates, the coaches, all the staff and directors, and the support of the fans.'

Real's number 7 is thrilled that the team has managed to score 102 La Liga goals and 148 across all three competitions, becoming the second-highest-scoring team in the Whites' history. (The 1959-60 team scored 158 goals in 46 matches.) 'I want to congratulate the team,' says Cristiano. 'The boss wanted lots of goals and to end on a high ready for the best possible start to next season.' Because, records aside, this season has not gone exactly as the Portuguese would have hoped and he is not completely satisfied. Of all the goals he scored, only one was decisive – the one in the final of the Copa del Rey, a stunning header in extra time which beat Barcelona goalie Pinto and enabled Real to claim their only title of the season.

But it's not enough for CR7. 'Real aspires to win all the titles and I would have preferred to score half the number of goals but win La Liga or the Champions League,' he explains in an interview with *El partido de las 12 – The Midnight Match*, a show which runs from midnight every night on the Cadena COPE radio station.

On balance, his personal star is on the rise. 'I have felt a lot more comfortable and you could even say this has been my best season.' He gives his performance and that of the team an eight or nine out of ten. But there's no denying that Real Madrid and Cristiano have had a difficult year thanks to their eternal rivals: Pep Guardiola's Barcelona and, above all, Leo Messi.

Chapter 24

Cristiano and Leo

'I don't compete against Messi, I compete against myself and
against all the teams in La Liga.'

Two footballers are sitting on a sofa, chatting. 'God sent
me down to Earth to teach people how to play football,'
says Cristiano Ronaldo. 'Don't be daft, I didn't send anyone
down to Earth,' replies Messi.

It's a joke which has done the rounds online and perfectly illustrates how the fans view the rivalry between the
Portuguese and the Argentine. Aged 27 and 24 respectively,
the two superstars share a similar career trajectory and
desire to win, but their style both on and off the pitch could
not be more different.

'Cristiano Ronaldo subscribes to Euclid's theory: the
shortest distance between two points is a straight line. Not
only that, you have to blast down that line at warp speed
until you reach the goal,' muses award-winning Spanish
writer Manuel Vicent in *El País*. 'Leo Messi prefers Einstein:
the shortest distance between two points is always a curve,
and the only way to arrive is if you zigzag unpredictably like
a careering swine trying to dodge the axe. Ronaldo inspires
passion – Messi, admiration.' And that's why they are considered the gods of the modern footballing world.

It is true to an extent that Cristiano likes to compete with
himself. When prompted to reflect on the comparisons

made with Messi, he replies: 'It doesn't bother me in the slightest. My personality and my style of football are completely different from his. I'm only interested in my football and winning with Real Madrid.' He insists he is not jealous of Messi, but there is no doubt that Leo is like the kryptonite to his Superman. The Argentine represents an obsession for him, his Achilles' heel. It's not a coincidence that from Spain, to Cyprus, to Bosnia, rival fans chant 'Messi, Messi, Messi!' at him. They know it will touch a nerve.

Leo has been compared with Cristiano for years. He is seen as his direct rival in the race to become the best in the world. And if the Portuguese publicly scoffs at the idea that he should feel any jealousy towards Messi and denies that privately he tries to break him down bit by bit, it is widely claimed that there has been an atmosphere of extreme tension between Cristiano and the 'little one', as he is known, ever since he toppled the former Ballon d'Or off the number one spot.

Real Madrid insiders say that seeing Cristiano Ronaldo in front of the TV watching Messi play is priceless. When his agent Jorge Mendes is watching with him, he tries to calm him down by saying that people don't understand anything about football, that the Barça number 10 doesn't deserve to be the best in the world.

It is true that in the 2010-11 season Cristiano has left Leo in the dust in La Liga, scoring nine goals more than the Argentine. But Messi didn't really consider himself to be in the running for top goal-scorer, preferring instead to prepare for and focus on the Champions League final.

Cristiano has scored more often and in a wider variety of ways. He has also been fouled more often. But Messi is ahead in terms of runs and passes, as well as being the king of assists (nineteen, to Ronaldo's nine). In the three main competitions the two are neck and neck on 53 goals, although the Flea has taken home the Liga and Champions trophies that Ronaldo so desired. They have just gone head to head again in their third consecutive Ballon d'Or duel, the prestigious trophy that Cristiano won first and wants to win twice more in the next five years.

The comparisons between CR7 and the Flea have been made constantly ever since the two started to shine at Man United and Barcelona. It began as a football rivalry but has since transferred to all aspects of their lives. There are university courses which analyse and compare their exposure in the media, and there is even a brand war. Cristiano endorses Nike, Messi Adidas; Cristiano wears Armani, Messi wears Dolce & Gabbana; Cristiano has a Time Force watch while Messi's is Audemars Piguet; when it comes to what they put in their cars, the Portuguese uses Castrol while the Argentine prefers Repsol; and finally, the White number 7 drinks Soccerade, while the *Blaugrana* number 10 drinks Gatorade.

According to *Sports Illustrated* Messi wins in the financial stakes, making 31 million Euros a year to Ronaldo's 27.5. But Cristiano is ahead on social media, with more than three million Twitter followers and 30 million Facebook fans, just a bit behind some of the biggest popstars like Lady Gaga. Messi only created his Facebook page in the spring of 2011, and as a result he is lagging behind with only seven million fans.

But all these comparisons bring us back to the same question: who is the best? It's a question asked thousands of times in the newspapers, on the radio, on TV and on blogs, and everyone from coaches, footballers, pundits and plain old fans have been swept up in the debate. Everyone has their own opinion.

Former Barça coach and three-time Ballon d'Or winner Johan Cruyff maintains that Ronaldo is a 'more physical' player, while Messi is technically more gifted. The ex-Netherlands player thinks it would be difficult for the Portuguese to reach the heights of Pelé, Maradona, Di Stéfano – all very technical players. Former Real and current England coach Fabio Capello says: 'It's difficult to decide which one is better. They are both very good but in different ways. Messi is unpredictable, no one is capable of doing what he does. But Cristiano is very powerful and has incredible speed.' But when asked who he would choose for his squad, Capello jokes: 'Cristiano speaks English. But Messi speaks football.'

'For me, Messi is the best, but both of them are up there on the list of greats,' says Sergio 'El Checho' Batista, former Argentine manager. 'Leo has amazing skills, he's incredibly talented, and he has a left-footed shot that many players envy. Cristiano hits the ball very well, he is strong and he moves very fast.'

'They are both top players,' agrees Portugal manager Paulo Bento. 'If they didn't play in the same country there wouldn't be a debate about who was better. I am proud to coach a player like Cristiano, he is the consummate professional.'

Real Madrid captain Íker Casillas is convinced that 'they are the two best players in the world. Some people prefer the strength and power of Cristiano's headers, other prefer Lionel's speed and dribbling. I choose Ronaldo, since he's my player.' Valencia defender Ángel Dealbert also prefers Cristiano: 'He is a more complete player than Messi, in the sense that he plays equally well with both feet, and his head. He can push forward and he can shoot. Messi loses points when it comes to headers and playing with the right foot.'

But former Real Madrid player José María 'Guti' Gutiérrez feels that 'Cristiano has fallen short of the mark in some important matches, something Messi never does. The real superstars are the players that can rise to the occasion at the highest level.' Brazilian prodigy Neymar who plays for Santos says he likes both players: 'They are the icons of the footballing world, but at the moment Messi is the best player in the world.'

Opinions, statistics, videos – and even marks out of ten, as if they were still in school. But everything serves to add to the discussion and help clarify the debate. A number of years ago, for example, the *Guardian* asked former Northern Ireland striker Gerry Armstrong and former England striker Trevor Francis (now both TV commentators) if they thought Cristiano was better than Messi. Francis said no, while Armstrong said yes.

Madrid sports paper *Marca* tries to make a decision based on technical ability alone:

Performance with the team:
Cristiano Ronaldo 7-8 **Lionel Messi**

Individual technique:
Cristiano Ronaldo 9-9 Lionel Messi

Physical fitness:
Cristiano Ronaldo 10-7 Lionel Messi

Speed:
Cristiano Ronaldo 9-8 Lionel Messi

Dribbling:
Cristiano Ronaldo 8-10 **Lionel Messi**

Shooting:
Cristiano Ronaldo 9-8 Lionel Messi

Passing:
Cristiano Ronaldo 9-9 Lionel Messi

Leadership:
Cristiano Ronaldo 9-7 Lionel Messi

The result is obvious but it should also be disregarded because it should be made clear that *Marca* is a publication primarily read by Real fans and always takes the side of 'the White House'. It is unlikely that Messi would ever win in one of their comparisons.

Italian paper *La Gazzetta dello Sport* also scores the two out of ten:

Tactical abilities:
Cristiano 8.5, Leo 9

Dribbling:
Cristiano 9, Leo 10

Speed:
Cristiano 9, Leo 9

Headers:
Cristiano 7.5, Leo 6

Right foot:
Cristiano 9, Leo 8

Left foot:
Cristiano 8, Leo 10

This time Messi wins by just one point.

CR7 versus Messi has earned its place as a classic derby. Sport is fuelled by rivalries between athletes, teams and countries, as well as by comparisons between different periods in each of their histories. Memory is a fundamental element of the game and pitting one person against another is a favourite pastime which has always divided world media opinion. Boxers Ali and Foreman, racing drivers Prost and Senna, Italian cyclists Gino Bartali and Fausto Coppi, tennis stars Borg and McEnroe, basketball players Magic Johnson and Larry Bird, motorcycle racers Valentino Rossi and Jorge Lorenzo, athletes Carl Lewis and Ben Johnson …

But in football it is rare to find a player considered to be a 'great' who can also be overshadowed by a contemporary. Pelé, Cruyff, Maradona and Di Stéfano never overlapped in terms of their time at the top. But now there is a personal duel between two stars which has become a one-on-one ever since the Portuguese arrived in La Liga. And the last season has been a rollercoaster of a ride, over the course of five derbies and a friendly between Portugal and Argentina.

The *Clásico* drama begins on Monday 29 November 2010. It is a strange day for a Barça-Real match, but there are general elections in Catalonia on the Sunday, so it is better not to compound the politics with added drama. Adverts about the game have hailed it as the most closely matched *Clásico* for years, indicating the possibility of a transfer of power from Barcelona to Real Madrid. Why? Because, they say, Cristiano is better than Messi, because Mourinho is not Manuel Pellegrini, nor is he Bernd Schuster or Juande Ramos or even Fabio Capello.

The Portuguese coach is the one who was capable of crushing the *Blaugrana*'s collective efforts from the Inter dugout just six months earlier, denying Guardiola and co. their ticket to the Champions League final in Madrid. He is the man chosen by the Real president as the antidote to the Catalan magic. A coach who, from the highest position in La Liga (unbeaten, and one point ahead of Barça on 32), questions Barcelona's successes and accuses the referees and rival managers of handing them all the power.

Cristiano limits himself to saying that the blue and claret team play more of a 'tiki-taka' game and the Whites play with the sole objective of scoring as quickly as possible. He says that Barcelona are still an extremely difficult team to beat, even if they haven't won six titles this year. 'They are just as good as they have always been over the last few years, a very strong team, especially at home. They have demonstrated that they can give us a run for our money in La Liga.' He doesn't mention Lionel, preferring to emphasise how well Real Madrid have been doing: 'We know that we are in a good place. That's why it will be a good match. May the best team win at the Nou Camp. And the best team will be Real Madrid.'

Sadly, Cristiano loses his bet. On 29 November at the Nou Camp, Barça teach their visitors a lesson in majestic football, while the Whites have no idea how to respond to the back-and-forth style of play which leaves their formation in tatters. By the end of a cold and rainy night at the Nou Camp, the goals number five and they could have easily been six, seven or eight without anyone calling foul play. Real Madrid is drowning in deep, cold waters. Cristiano Ronaldo has been almost invisible. He is forced to run against the current, waiting in the pouring rain for passes which never arrive. The only moments worth noting are a free kick from 45 yards which is just wide and a one-on-one with Valdés which goes nowhere.

Other moments are noteworthy for the wrong reasons, after the tension of the match causes him to lose his nerve and get himself into trouble. After the ball goes out and lands near the home team's dugout, Pep Guardiola recovers it, dummies a throw-in, and then drops it back on the ground ready for Cristiano, who has just arrived to pick up the ball and continue the game. The Portuguese responds by pushing the rival coach, who staggers backwards. Andrés Iniesta and Víctor Valdés intervene: cue insults and more pushing. To prevent the situation from getting out of control, referee Iturralde González quickly shows Cristiano the yellow card. The fans in the stands start to whistle at him, which only makes him face up to his opponents with more rage. But he still can't get past Alves and Abidal.

Nothing else remarkable happens, save for a moment of crossed wires with Mou. The number 7 goes over to the dugout to ask for instructions – or perhaps for the magic solution to the problem. But the Special One remains stony faced, and sits down on the bench without saying a word. Ronaldo is left to face his problems on the pitch alone and that's the end of that. He has failed to score in a single one of the six matches he has played against Barça so far.

But Messi hasn't scored either. He has never scored against a team managed by Mourinho, be it Chelsea, Inter or Real. This match breaks a run of ten consecutive games in which he has scored, but he has been generous and helped set up goals three and four for David Villa with surgical precision. The Flea has ruffled Carvalho, Lass, Pepe and Sergio Ramos's composure, and after a senseless foul on the Argentine in the 92nd minute and a punch-up between Puyol and Xavi, the red card finally comes out. Ramos has lost control, which is not unusual in such a game of nerves, particularly when the Whites know that Mourinho's game plan is still under construction, his ideas still need fine tuning, and he still doesn't know how to beat his eternal rivals.

Cristiano Ronaldo leaves the stadium without offering any statement or any explanation as to what went on out there. Captain Casillas also stays quiet.

Interestingly, this is the first time a team led by Mourinho has been beaten 5-0. At the press conference, the manager assumes an air of calm for once. 'It is a very easy defeat to get over,' he says. 'It is not one of those games where we deserved to win and then lost, or where we continually hit the woodwork. There was one team that played well and another that played badly. You have to be good natured. When you win important titles then you have a reason to cry with happiness. When you lose like we did today you don't have a right to cry, you have to get back to work. We'll live to play another day.' But the Special One will have to wait almost five months for another shot at Barça, and then it will be the first in a marathon of *Clásicos* – four in less than a month.

But first, on 9 February 2011, Cristiano and Leo will meet in Geneva in a Portugal-Argentina friendly to continue their unresolved duel. The enormous sense of anticipation surrounding the match means the 33,000 tickets are sold out in minutes and are now going for at least 600 Euros online, six times the original price. The match will be broadcast across five continents and will be followed by 250 journalists from sixteen countries. The two main protagonists have not made prematch statements, while the two coaches try their best to emphasise that this match is Portugal versus Argentina, not Ronaldo versus Messi – with little success.

Referee Massimo Busacca blows the whistle and seven-times world Formula One champion Michael Schumacher takes the honorary first kick. After nineteen minutes of play, Messi delights the crowd with one of his famous slaloms. He takes off from the left hand side of his own half, dodges past opponents, and offers the ball to Di María with a sharp pass which evades the Portuguese defender. The Real player crosses the ball into Eduardo's goal: 1-0 to Argentina.

Shortly afterwards Cristiano equalises, more by chance than on his own merit. On the edge of the area, Nani manages to confuse the Argentine defence. His pass doesn't quite reach Almeida and the ball ends up dead in front of goal. Cristiano only has to beat Romero to the punch to make it 1-1. Now the fans have really got themselves a show and it's clear that the *Albiceleste* number 10 and the Red and Green number 7 are the real stars. The other twenty men on the pitch are secondary by comparison.

But in the 60th minute, Portugal coach Paulo Bento replaces Cristiano with Danny. The Portuguese think the match is more or less over. But the Argentines are hungry for results, and they push forward in search of the victory. In the final minute, Coentrão provokes a penalty, giving Messi the chance to score, win the match, and level the score with Cristiano. The show is over and it's time to return to the daily grind of the Spanish championship.

On 16 April 2011, it's the return leg of the *Clásico* at the Bernabéu. Nothing has changed since the last round: Pep Guardiola's team are still top of La Liga. With sixteen consecutive wins they have broken the record previously held by the 1960-61 Real Madrid team (which included Puskas, Di Stéfano, Gento and Santamaría), and they have an eight-point lead at the top of the table. Four days earlier they beat Shakhtar Donetsk to go through to the Champions League semi-finals, where the draw has dictated that they will play Real yet again.

Real have knocked out Olympique Lyonnais in the final sixteen, breaking the curse and making it through to the quarter-finals after 2,562 days, 74 players, nine coaches and five presidents since the last time they made it to this stage in the 2003-04 season. In the quarters they dispatch Spurs with ease, 4-0 at home, 0-1 at White Hart Lane.

The Whites are starting to feel the wind in their sails and the fans are already dreaming of their tenth European cup – a trophy which hasn't graced the glass cabinets at the Bernabéu since Zidane scored an incredible volley in Glasgow in the 2002 final. But before they can go out onto the famous Wembley pitch, there is the small matter of having to play an additional *Clásico* against their archenemies. The home leg will be on 27 April, and the return leg on 3 May at the Nou Camp. In addition, they have to play Barça in the final of the Copa del Rey on 20 April.

Let's start with the 32nd Liga match day, the last chance for Mourinho's team to get back into the race for the title. Eight points is a lot but who knows … a victory for the Whites could help to bring down their rivals' morale and could have an effect on the remainder of the season. On 3 April, Real Madrid suffered a devastating loss against Sporting Gijón which put them further out of reach – Mourinho's first home league loss in nine years. But the *Clásico* is another story.

Mourinho has been preparing for this as though it were a stage production. The night before the derby, he appears at the press conference in Valdebebas and does not utter a word. He lets Aitor Karanka, his second in command, do all the talking. He doesn't even greet the journalists and some of them leave as a sign of protest. In response to the Madrid manager's silence, Guardiola offers some praise of the opponent's game: 'I have never seen a team as good as this Madrid team. In four or five seconds the ball can go from Casillas to the opponent's goal. They are better and stronger than they were the last time we met, they shoot more, they pass more, and in the second half of the year they have spent more time playing as a team. They use a diverse range of tactics which makes them more difficult to control.' And with regard to the coach he adds: 'Mourinho is very powerful. He knows how to play a wide range of styles. We should watch closely because this dictates the way we attack and defend.'

The Special One's presence has intensified the atmosphere. He will undoubtedly be the decisive *Clásico* protagonist off the pitch. On the pitch, that role belongs to Messi. The little number 10 has achieved a fantastic score of 48 goals in 45 matches. He is the highest scoring Barça player in a single season, beating Ronaldo Nazário's 1996–97 record. And in the race for top goal-scorer he is ahead of Cristiano by thirteen goals. But the Portuguese has been decisive for Real Madrid in the Champions League, scoring against Spurs in the quarter-final at White Hart Lane.

At the Bernabéu, both players are hoping for memorable firsts: Cristiano has never scored against Barça, and Leo has never scored against a team managed by Mourinho, despite this being his ninth attempt. The manager is hoping to avoid a repeat performance of their last encounter. He's worried about the possibility of Real facing a similar humiliation, only this time in front of the home crowd. That really would be screwing things up, to borrow the expression from the 1978 World Cup-winning Argentine coach Cesar Luis 'El Flaco' Menotti.

He leaves playmaker Özil on the bench, along with Higuaín, Adebayor, Benzema and Kaká, and instead creates a defensive line with plenty of men behind the ball and Pepe as a central barricade. The idea is simple: block the opponent's game. It is a *Catenaccio*-style defence tactic worthy of the Italians. The only way to win is from set pieces or counterattacks. For Cristiano, leading the defence operation is a tricky business, especially since his team-mates are very deep, a long way from the Barça goal. But by the end of the first half, he has managed a shot at goal, after a corner which is headed to him by Ramos. He almost manages to head it in, but Adriano blocks it just below the crossbar.

After the break, he is straight back into the action with a direct free kick which deflects off Valdés' right post. The game is just starting to warm up when Albiol fouls David Villa right in front of goal, earning himself a red card and a penalty for Barcelona, which Messi puts away without any problem. Half an hour later it's Cristiano's turn to level the score from the penalty spot. He shoots and scores – finally, his first goal against Barça after seven matches. It's 1-1 at the close, after a weak and unpleasant game all round.

The draw leaves Barça an arm's length away from their 21st Liga title, giving Real confidence in terms of what's to come. So much confidence that the fans at the Bernabéu celebrate the draw as though it is a win. But the rough match has unleashed a string of controversies.

The first is prompted by Mourinho, as always, who criticises the referee at the press conference and paints a picture of a web of hidden powers which penalise any team he manages, be it Chelsea, Inter or Madrid. 'I'm tired of finishing every match against Barça with ten men. It was a very balanced game while we each had eleven. And then, as so often happens, with eleven against ten it's practically mission impossible against a team whose possession of the ball is the best in the world. Once again, I am witnessing unbelievable double standards on the part of the referees.'

Mourinho aside, there is another controversy which must be taken more seriously. This time it's Leo Messi in the spotlight, for kicking a ball into the stands. The ball runs away from him on the touchline, and instead of letting it go out, he sends it flying, hitting some fans in the crowd. The referee doesn't caution him, but the fans voice their disapproval. 'Are you crazy?' exclaims Pepe, rushing over to him. The fans are amazed, they cannot believe what they have just seen. What's going on with that Rosario boy? He rarely loses his cool on the pitch. Why did he pull such a nasty stunt?

The boy in question gives no explanation and he doesn't seem to apologise either. His team-mates come to his rescue. In his defence they cite the extreme tension on the pitch, Leo's sense of frustration in the face of Pepe's close marking, and they highlight the Real midfielder's five fouls against their number 10 without so much as a booking.

It's 20 April, the day of the Copa del Rey final in Valencia. More importantly, it's the day that Cristiano scores the fans' favourite goal of the year – the goal which brings Real their only title of the season. But the goal doesn't come for more than 100 minutes. He starts in the number 9 position, which is not where he feels most comfortable. He doesn't like receiving the ball with his back to the goal and it's difficult being the only centre forward on the pitch. He has to run back and forth to help his team-mates get the ball forward, and it is starting to wear him out. Eventually, towards the end of the first half, he gives a great assist to Pepe, who hits the post.

Throughout the first half, Real have dominated the entire pitch and Barça have not even managed a single shot at goal. But Ronaldo has been looking lonely out there, and in the second half, when Barça get themselves back on track and back in sync, he looks even more isolated. At the end of an intense 90 minutes of excellent football, the number 7 has still only had one shot on target. He will have to wait until extra time, until the 100th minute, to break his long and drawn out Barça dry spell.

Di María plays a one-two with Marcelo and sets off on a run, igores Alves and unleashes a powerful cross from the left hand side. Cristiano leaps into the air above Adriano and, demonstrating his ability to dominate in the box that he learnt at Man United, sends the ball flying into the net with a powerful header. Barça goalie Pinto can do nothing to stop the shot. The spectacular goal brings home Real's first Copa del Rey in almost two decades.

This time Barça are well and truly defeated, and not just because of the result. Leo had tried to get things moving from whatever position he happened to be in, but he always found himself tangled in a web of Real defenders. He controlled the ball far too much without any execution, and his dodging and feinting was completely ineffectual. After the break things had improved, and he even made one fantastic deep pass to Pedro – although the linesman ruled the subsequent goal offside. The match has been a failure as far as Leo is concerned. It's also the first defeat in a final for Barça under Guardiola's reign.

Seven days later, it is the first leg of the Champions League semi-finals. In the press conference at the Bernabéu the day before, Pep Guardiola loses his rag. Mourinho had sent him some message or other about the quality of the refereeing at the Mestalla match and the choice of referee for the semi-final, and Pep explodes, ranting for more than two minutes. This is unheard of for the coach. 'Since Mr Mourinho has addressed me in such familiar terms and called me "Pep", I'll call him "José",' he begins. 'At 8.45 tomorrow evening, we have a game to play. He has already been winning all year off the pitch. Let him have the Champions League. He can take the trophy home with him. We will be playing, whether we win or lose. Normally, he wins because his career is guaranteed. We are happy. With our little victories, which everyone admires, we are happy. In this room, he's the bloody boss, the goddamn master. He knows more than everyone else put together. I have no desire whatsoever to compete with him.'

The next day, Lionel Messi is back in charge. Two successful plays, and two goals by the Argentine. The first is thanks to a great pass from Afellay, and the second is after an impressive zigzag up the pitch all the way to the goal. It's more than enough to bring down a Real Madrid team which has resorted to conservative tactics and possessive guarding of the area – it's more or less what happened in the *Clásico* in La Liga.

They spend all their time trying to block Barça's game but they don't make any attempt to play their own. So much so that after a quarter of an hour, Cristiano Ronaldo is desperately waving his hands in the air, signalling to his teammates to move out of their positions, pass him the ball and help him out by creating some chances for him. At the end of the first half, he is the only one who has conjured any decent opportunities for Real, including shots from afar which have Valdés on the back foot. But compared to Messi he is lagging far behind, leaving the Argentine to dominate yet again.

Meanwhile, Mourinho is determined to take centre stage at the press conference. And once again, he outdoes himself in his attempt to create a scene. 'Real Madrid is out of the Champions League,' he says. 'We will go to the Nou Camp with our pride intact, with total respect for our footballing world, albeit a world which every so often makes me feel a little bit disgusted. We will go without Pepe, who didn't do a single thing wrong, and without Ramos, who didn't do anything wrong, and without the coach, who is not allowed to be in the dugout ... with a scoreline which is practically insurmountable.

'And if by chance we score a goal over there and we get a little closer to staying in it, I'm sure they'll quash us all over again. My question is, why? Why aren't other teams allowed to play against them? I don't understand it! If I told the referee and UEFA what I think about what has gone on here, my career would be over immediately. I don't know if it's because they're patrons of UNICEF, or because they smile more sweetly, or because Villar [president of the Spanish Footballers' Association] has so much clout within UEFA. The fact is that they have something which is very difficult to come by – power.

'Why was Pepe sent off? Why weren't Chelsea given four penalties they deserved? Why was van Persie sent off? Why was Motta sent off? Where does this power come from? Their power should be due to their footballing talent. That they do have. They should win because of that. It must taste very differently to win the way that they win. You have to be really rotten to enjoy that kind of win. Guardiola is a great manager, but he has won a Champions League that I would have been ashamed of winning. He won it thanks to a scandal at Stamford Bridge. And this year he'll be winning his second thanks to a scandal at the Bernabéu.'

It's a tirade which will again cost him dearly. UEFA's Commission for Control and Discipline will later fine him 50,000 Euros and suspend him for five matches. But in the meantime the coach has laid all his cards on the table, making it clear to his colleagues and players where they should stand on the issue.

Cristiano tows the line. 'You all saw what happened. When we both had eleven men we might not have been playing that well but at least we had the match under control,' he says during a post-match analysis. 'But it's always the same against Barcelona. Is it a coincidence? A 0-0 score-line wouldn't have been a bad result, we could have scored the away goal in the second leg. Besides, we were going to bring on Kaká and try to attack a bit more in the last twenty minutes. But then Pepe got sent off ... We all feel sad about it because it's always the same against this team. And this always happens to the coach whenever he plays against them.'

He also criticises Wolfgang Stark, the German referee: 'There was nobody I could turn to. There was absolutely no point in trying to talk to him because the red card was a done deal.' When asked about Messi, he plays down his rival's performance: 'Messi? Well, he was playing against ten men, that's always easier. I wish I could have been play-ing against ten men like he was.' And when it comes to his thoughts about the return leg, like his coach and fellow compatriot the number 7 is under no illusions: 'It's already 0-2 and we'll be playing away ... anything can happen in football but that's going to be a tough ask.'

On 3 May at the second leg of the Champions League semi-finals at the Nou Camp, Mourinho is not even in the stands. He watches the match on TV from his hotel room. And he witnesses his team being more daring and ambi-tious than in the other derbies. They have Barça on the back foot and in the first quarter of an hour they manage to keep them firmly in their own half. But gradually Barça start to chip away at their usual game. Messi finally comes face to face with Casillas, who miraculously manages to block three attempts in five minutes, to keep his team out of danger.

After half-time, the Whites come back onto the pitch with renewed energy and determination. Cristiano, who up until that point has not had any good crosses and has only managed some ineffectual dribbling, finds himself in the centre of the most controversial moment of the match. Tackled by Piqué just as he is passing the ball to Higuaín, he stumbles and falls, bringing down Mascherano in the process. Higuaín goes on to score, but the goal is disallowed as the linesman only saw the second part of the play and calls a foul against Cristiano.

But the near-miss is enough to shock Barça into getting things moving and after an assist from Valdés via Iniesta, Pedrito faces up to Casillas to put the *Blaugrana* in the lead. But Real haven't given up. Di María shoots, hits the post, recovers the rebound and passes to Marcelo who equalises. The final twenty minutes are intense, but there are no more goals as Barça manage to get the game back under control.

Messi may not have scored this time, but he has run about eight kilometres and he has done well to keep up the pressure. He provokes a warning against Carvalho and yellow cards on Xabi Alonso, Marcelo and Adebayor. He is fouled twelve times and he looks absolutely shattered. With or without the goal, he has been the definitive player in the 1-1 match which sends Barça on their way to Wembley. On 28 May, at the home of English football, they will go on to win their fourth European Cup, beating Man United 3-1. But for now, Messi is happy just to be carried along by the atmosphere at the Nou Camp as his team celebrates the victory and the end of an exhausting month of derbies. And just when it seems like the excitement is about to become too overwhelming for him, Pep Guardiola comes over and envelops his star player in a bear hug.

Meanwhile, Real waste no time in complaining about referee bias and that network of hidden power which has once again favoured their rivals. Everyone, from Karanka to Iker Casillas, seems to have learned Mourinho's tirade by heart. 'We knew that something like this would happen, and once again we have been proven right,' insists Cristiano. 'Higuaín's goal was good. There have been so many issues. Think about what happened at the Bernabéu when Alves was messing around [and got Pepe sent off] and what has happened today. Barça have a great team, but there is something else going on here. I don't want to suggest any kind of corruption, but it bothers me.' He is also quick to accuse Mascherano of making it look like he committed a foul when he didn't. 'He wasn't like that at Liverpool. He can only have learned these tricks at Barcelona.'

All the squabbles have built up thanks to a tense first leg, a month of being at such close quarters and all the preaching from Mourinho. But a month later the dust has settled. Over in Portugal, Cristiano is feeling more philosophical: 'We can't go on feeling sorry for ourselves. We had the ability to win and we didn't pull it off. It wasn't only down to the refs. A lot of things happened this year in La Liga and the Champions League, but I don't want to dwell on all that now.'

Regarding Barcelona, he adds: 'They played better and they didn't win by accident. They won because they were better.' His goal now is to beat them. 'No match is impossible. Barça are a great team and they have a great coach, but we'll get there in the end,' he promises. 'The things which are harder to achieve always taste sweeter when you achieve them.' Like beating Leo Messi, perhaps? The Argentine has clinched the 2010-11 season 2-1. But the battle continues. Who will win? Watch this space.

Chapter 25

Cristiano and Mou

'The boss is first and foremost my friend, secondly, my coach and thirdly, someone I greatly admire.'

Best male athlete: Cristiano Ronaldo. Best coach: José Mourinho. They are crowned the winners in the male sports category of the sixteenth edition of the *Globos de Ouro* – the Portuguese Golden Globes. Created by *Caras* magazine and *SIC* TV channel, the awards celebrate the nation's cinema, theatre, fashion, music and sports stars.

Thanks to his record tally of goals scored in La Liga, Ronaldo has beaten four-times World Rally Champion Armindo Araújo, Benfica's Fabio Coentrão, who will soon be joining Real Madrid, and European judo champion João Pina. Mourinho has beaten Benfica's Jorge Jesús, Sporting's Domingos Paciência, and Rui Rosa, the national judo team coach. It's his second consecutive win: he received recognition in 2010 after his Champions League title-win with Inter Milan.

The gala takes place on Sunday 29 May 2011, although neither of two Real winners is present at Lisbon's Coliseu dos Recreios concert hall. Ronaldo is with the national team, preparing for an upcoming Euro 2012 qualifier against Norway. He is represented at the gala by his sister Katia Aveiro. Mourinho has stayed in Madrid to plan ahead for the coming season. He has been handed a significant amount of control since the departure of the club's general manager, Jorge Valdano. He is represented at the gala by his friend João Graça. The *Globos de Ouro* is one of many awards schemes to recognise Cristiano and Mou, both Portuguese idols in their own right. Now colleagues in Madrid, they have maintained a close – though often fraught – relationship.

In April 2010, Mourinho's Inter Milan beat Barça 3-1 at the San Siro in the first leg of the Champions League semi-finals. During a press conference at Valdebebas, the media want to know Cristiano's opinion about his compatriot. 'I'll be honest with you: I like people who have a winning mentality,' he replies. 'But I am very happy with Pellegrini's achievements and that's all I have to say for now.'

A few weeks later, rumours are circulating in the 'White House' that Mourinho is set to become the new Real manager. *Sky Sports News* is reporting the story as if it's a done deal. 'He's a very special coach,' comments Ronaldo. 'He has demonstrated that he is one of the best in the world. Perhaps some people don't like his personality, or the fact that he is so revered. I know him very well, and I like what I see. I know his character: he's a winner.'

When asked whether he would like Mourinho to win the Champions League with Inter and then come to Real he replies: 'This is not the time to discuss the matter. Right now I am only interested in having a good World Cup with Portugal, not what is happening with transfers or the future of Real's managerial position. I would just like to wish him luck in the Champions League final. He's a fellow Portuguese sportsman, that's why I want him to win.'

On 22 May, Mourinho's team lifts the trophy at the Santiago Bernabéu after beating Bayern Munich 2-0. Four days later, Florentino Pérez announces Manuel Pellegrini's dismissal and confirms the addition of José Mourinho to the Real Madrid dugout. By this time, Cristiano is in South

Africa with the national team. He is delighted with the news. 'I like coaches who have a desire to win,' he tells *Público* newspaper. 'The trophies Mourinho has won with his previous clubs speak for themselves. I hope to be able to celebrate winning many more with him. The desire to win titles was one of the reasons I moved to Real Madrid. And I am extremely confident that we can achieve great things.'

Meanwhile, the man in question is busy singing Ronaldo's praises in an interview with *Marca*. 'Cristiano is phenomenal. No one should complain if he wants to spend his vacation with Paris Hilton, go to Los Angeles or buy himself a Ferrari. Someone who works as hard as he does is on another level professionally. He is football history in the making. All he needs to do in order to be like Pelé, Maradona or Di Stéfano is win more titles.'

The Special One knows that Cristiano's first season at Real Madrid hasn't turned out quite the way he wanted, and the manager has no hesitation in bringing it up. 'He hasn't won any titles,' he points out. 'I don't think he is satisfied with just having a great season or scoring 26 goals in La Liga.'

It's clear that Mou knows his future player very well. He has known Cristiano since the latter was a teenager at Sporting Lisbon. 'It was in a game against [Portuguese team] União Desportiva de Leiria,' Mourinho recalls. 'We were going to train afterwards, so we stayed to watch the match. Then he walked past, and I said to my assistant: "There goes Van Basten's son." He was a striker, his movements were very elegant and he had great technical skills. He reminded me of the Dutchman. It's strange … I didn't know his name, but I have to admit that he astonished all of us because he stood out much more than anyone else on the team.'

Since that first day their paths have crossed many times. First, in the Portuguese *Primeira Liga*, where Mourinho wins two league titles and one Champions League with FC Porto. Meanwhile, Ronaldo is just breaking into Sporting's first team. Next it's on to the English Premier League, with Mourinho in the Chelsea dugout and Cristiano wearing number 7 for Man United. Cristiano comes to England in 2003 and within two years he has made a name for himself. In June 2004 Mourinho arrives at Stamford Bridge and wins two successive league titles.

The reporters start asking Ronaldo if Mou is stealing his thunder as England's star Portuguese import. 'We're talking about a manager and a player, each with their own role to play,' he tells the Portuguese press at the end of the 2005–06 season. 'Mourinho is a great coach, he's one of the biggest names in the Premier League. But there's plenty of room for me. It's important for Portugal to have two people who are so talked about, although for very different reasons. We only really meet when our teams face each other, but we're on friendly terms.'

But a year later, there is talk of a 'war of words' between the two. Looking back now on the disputes he had with the coach, Cristiano insists it is all water under the bridge. But at the time, the story was so well documented that it 'bled rivers of ink', to quote the common Spanish idiom.

By Sunday 22 April 2007, the race is on between Man United and Chelsea for the Premier League top spot. The Blues have just drawn at Newcastle, where the referee denied them a penalty. Meanwhile, the day before at Old Trafford, the Red Devils were granted a reprieve when a foul against a Middlesborough player should really have cost them a penalty.

At the Chelsea press conference, Mourinho is frustrated: 'There's a new rule in English football. Don't give any penalties against United, and don't give any penalties in favour of Chelsea.' He adds: 'I don't think I should be criticised for making a truthful observation … If someone wants to pun-ish me, let them punish me. It would be the end of democracy and a return to some very archaic attitudes.'

And with that, a war erupts between Mourinho and Man United. The first to respond is Cristiano Ronaldo, who has just been awarded the Player of the Year award on 22 April. 'I really don't want to be dragged into Mourinho's complaints over referees – everybody knows how he is,' he tells Portuguese broadcaster RTP TV. 'He always has to say something because he can't admit his failures.'

Mourinho responds immediately. 'Ronaldo is a great player, perhaps the best in the world. But he needs to be mature enough to accept that you cannot argue against the facts. If he says it's a lie that Manchester United have conceded penalties that were not given, then he's lying. And if he lies he will never reach the level to which he aspires in football.'

Sir Alex Ferguson comes out in defence of his star player at a press conference, talking non-stop about the Chelsea manager's antics. 'He has no respect for anyone but himself. I am surprised no action has been taken against him. He just seems to go on, and on, and on. José Mourinho seems to be on some sort of personal crusade about regulations and honesty and suspicion in the game. Everyone is entitled to have a comment or opinion. Ronaldo has an opinion. That doesn't mean to say he is a liar. [Mourinho] is on about us changing the regulations. I would like to know who is doing it. Is it us? The FA? The Premier League? UEFA? I really feel he has been let off lightly with those comments.

'Jesus, God. It is a rant all the time now. I don't think it is fair to the game,' he continues, adding: 'We all get good and bad decisions. Does he remember the goal Paul Scholes had disallowed for offside when we played against Porto in the European Cup? We didn't like it and we complained.

But we didn't go to war on it.' Ferguson also expresses his concern about putting added pressure on referees. 'The thing is, José is a very clever man. In some people's eyes he is a hero. I don't know who is a villain and who is a hero … It is a calculated move. We have four games to go now. If we get a penalty kick against us in that time, Mourinho wins that war. That is wrong.'

Enter Carlos Queiroz into the arena, Ferguson's right hand man at the time. 'Mourinho has his own style. He always tries to divert everyone's attention to the points which are convenient for him. These are his tactics and that's the way he is. We are different because we are humble enough to recognise the merits of our rivals.'

After a 2-2 draw at home to Bolton, which leaves Chelsea trailing United by five points at the top of the table, Mourinho renews his attack on Cristiano. 'It's a game where a kid [said] some statements … not showing maturity and respect, maybe a difficult childhood, no education, maybe the consequence of that. Sir Alex felt he had to protect his boy. But [that's] normal … I have no problems with him [Ferguson]. I have no problem with the boy.'

The United coach is indignant. 'It is really below the belt to bring class into it. I don't know why he has done this. Maybe he is trying to unsettle the boy. Just because you come from a poor, working-class background does not mean to say you are not educated. What Ronaldo has are principles – that is why he has not responded to it. Other people are educated but have no principles.'

Ferguson wants this back-and-forth to end. Eventually, the Special One backs down and apologises to Cristiano. 'Mourinho has apologised to me and now I have no problem with him,' the player confirms. 'As far as I am concerned, the whole thing is now in the past.'

Agent Jorge Mendes later reveals that the apology has been made over the phone, just before the Premier League match between Chelsea and United. A few weeks later on 19 May, the two clubs are due to meet again in the FA Cup final at Wembley. On the eve of the match, when asked what message he would like to convey to Ronaldo, Mourinho responds: 'Play good, no injuries, because I don't like injuries in my players or opponents. And as the [great] player he is, he wants to be fair with his opponents.'

Mourinho leaves Chelsea on 20 September 2007, and the dispute is well and truly over. Cristiano even misses him, noting that without his guidance, Chelsea are 'a completely different team. You can never write Chelsea off, but I have a feeling that this will not be a good season for them,' he tells Viennese newspaper *Heute*.

Three years later, Mourinho and Ronaldo cross paths once again at Real Madrid. And this time, the player's first impression of his new manager is excellent. He says that Mou is almost faultless as a coach. 'The way in which he won the Champions League with Inter is proof of that. I watched a number of the Italian team's matches last year and Mourinho was a decisive factor in them winning the Champions League, the league and the cup.' He has put his trust in the new coach, promising that 'this year, we will work together to win every competition. Mourinho has already won titles with Inter and Porto. He can do the same here.'

In October, after Real Madrid beat Milan 2-0 in the group stage thanks to a goal from a Cristiano free kick, the star player confirms that everyone is happy with Mourinho. 'When things aren't going well it's only natural for people to be down about it. But this season is going fantastically. Thank God everything is going so well. Mourinho is fantastic. I am grateful that he came here because with his experience and with all the titles he has won, it is a pleasure to work with him. I always said that I wanted to be coached by Mourinho and now it has become a reality. I'm not the only one who is happy – my team-mates are also thrilled to be playing for him. I hope we win the Champions League.'

For his part, Mourinho considers Cristiano to be untouchable: his place in the starting line-up is never contested. He describes him as a 'hardworking, modest and down-to-earth player', noting that the public perception of Cristiano is 'completely different to who he really is as a person'. As far as Mourinho is concerned, his fellow countryman is the best in the world. 'There are two choices: Cristiano or Messi. If you think Cristiano is the best, then Messi is the second best. And vice-versa. But to me it's obvious: Cristiano is the best.' The Special One is convinced that CR7 will stay at the top for many years to come, saying that no other player will come close to matching Cristiano's abilities in the near future.

On 10 January 2011, Lionel Messi is named the winner of the 2010 Ballon d'Or at the Zurich Opera House, beating his Barça team-mates Andrés Iniesta and Xavi Hernández to take home his second consecutive trophy. Cristiano is not one of the three finalists. The following year he will come second, and Messi will make it three in a row.

Meanwhile, José Mourinho goes up on stage to collect the prize for best manager of 2010, having beaten Spanish coach Vicente del Bosque and Barça's Pep Guardiola. The Real coach weighs in on the results: 'For me, Messi, Iniesta and Xavi are players on another level. And when a player on another level such as Messi wins, everyone should respect it. Obviously, I would have preferred Sneijder to win after everything he's done in the past year, or Cristiano Ronaldo because he's one of my current players, or Diego Milito, but I have to respect the choice that has been made.'

Once again, Mou doesn't hesitate in piling on the praise where his star pupil is concerned. In fact, he has defended him all year from criticism and provocation. Back in September, Cristiano was frustrated because the Bernabéu crowd kept whistling every time he touched the ball during a match against Osasuna. He asked the fans to divert their energy into supporting him rather than whistling at him. The Special One came to his rescue: 'He is a kid who puts his body and his future on the line when he plays for us, he assumes all the risk. All he asked for was a bit more understanding between the team and the fans. And he asked nicely.'

In February, after a scuffle between Cristiano Ronaldo and Walter Pandiani just before half time in another Osasuna match, his opponent comments that he has a screw loose. Mou responds: 'Pandiani had his minutes of fame today talking about Cristiano. He should pay for that kind of advertising. Prime-time publicity like that is usually very expensive. He's smart, he got it for free, he got his moment of glory.' Pandiani's response is equally biting: 'His daddy had to come out and defend him. I don't need publicity! I've been playing in Spain for eleven years, I don't need anything from those two.'

True to his style, Mourinho grumbles about the referees on numerous occasions, claiming that the same defenders who seem almost afraid of certain star players nonetheless 'come down hard on Cristiano'. Ronaldo takes up the same argument after a kick from Dinamo Zagreb defender Leko in the first match of the 2011–12 Champions League. 'The referees never protect me,' he claims. 'Some people get star treatment – no one ever touches them! In my case, they could knock me down with a pole and nothing would happen to them. I don't understand it!' The allusion to Messi and Barça is obvious.

And speaking of Barça, it's after a match against the rivals on 27 April 2011, the first leg of the Champions League semi-finals, that Cristiano and Mou have their first major disagreement since his arrival at Real. 'As an attacking player, do you like the way your team played today?' the reporters ask Cristiano after their 0-2 loss, referring to their defensive performance. In his usual honest way, he replies: 'No, I don't like it, but I have to adapt to it because that's the way we play.' His succinct response is a little too blunt and it will undoubtedly spark a debate in the press.

Mourinho is not amused. It's the first time he has received criticism from the Real dressing room – and it has come from none other than his star player. 'He can say what he wants, that's his opinion. I don't have a problem with it,' Mou tells the press at Valdebebas. Case closed, or so it seems.

But three days later he punishes Cristiano by leaving him out of the line-up in a vital Liga match against Zaragoza. 'It was a technical decision,' Mou explains, claiming that he wanted to rest Ronaldo before the return leg against Barça at the Nou Camp. But nobody believes him. In the entire season, the White number 7 has only been benched once for technical reasons, during a trivial Copa del Rey match against Levante in December. The move is seen as punishment for criticising Mourinho's game strategy, a way of teaching the player to keep his mouth shut.

Cristiano is indignant about the treatment he has received and Mourinho is reportedly furious because his protégé has publicly criticised his tactics. According to *El País*: 'During the prematch preparation the night before the Barça game, it was clear to the entire Real Madrid camp that there was a lot of friction between the two. According to one source, Mourinho even brought it up in front of the others, saying: "Don't complain about our defensive strategy Cristiano. You know it's your fault if we have to play that way, because you don't want to defend."'

Mourinho is convinced that if Cristiano is the top goalscorer in the world, it can only be thanks to his managerial strategy. His formation has been built around the striker, allowing him to receive the ball without overexerting himself and save his energy for running and scoring. He certainly doesn't want to hear any criticism from the one player around whom he has carefully constructed his team. What started as a quibble has turned into a full blown dispute. The press are only too happy to take full advantage of the story, going into depth on each side of the debate. They even go into the archives to drag up the famous 'war of words' that the two had back in England. They start referring to this new rift between the two Real stars as the beginning of the end.

But that's a little too dramatic. By the end of the season things have calmed down. When Spanish radio network Cadena COPE asks Cristiano if the Zaragoza match was Mourinho's way of punishing him, he replies: 'I don't know. You will have to ask Mourinho. When he's next on air for an interview, ask him.' And he takes great care to play down the comments he made after that infamous Barça match. 'It's all in the past now. I have talked to my teammates and the coach about it,' he explains. 'Sometimes we shouldn't speak our mind so easily. Sometimes we say things we shouldn't. I didn't mean to offend anyone, I was just frustrated after Pepe's sending off. Sometimes I say things I don't really mean. But that chapter is closed now and everything is fine. Nobody's perfect.'

He has resorted to self-deprecation, but at least he has restored the balance in his relationship with Mou. 'I was thrilled when I heard that he was coming to Madrid. Not just because he's a Portuguese coach – that's not the most important thing. The best part is the fact that in every league he has joined, he has demonstrated that he's the best. For me, the top people are those who can show that they are capable of doing great things in more than one league. If you are good in Portugal, you have to be good in Spain and Italy as well. To me, he's the best because he has won every championship in which he has coached. He has a strong winning mentality.

'I have heard many players speak about him, but only those who have worked with him really understand what a great manager he is. There are those who have no idea what goes on in the dressing room or in training, yet have an opinion of him. They either love him or hate him – it's similar to how people feel about me. As far as I'm concerned he's a great coach – phenomenal. I hope he will continue coaching me for many years to come.'

So who's better, Mourinho or Ferguson? 'They're different. You can't compare a Ferrari with a Porsche. Either you happen to like the Ferrari better, or you prefer the Porsche. Everyone has their own personal preference. They are the best coaches I have ever worked with. Mourinho has really impressed me with his training methods – they're the best I have ever seen. But no, you can't compare the two.'

At the start of the 2011–12 season, he elaborates further in an interview with *Marca*. 'The boss is first and foremost my friend, secondly, my coach and thirdly, someone I greatly admire. I am delighted to work with him and learn from him every single day.'

Chapter 26

Out of this world

Fate rests on two penalty shoot-outs.

But first, one more goal at the Nou Camp and Real Madrid have clinched La Liga – to the disappointment of Lionel Messi and Barcelona.

Let's start with the best bit – Ronaldo's most important goal since he arrived at Real. A powerful blast that secures the title for the Whites and reignites his dream of reclaiming the Ballon d'Or. The Real striker has been yearning for that prestigious individual prize ever since he took it from Messi in 2008.

It's 21 April 2012, Barça versus Real Madrid, 8pm at the Nou Camp. For the first time since La Liga 2008–09, the Whites have made it to the end of the season ahead of the *Blaugrana*. They are four points clear of Pep's team, 85 to 81, enough to seal the championship at the home of their rivals and end Barça's incredible three-season run. It's Barça's last shot at the title, it's *Clásico* number 184 and it's neck and neck – 86 wins each, 12 draws.

All the attention is on Cristiano Ronaldo and Leo Messi. 'The battle for La Liga isn't about two teams, it's about two players,' claims *Sport*. And it's not hard to see why: Ronaldo and Messi's performances have carried their teams. In 32 Liga matches, they have each scored 41 goals, equalling the record set by Cristiano in 2010–11. So far the Argentine has racked up six braces, five hat-tricks and one four-goal match. The Portuguese has scored five braces and seven hat-tricks. 'You've never seen anything like it. Never has La Liga had two such phenomenal players,' says *Sport*.

And tonight, they will be playing for La Liga, the top-scorer position, the Golden Boot and the Ballon d'Or. With the exception of the 2011 Copa del Rey final, it's fair to say Ronaldo has always lost when going head to head with Messi – be it at Man United or Real. And he lost the last Liga *Clásico*, on 10 December 2011 at the Bernabéu, when Barça came back from 1–0 down after Karim Benzema's goal in the 22nd second to win 3–1. Messi didn't score, but he had a hand in the goals. And Ronaldo missed two clear chances in two Real counterattacks.

But on 21 April 2012 it's a very different story, and Ronaldo proves decisive. He scores the final goal of the 2–1 victory, putting Mourinho's team seven points clear of their rivals. It's enough to ensure the title win. It comes in the 73rd minute, shortly after the equaliser from Alexis, breaking the flow of the *Blaugrana*'s attempted comeback. Mesut Özil gets the ball from Di María in front of the halfway line and crosses deep towards Cristiano. The number 9 breaks away from Mascherano and heads towards Víctor Valdés. He sends the ball to the right, beating the Barça goalie at the near post. It's an incredible shot, and Cristiano celebrates by running towards the Barça fans, signalling for them to calm down, mimicking the gesture Raúl once made towards them. 'Calm down, calm down, I'm right here,' he shouts, only too aware of what the goal symbolises. At the press conference afterwards he says: 'It was an important goal, but the team's victory as a whole was more important.'

Cristiano has scored once again at the Nou Camp, playing a crucial role in breaking Real's three-year drought.

And as far as the Madrid press are concerned, he has dethroned Messi. The Argentine has scored in his last ten Liga matches, but tonight he has been unrecognisable – not even a shot on target. It's unheard of for him. He has done his bit, initiating the play that led to Alexis's goal, but he hasn't influenced the match in the way everyone was expecting. Mourinho's game plan has kept him at bay.

With La Liga in the bag, Cristiano faces another challenge in just four days' time: the return leg of the Champions League semi-final against Bayern Munich, the penultimate step towards getting their hands on their tenth Champions League trophy. The whole of Madrid has been dreaming about it – and Real has been chasing it in vain for a decade, ever since Zinedine Zidane's winner against Bayer Leverkusen on 15 May 2002 at Glasgow's Hampden Park.

Mourinho's men know Chelsea awaits the winner in the final at the Munich Allianz Arena. Against all odds, Roberto Di Matteo's Blues have trounced reigning champions Barça in an incredible game. In the 43rd minute they went 2–0 down, after being reduced to ten men with John Terry's sending off a few minutes earlier. After their 1–0 victory in the first leg, their dream had quickly turned into a nightmare and a Barça win seemed inevitable. Two minutes later, on the stroke of half time, a lob from Ramires made it 2–1, and finally, in the 91st minute, Fernando Torres beat Valdés to finish it off. Barça's 81 per cent possession has proved worthless, as have the 47 shots on target over the two legs. Chelsea have had four shots on target and scored three goals, and now they are taking their *Catenaccio* defending to Munich. And where was Messi? He missed a penalty in the 47th minute that could have been decisive, and hit the woodwork on another occasion. It has undoubtedly been his worst night in quite a while.

'You'd better not miss', reads the front page headline of *Marca* the next day, accompanied by a shot of Messi's devastated face, and one of Cristiano celebrating his goal. And in red letters: 'Today, CR7, king of the Bernabéu, is entrusted with taking the team to the final after Barça's unbelievable defeat.' It's a bad move drawing the comparison, because history has a habit of repeating itself. Like Barça before them, the Whites choke. And Cristiano misses from the penalty spot, just like Leo, despite having netted his last 27 penalties. It's Real's first in the penalty shoot-out. He sends it to Neuer's right and the German goalkeeper blocks it, before denying Kaká and Ramos as well. Xavi Alonso is the only one who scores. Íker Casillas's two saves make no difference – the tenth Champions League trophy will have to wait until next year.

At the crucial moment, Cristiano has missed the penalty that could have put Real on an entirely different path. But, unlike Messi, he has made his mark during the previous 120 minutes. He has scored a penalty in the sixth minute and another in the fourteenth. With Real 2–0 up he moves ten paces back and waits for the Germans to falter so he can go on the counterattack. He wants to sit it out. It's a conservative strategy from Mourinho, which fails them in the end – despite Saint Íker's best efforts. Robben scores a penalty, which takes them on to the shoot-out. Goodbye Champions League. They'll have to make do with La Liga.

They still need to make it official, but it doesn't take much. On 2 May at San Mamés, the Whites dismantle Fernando Llorente and Marcelo Bielsa's Athletic Bilbao. Cristiano scores a header crossed from a corner to make it 3–0. Unfortunately, when the final whistle goes, the first thing he does is gesture rudely to Spain's Javi Martínez, who had been sent off after a double yellow. He says something to Cristiano, who reacts badly. 'You have to let the outbursts slide,' says Lions coach Bielsa. 'They've just won, they're champions fair and square, and they should celebrate that.' It's Real's 32nd Liga title. And it's quite an achievement for Mourinho, who has now won the league in Portugal, England, Italy and Spain.

It's Cristiano's first Liga win. At 7pm the next day, in front of thousands of fans in the Plaza de Cibeles, the whole squad pays tribute to their triumph. In the centre of it all, Cristiano fields questions from Real Madrid TV.

'It's your first Liga title with Real – how do you feel?'

'It's a feeling of great joy – I'm so happy. The fans deserve it. It's been an incredible season, the team has been phenomenal. We played really well and we deserve that trophy. There are still two games left, but we've achieved our goal.'

In the two remaining matches, Cristiano scores two more goals, taking him to a league total of 46 – one every 75 minutes. He has scored ten in the Champions League, three in the Copa del Rey and one in the Spanish Supercup – a total of 60 in the 2011–12 season with Real. He has steadily improved since the 33 he scored in his first season in Spain, and he has even beaten his record of 53 from the previous season. He has had a run of success unprecedented in the club's history, shattering records set by big names such as Puskas, Di Stéfano and Hugo. In his three seasons at Real he has scored 146 goals in 144 matches, an average of 1.02, and he holds the record for 100 goals scored in the minimum number of matches. He is the only player in La Liga to have scored against all nineteen rival teams in a single season.

No one in Real's 110-year history can hold a candle to his achievements. His track record in and around the box is stellar: 161 shots – one every thirteen minutes – resulting in

46 goals. It's an impressive tally, although not good enough to bag his second consecutive top goal-scorer title, as Messi has managed 50 Liga goals. The Argentine has had an unstoppable year. He has flattened the competition with a total of 73 goals, a watershed in footballing history. But as the ever-practical Mourinho points out, they are goals that led nowhere.

The Portuguese, on the other hand, has won La Liga, and has emerged as a true Real leader. He has worked the hardest for the team in both defence and attack, and has played a big part in the 121 goals that made them champions, with twelve assists as well as all his goals. He threw himself behind the team from the first day of the season and came to the rescue when Real needed it the most – like against Sporting, or at the Vicente Calderón against Atlético Madrid. He has scored from every angle: left-footed, right-footed, headers, and even one with his heel against Rayo in Vallecas – an incredible goal. It has undoubtedly been his best season since he arrived in the Spanish capital in July 2009, and Real have finally triumphed over a seemingly invincible Barça. José Mourinho can finally stop having nightmares about Pep Guardiola, Ronaldo about Messi, and the Whites fans about the Barça fans. Bit by bit, Ronaldo has made the Bernabéu his home, from the whistles of the previous years, to the rapturous applause. The fans have gone from critiquing him to chanting his name.

Now it's time to conquer his home country, once and for all. Euro 2012 begins on 8 June in Poland and the Ukraine, and Portugal have never won. Despite having had great players, from Mário Coluna, the 'Black Panther' Eusébio and Fernando Chalana, to Paulo Futre, Luís Figo and Rui Costa, the trophies have always been just out of their reach. In the 1966 World Cup, Eusébio was the top goal-scorer with nine, but Bobby Charlton's England beat them in the semis. In Euro 2004, against all odds, Otto Rehhagel's Greece defeated them in the final in Lisbon, in front of the home crowd. And in the 2006 World Cup it was a Zinedine Zidane penalty that denied Figo and Co. their ticket to the final. Portugal have a history of coming second, third, fourth – never the champions.

Things aren't looking good this time either. Despite being ranked fifth by FIFA, and despite having Cristiano in the side, the pundits claim Portugal is even less consistent than when led by Figo, Rui Costa or, later, Deco. On top of that, they have drawn Group B, the group of death. They will have to face World Cup runners-up Holland, tournament favourites Germany, and Denmark, who can always put up a good fight. They need Ronaldo to play like he does in Madrid and score an avalanche of goals – something he has yet to do for his home country. He has scored 32 in 90 international fixtures, an average of 0.36. And in the big matches he has scored just five: a total of three in Euro 2004 and Euro 2008, and one in each of the 2006 and 2010 World Cups.

The Portuguese fans want to see him demonstrate the leadership skills he has honed in Madrid. They want a Cristiano in the mould of Maradona in the 1986 Mexico World Cup, a captain who can guide his team to the trophy. But in the first two matches he doesn't live up to Portugal's expectations. On 9 June against Joachim Löw and Mesut Özil's Germany, he goes unnoticed. He plays on the left, marked closely by Boateng. He gets very few passes and barely has any opportunity to use his speed and show his potential for explosiveness. Meanwhile, Bayern striker Mario Gómez gets a chance at a header – and he doesn't waste it. The Portuguese team only manage to fight back in the last ten minutes, out of sheer fear, and Silvestre Varela almost manages an equaliser in the final minute. 'We were unlucky,' says Cristiano at the final whistle. 'Nothing is perfect. In 2004 we also started out on the back foot and we ended up going to the final.'

The second match is against Denmark on 13 June in front of 28,000 at the Arena Lviv, and it's a disastrous night for Ronaldo. He can't connect with the ball, his shots are disappointing, and he misses obvious chances. It seems as though he has lost all the magic in the box. He shoots like an amateur, and his defending is even worse – particularly when Denmark get their first goal. He has two clear chances and fails miserably both times. It's his worst ever outing in the national shirt. Luckily, with three minutes to go until the final whistle, Varela converts one of the captain's botched attempts into a goal that is deserving of the victory. Portugal have hung on to their chance of going through. But Cristiano is not having a good time. He has racked up thirteen shots in the tournament, but none of them have made it into the net. His footwork has not been particularly good either. He has gone five games without scoring, his longest drought all season. It's a weight on the shoulders of a goal-obsessed player like Cristiano Ronaldo, who feels he is being watched and judged by his entire country, not to mention the rest of planet football.

He is annoyed with himself – and with the fans, who are chanting Messi's name. 'You know what Messi was up to this time last year? Getting knocked out of the quarter-finals of the Copa América,' he grumbles. It's neither here nor there, but it reveals, once again, just how much his eternal rival weighs on his mind and how much he feels the pressure.

Back in Portugal there is plenty of criticism, and not just about his performance, but about his outbursts, and his conduct on the pitch – such as his criticism of his colleagues when things aren't going well. He is accused of egotism, of thinking too much about himself and the Ballon d'Or, and not enough about the team. 'He is not mature enough to be the captain, it was irresponsible of Scolari. Now nobody can keep his ego in check,' former Portuguese Football Federation director António Simões tells *Diario de Noticias*. 'And that's detrimental for the team, and for Cristiano himself.'

His team-mates defend him to the hilt. 'There's nothing wrong with Cristiano,' declares Varela. 'He's our captain and he gives his all to the team every day. He has sacrificed so much for Portugal.' Real team-mate Pepe excuses his blunders in front of goal, saying 'even the best people miss'.

Everything changes on 17 June in the deciding match against Holland. Cristiano demonstrates his class, destroying the Oranges' defence and sending Portugal through to the quarter-finals with two goals. This time it's a stellar performance: twelve shots on target – the best stats in the tournament's history – plus he has run 10,139 metres, dribbled, headed, crossed, assisted … and scored. His first goal is in the 28th minute. He gets the ball from João Pereira, controls it, and sends it flying past Stekelenburg, bringing the score level after Van der Vaart's goal. Then, in the 74th, Moutinho recovers the ball after an incredible steal and Portugal make four rapid passes to move it up the field in just eight seconds. Ronaldo gets the ball from Nani after a 50-metre sprint, and calmly puts it past Dutch defender Van der Wiel, while the goalie looks on helplessly. It's a Real-style move – one Cristiano always executes with aplomb. Only the woodwork will deny the captain his hat-trick, but by then it hardly matters. He is well and truly back.

He has obliterated the Dutch, and four days later beats

the Czech Republic as well. It's 0–0 with eleven minutes to go. Twice, Cristiano has come close to overpowering goalkeeper Petr Čech. The first is just before half time: a right-footed shot that slams into the left-hand post. The second, just after the break, is a free kick that also hits the woodwork. The goal finally comes in the 79th minute – right-footed cross from Moutinho, Cristiano charges towards the penalty spot, towards Gebre Selassie, then dives forward for the header, and beats the outstretched hands of the goalie of the year who had denied Messi a spot in the Champions League final and then denied Bayern Munich the trophy just weeks earlier. Cristiano has succeeded where they failed, and it's enough to take Portugal through to the semis.

It's a well-deserved victory. The Portuguese have had twenty shots on target, including eight from Ronaldo, who has undoubtedly been the decisive player. 'It was a team victory. We won because we had such strong cohesion in midfield,' he says afterwards. 'We played a solid game and had plenty of chances. The Czech Republic didn't really have any. Now we're just hoping for a great opponent in the semis.'

The following day, the Portuguese press, the world's media, rivals and friends all weigh in on CR7's talents. 'Best in the world', says the *Record* front page. 'Unstoppable!' screams *A Bola*. 'Worth his weight in gold', writes *O Jogo*. 'He's overtaken Messi', reads the headline in *La Gazzetta dello Sport*, while *L'Equipe* insists he can beat Messi to the Ballon d'Or if he keeps up that type of performance.

'Cristiano is an incredible finisher,' says Czech Republic coach Michal Bilek. Goalie Cech adds: 'It's not easy to stop him. I couldn't do anything about that goal.' 'Did you see it? He's on another level,' says Fábio Coentrão. 'He's not just the best in the world. He's out of this world,' adds Pepe. José Mourinho will echo these words months later, musing on the eternal Messi/Ronaldo comparison. 'Cristiano wasn't born in Madeira, he was born on Mars. He's not of this Earth. So he's the best in the universe.'

On 27 June, it's the semi-final against Spain in Donetsk. 'It doesn't matter who our opponents are because we keep getting better and better and our goal is simply to get to the final,' Cristiano has said. Nonetheless, perhaps he would have preferred to avoid the familiar duel with Spain. Vicente del Bosque's Reds knocked out Portugal in the final sixteen of the World Cup in South Africa, plus he'll be facing Real team-mates Álvaro Arbeloa, Alonso, Ramos and Casillas, who know him all too well and will try to put the brakes on in any way they can.

He is no stranger to duels with Arbeloa, as the latter was at Liverpool when Ronaldo played in England. Before the match the Spaniard declares: 'Cristiano is mentally and physically demanding. And you know that over the course of 90 minutes there will be some plays you just won't be able to stop.' Del Bosque, for his part, remembers that day in Cape Town when they beat Portugal to the quarter-finals. 'But he wasn't his usual self, he had a lot of help.' But, more importantly, he hasn't forgotten the encounter in Lisbon in 2010, when Portugal beat Spain 4–0. 'They were far superior,' he says.

Portugal manager Paulo Bento is convinced that 'there will be moments in the match when we will dominate. We want to retain possession, attack with courage and patience, and keep it together when they have possession. Our aim is not to spend the match on the defence – we want to create big problems for our opponents.'

And to some extent, Bento gets his wish: Portugal stand up to the world champions. They refuse to concede an inch, and prove themselves physically and strategically capable of blocking the plays of a tired and unimaginative Spanish side. But they don't seem to be making use of Ronaldo, their secret weapon. The captain doesn't get many chances. He causes a stir in the Reds' defence, but he doesn't make many inroads. His attempts to cut in to the centre are always denied by Arbeloa and Sergio Ramos – who gets a yellow card for blocking him with his chest. And Cristiano's three free kicks come to naught, over the bar, into the stands.

After a foul against Nani, Cristiano and Meireles launch a surprise counterattack against the Spanish defence. It's three against three. Meireles crosses to Cristiano, unmarked on the edge of the area. The entire stadium and everyone watching on TV hold their breath, thinking this will be his fourth Euro goal, the one that takes Portugal into the final. But it goes over the bar. Maybe it's because Piqué was closing in and he had to take his shot too quickly. Maybe it just wasn't a clean strike. Who knows?

Extra time. Iniesta pushes Spain closer to the elusive goal, while Ronaldo is left begging for a cross that never comes. The whistle goes without a single shot on target from the Madeiran. He has only managed seven attempts: five misses and two runs that were blocked by the defenders.

Time for penalties. Cristiano plans to take the fifth, but he never gets the chance. By then, Cesc Fàbregas has already converted the winning spot-kick to put Spain through to the final. 'So unfair!' Ronaldo mumbles to the cameras.

Later, he says: 'The luck was on their side and I congratulate them. I'm sad because that's two semi-finals I've lost this year – both on penalties. But we can still be proud: it was a very balanced game, which came down to penalties. And then, it's a question of luck.' When asked who decided he should step up last, he replies: 'The coach, the team, all of us. In the end, I did everything I could.'

Chapter 27
A great leader

'All that matters is what Real Madrid does and what I do.'

'It could be that I'm a little bit sad. I don't celebrate goals because I'm unhappy.'

Why are you unhappy?

'Everyone knows why.'

Are you disappointed because you didn't win the title of best player in Europe?

'No, it's not that. That hardly matters. There are more important things than that.'

Is it personal or professional?

'Professional. I'm not going to talk about it anymore. The club knows why.'

It's Sunday 2 September 2012, the third match day of La Liga. Cristiano Ronaldo has scored twice against Granada at the Santiago Bernabéu, taking him to 150 goals with Real. When his left leg begins to hurt, he heads towards the dugout. The game is still in play as he goes into the dressing room. He is not there to celebrate Real's third goal. He hasn't even celebrated his own.

Following the match, he makes an appearance in the press area, and it's there that he drops the bombshell. A few words about sadness are enough to make headlines in tomorrow's papers, fuel hours of radio and TV air-time, and worry the club and the fans. But the question remains: why is he unhappy?

Some ask whether a rich, good-looking celebrity has the right to discuss his sadness with the world, given all of Spain's current troubles. Since the start of the season, things have gone pretty well for CR7 from a sporting point of view. In the Spanish Supercup at the Nou Camp on 23 August, for example, Real goes up against Barcelona in another *Clásico*, which the Catalans win 3–2. Cristiano opens the scoring with a great header. Barça respond with goals from Pedro and Xavi, and a Messi penalty. In the 85th minute, when a 3–1 result seemed inevitable, a big error by goalkeeper Víctor Valdés enabled Di María to make it 3–2, leaving it wide open for the deciding leg.

On 29 August at the Bernabéu, Real have already scored their first by the ninth minute. Pepe sends in a long pass, Mascherano can't get to it, and Higuaín beats Valdés with a shot between his legs. And Cristiano scores the second after another Barça defensive error, this time from Piqué. Once again, Valdés has to watch as the ball flies between his legs.

Messi has been in the background during the first half. But after the break, he scores from a free kick, unexpectedly throwing the game open once again. Barça are a man down after Adriano's sending off and they seem weaker and more uncertain than usual. But they are still creating chances. Real are struggling, but they manage to hang on thanks to Casillas. The Whites have left Messi and Barça in the dust to take home their first trophy of the season.

The following evening, CR7 attends the UEFA football gala in Monte Carlo, where the 2011–12 European player of the year will be announced. Thanks to his Liga title and a good Euro 2012 performance, the Portuguese striker is as deserving as anyone and is undoubtedly one of the favourites. But the trophy goes to Andrés Iniesta, who with nineteen points beats Cristiano and Leo Messi, tied on seventeen. On hearing the result the Real number 7 looks a little miffed. But he has maintained that it's not the reason for his unhappiness. Perhaps it's the fact that La Liga has not got off to the best start – Real drew the first match with Valencia and lost the second to Getafe. But apparently it's not that either.

One thing's for sure, the club are well aware of his position. The Saturday before the Granada match, Cristiano speaks to Florentino Pérez to tell him he is unhappy, that he wants to leave. His team-mates have seen him looking downcast and those closest to him say he seems despondent and lacking in motivation. Aside from the comments and opinions of the football pundits, the debate about what's eating Cristiano spills over into the wider media. Everyone has a theory. Some claim he wants to review his contract to bring his salary in line with those of Zlatan Ibrahimović and Samuel Eto'o, who earn more than him at Paris Saint-Germain and Anzhi Makhachkala. Others say he has reportedly received an offer from Manchester City that is making the Real directors nervous. Some seem to think he has used the same tactic as his compatriot José Mourinho to win more protection, support and status from the club, more recognition from his team-mates of his work and leadership skills, and more adulation from the fans. Despite Cristiano's assurances to the contrary, there are those who are convinced it must be something personal bothering him that he does not want to reveal.

Both friends and rivals intervene in the debate. 'Everyone has the right to feel unhappy now and then, even Cristiano. We can't be happy 24/7, 365 days a year. He's a human being just like the rest of us, and he will go through ups and downs,' says Real right-back Álvaro Arbeloa. 'He may not have the same difficulties as the average Spaniard, but he has the right to be unhappy.' And he affirms that 'if Cristiano needs support from his team-mates, then of course we will support him. And so will the club, if he needs it. And if he needs affection from the fans, I'm sure he will get that too.' Leo Messi stays out of it, declaring solemnly: 'You shouldn't ask me about Cristiano. It has nothing to do with me.'

The mystery is partly resolved by a message posted by the footballer himself on his Facebook page while in training with the Portuguese team in Obidos. 'That I am feeling sad and have expressed this sadness has created a huge stir. I am accused of wanting more money, but one day it will be shown that this is not the case.' So it's not about the money. Meanwhile, Cristiano makes clear that his 'motivation, dedication, commitment and desire to win all competitions will not be affected. I have too much respect for myself and Real Madrid to ever give less to the club than all I am capable of.'

But the reasons behind his unhappiness remain unknown. Things die down over time, and eventually the discussion disappears off the front pages of the papers. Only at the end of the season does Florentino Pérez offer his version of events. In an interview with Cadena Ser radio station, the Real Madrid president explains: 'Cristiano told me he was unhappy and I told him that we were going to do everything possible to make him happy because he is the best player in the world. I don't know if he had an offer from Paris Saint-Germain. He hit a rough patch, that's it, nothing happened. Lately his performance has been spectacular.'

No one can argue with that, because Cristiano has had a fantastic season. He has scored no fewer than 55 goals in 55 matches – 34 in La Liga in 34 games, seven in the Copa del Rey, two in the Spanish Supercup and twelve in the Champions League. He has netted a total of 201 in 199 matches across all competitions since he signed with Real in 2009, making him the sixth-highest goal-scorer in the club's history. In just four seasons he has overtaken great players such as Amancio Amaro, Emilio Butragueño, Pirri and Paco Gento. He has become the highest-scoring Portuguese player in European competitions with 52 goals, beating records set by Eusébio and Real legend Alfredo Di Stéfano. He scored 35.6 per cent of the Whites' goals in the 2012–13 season, way ahead of strikers Karim Benzema (20 per cent) and Gonzalo Higuaín (17 per cent). Incredible figures. And in the last season he has been the driving force behind Real Madrid, the hero of many matches, the player with the most guts and enthusiasm, who has pulled the results out the bag. He has become an authoritative leader on the pitch and in the dressing room and has been ready and willing to take on whatever challenge is thrown his way.

The next *Clásico* rolls round after the Supercup, on 7 October 2012. This time it's a Liga game at the Nou Camp. It's early in the season, but already it's a crucial game. After just seven matches, Barça are eight points ahead of the Whites. Mourinho's men need to close the gap. Just one defeat could ruin their championship prospects. Cristiano has already scored twelve goals, eight of which were in the last four fixtures, including hat-tricks against Ajax in the Champions League and Deportivo de La Coruña in La Liga. Rival Messi has scored ten goals so far this season, but has not scored at all in the past three matches.

This time, both Leo and Cristiano are on form, putting on a stunning performance in an intense match that delights the 400 million live TV viewers. The Portuguese gets one past Valdés in the 23rd minute, with a sharp shot that tucks in at the left post. The Argentine replies in the 31st. Pepe fails to clear a cross from Pedro, the ball lies dead momentarily, and the number 10 shows Casillas no mercy. And he keeps up the pace in the second half. Xabi Alonso fouls him on the edge of the area, and the referee spares him the red. Leo retrieves the ball and takes a left-footed free kick, clearing the wall and beating the goalie with a beautiful strike to make it 2–1. Five minutes later it's Cristiano's turn. After a pass from Özil, he dashes away from the defenders and finishes it cleanly. 'Messi and CR7 show with their doubles why they are from another planet,' reads the *Marca* headline the following day. It ends 2–2, and there's everything to play for in La Liga.

But that won't last long. As Real draw with Espanyol on 16 December, Barça are making a comeback against Atlético Madrid. A great goal from Adriano and two from Messi put the *Blaugrana* thirteen points ahead of the Whites. José Mourinho has already given up on the title. But he hopes the team will up its Liga game, if only because 'it will also help us to do better in the Copa and the Champions League, where we have the chance to come out stronger'.

Barcelona will indeed go on to win the 2012–13 Liga trophy, thanks to another Real draw with Espanyol, on 11 May 2013 at the Cornellà stadium. Barça are declared champions four match days ahead of the end of the season. It hardly matters that on 2 March, Real defeat them for the first time since the 2007–08 season with a 2–1 win at the Bernabéu. An incredible first half of the season – eighteen wins and a single draw, 55 points out of a possible 57 – means Tito Vilanova's men have a huge cushion to fall back on. They finish the season with 100 points to Real's 85. In the end it will be a fairly meagre year for Cristiano, lacking in individual as well as club titles.

On 7 January 2013, alongside Messi and Andrés Iniesta, he will discover who has won the 2012 Ballon d'Or at the

FIFA gala in Zurich. In the November, he had given a lengthy interview to *France Football*, in which he spoke in about his season and the prestigious trophy. When asked whether he deserves the Ballon d'Or, he replies: 'I don't know. It's not up to me. There are people who vote – coaches, captains. It's out of my control. We will have to wait to see the results of the vote.' But when the reporter persists, asking whether he would vote for himself if he had the chance, CR7 is in no doubt. 'If I could, of course I would vote for myself.'

On the big day, Cristiano is the last of the nominees to touch down in Switzerland, accompanied by a delegation from Real Madrid and his girlfriend Irina, who looks likely to be the toast of the gala in a stunning black gown. In front of the photographers, at the joint press conference with Leo and Andrés, Cristiano is presented with a New York Yankees baseball cap, a blue raincoat and a grey T-shirt. He is the most talkative of the three. He insists that the Ballon d'Or 'is not a life-and-death prize. Life goes on after this trophy. I have a clear conscience because my mission is complete. We won La Liga and the Supercup.' On the subject of Messi, he says: 'It's not a personal duel. Both of us are just trying to do our jobs and give the best possible performance.' Leo agrees: 'He's right, we only try to do the best we can so that our teams win.'

The only controversial moment comes when he is asked about his vote. 'I didn't vote. I had a bit of a knock in training with the national team and they sent me home.' Who would have got his vote? 'That's private.' When asked the same question, Messi responds: 'Of course I could have voted for CR7, he's an incredible player. But I prefer to vote for my team-mates.' He reveals he has voted for Kun Agüero, Xavi and Iniesta.

Just before 8pm, 2006 Ballon d'Or winner Fabio

Cannavaro opens the envelope, as the cameras focus in on the three finalists. There is a brief moment of suspense, before the former Italy captain proclaims: 'Lion Messi'. Andrés Iniesta turns to congratulate his team-mate, while Cristiano looks disappointed. Messi is the first player in history to win a fourth Ballon d'Or, the accolade recognised as rewarding the best player in the world. He overtakes legends and three-time winners Johan Cruyff, Marco van Basten and Michel Platini. Barça's number 10 has received 41.6 per cent of the votes, beating Cristiano's 23.68 per cent and Iniesta's 10.91 per cent. Leo's 91 goals have counted for more than Cristiano's Liga or Supercup victories with Real, or Iniesta's UEFA Euro 2012 trophy with Spain. Another frustration for Cristiano.

30 April 2013. It's the return leg of the Champions League semi-finals at the Bernabéu. Real are wishing, hoping, praying for an epic recovery to avoid a knockout. In the first leg against Jürgen Klopp and Robert Lewandowski's Borussia Dortmund, Real were overwhelmed, and the game ended 4–1. Real's only goal, their sole glimmer of hope, was scored by Cristiano. He was only able to keep up the fight against the powerful Germans for around 40 minutes and equalised just before the break thanks to a pass from Higuaín and an error from Hummels. But despite his best efforts, he is unable to protect Real from a beating in the second half.

Faced with a difficult return leg, everyone has put their faith in CR7 who, in spite of injury niggles, still has all the requisite talent, class, heart and natural competitiveness. He has demonstrated as such with his twelve goals in eleven matches in the tournament. And he has proved himself in challenging situations, such as in the final sixteen against his former Manchester United team, or in Istanbul in the second leg of the quarter-final against Galatasaray. On 13 February at home to Man United, Cristiano equalises in the 30th minute. Di María sends in a high pass at the far post, Evra miscalculates the trajectory and Cristiano is ready. He beats him in the air with an impressive leap and his magnificent header flies in at De Gea's left post. It's a phenomenal goal, for which he later apologises to the English fans. 'Man United was my home for many years. They took me in when I was a kid and I care about them a lot.'

At the final whistle, Sir Alex Ferguson goes over to hug his former player. 'I am proud to see how he has flourished,' he says at the post-match press conference. 'I don't know how you can describe a goal like that. I blamed Patrice Evra for not challenging for his goal until I saw the replay and felt a bit stupid. His knee is about as high as Evra's head – phenomenal. I've seen it before, in Rome [against Roma in 2008], and I don't think any other player in the world can do that, certainly not Messi.'

Two weeks later at Old Trafford, Cristiano is the hero once again, beating Rafael to score Real's second goal and take them to a 2–1 victory. And in the quarter-final against Fatih Terim's Galatasaray at the Türk Telekom Arena, he scores three, leading a historic battle amid the noise to make it 3–2 and help Real avoid elimination. Given the way the tournament has gone, and the type of season he has had, it's understandable to think that the number 7 could pull off yet another miracle and take his club through to the Champions League final at Wembley. But this time, it's beyond their reach.

They get off to an explosive start and, despite squandering three chances, look close to taking down Dortmund in a final push. They win 2–0, but it's the Germans who are celebrating after winning on aggregate. Cristiano is disappointed not to have been able to score, apologises to the fans yet again for not making it into the final, and congratulates Dortmund. 'Real Madrid will have their chance to win their tenth trophy,' he says. 'Not this year, but maybe next year.' And he adds: 'Not only now, but right from the beginning of the season I have felt good. I feel comfortable. The fans have been good to me. I'm OK.' The unhappiness has finally disappeared.

On 17 May 2013 at the Santiago Bernabéu, Real Madrid play Atlético Madrid in the final of the Copa del Rey. It's the Whites' last chance to win something. Mourinho's men have made it this far after beating their eternal rivals in the semi-finals, thanks to Cristiano. After the first leg finished 1–1, Cristiano runs rings around Barça in the return leg on 26 February at the Nou Camp, in front of a 95,000-strong crowd – who whistle non-stop throughout the match. The defenders can't find a way to stop him and no one else on the pitch can hold a candle to him. And he wins his duel with Barça's number 10, who seems barely present. Meanwhile, Cristiano is omnipresent: he runs the length of the pitch and takes nine shots, including five on target and two goals. One is a penalty after a clear foul by Piqué. The other is from a play that starts deep in Real's own half: a precise pass from Xabi Alonso, a run by Di María, and Cristiano steps in at the right moment to beat goalie Pinto. It's his eighth goal in his last six visits to the Nou Camp – even better than Alfredo Di Stéfano's record during his Real heyday. He is the Barça fans' worst nightmare.

Having dealt with his most dangerous opponents, he turns his attention to Atlético Madrid, who haven't won a derby with their local rivals for fourteen years. Their two Liga matches have been uneventful: Real won 2–0, and later 2–1 – when their minds were on Borussia Dortmund. True,

Cholo Simeone's team has put on some good performances in Europe in recent years, but Real are the favourites for the consolation title that could help to alleviate some of the pain of the season's losses, while Atlético are just hoping to break their derby curse.

In the fourteenth minute Cristiano silences the Red and White fans. From a Luka Modri corner, the ball flies between the penalty spot and the little box in front of goal. The number 7 goes up for it over Diego Godin and heads the ball in at the post, where goalkeeper Courtois can't get to it. It's his ninth in nine matches against Atlético, and Real's only goal in the first half. On Mourinho's instructions, they close ranks deeper into their own half, as on many other occasions when they have been in the lead. From here onwards they await their chance to seal the match with a counterattack. But Atlético have other ideas, and they equalise thanks to a smooth play by Radamel Falcao.

In the half-time break, Mourinho decides to change tack and go for the victory. Three shots come off the post, including a free kick from Cristiano, which has him raising his arms in frustration. And then it gets complicated. Referee Clos Gómez gives Mourinho a red card in the 75th minute and Cristiano is left to battle on to the end of the match and into extra time. He is not happy about the way the Atlético players are marking his team. Wound up, he gets in a scuffle with the captain, Gabi, as they both vie for the ball, and ends up swinging his foot up towards Gabi's head. Straight red card in the 114th minute. He makes his way off.

Íker Casillas tries to cheer him up on the bench. But Atlético are up 2–1 thanks to a header from Miranda, and they go on to lift the Copa del Rey. Cristiano does not go up to collect his runner-up medal from King Juan Carlos, instead disappearing into the bowels of the Bernabéu.

Those 114 minutes are the last of the 2012–13 season for Cristiano Ronaldo. He won't be playing any more matches due to back pain. On 1 June, the 38th and final match day of La Liga, he makes an appearance on the pitch at the Bernabéu during the match against Osasuna. Dressed in a white T-shirt and jeans, he receives the prize for healthiest Real Madrid player.

It's also time to bid farewell to coach José Mourinho amid whistles and applause. After three years in the dressing room, the Special One is off. The Premier League and Chelsea await, as he finishes a season that he says has been the worst of his career. CR7 seems to have distanced himself from his mentor and friend. After the defeat in the Champions League semi-final, he even said that he did not mind whether Mourinho stayed on or not. 'I don't need to worry about others. All that matters to me is what Real Madrid does and what I do.'

Mourinho has gone, and Cristiano remains. He has two years left on his contract and is not going anywhere. 'I wouldn't sell him,' says Florentino Pérez. 'Not for a billion euros.'

Chapter 28

Five long years

'Good evening. There are no words to describe this moment ...' Cristiano Ronaldo pauses, overcome with emotion. Tears in his eyes, a lump in his throat, he is unable to speak. The audience breaks into applause, giving him a moment to gather his composure and dry his eyes before continuing. 'Thank you to all my teammates, both at the club and the national team, and to all my family who are here tonight ...' He breaks off, overwhelmed once again. 'This is an incredible honour. Everyone who knows me knows how difficult it has been for me to win this trophy. I would like to thank my agent and my president, and everyone who is here tonight. And I would also like to pay tribute to Eusébio and to Mr Nelson Mandela, who have been very important to me. My girlfriend is here tonight, along with my mother and my son. This is the first time my son has seen his father win a Ballon d'Or ... and ... forgive me, this is a very emotional moment for me. It's difficult for me to speak. Thank you everyone.' The tears prove too much, and the ceremony ends with music and more applause.

It is 13 January 2014. The venue is the Zurich Palace of Congress. At ten to eight, FIFA Ballon d'Or gala hosts Fernanda Lima and Ruud Gullit invite *L'Equipe* newspaper president François Morinière, UEFA president Michel Platini and Pelé onto the stage. O Rei is tasked with opening the envelope to reveal the winner. The cameras zoom in on the three finalists: Cristiano, Lionel Messi and Franck Ribéry. The Frenchman is wearing a black jacket and bow tie, the Argentine sports a rather loud crimson Dolce & Gabbana jacket, while CR7 is in shiny black. All three are focused on the stage. Pelé keeps them in suspense, smiling and waving the card, before finally announcing: 'The winner is Cristiano Ronaldo.'

The Real number 7 and Portugal star bows his head for a moment, then turns to kiss Irina before making his way towards the stage. He shakes hands with FIFA president Joseph Blatter, hugs Pelé, and greets Platini and the *L'Equipe* president. Cristiano Ronaldo Junior comes up from the stalls to join him on stage. Pelé picks him up while his father receives the Ballon d'Or trophy from Blatter. When it's Cristiano's turn to speak, his heart is in his mouth. 'They were real, genuine tears', he will say later. 'When my son came up on stage my emotions got the better of me – even more so when I saw my family crying. I didn't want to cry, but I'm not made of stone.'

After five long years Ronaldo has reclaimed the Ballon d'Or, crowning him the best in the world. When he first won it in 2008, he was just 24 and seemingly unrivalled. But Messi's unstoppable rise in the subsequent months and years began to highlight his own limitations. Four seasons, four consecutive Ballon d'Ors for Messi and a long and difficult wait for Cristiano. Years of hard work and goals – 403 for club and country, including an unprecedented 69 in 2013 – and a slew of records have helped him win back the trophy from his eternal rival in one of the closest races in the history of the award. Cristiano has 1,365 points (27.9 per cent of the votes) against Messi's 1,205 (24.7 per cent) and Ribéry's 1,127 (23.3 per cent). Coaches, captains and journalists from 209 countries have acknowledged the Portuguese's perseverance, faith, willpower and goal-scoring capacity, and his personal achievements have made up for a lack of success at team level. He is not the first footballer to have clinched the golden ball without winning any titles during the year – others to have done so include Stanley Matthews in 1956, Dennis Law in 1964, Gerd Müller in 1970, Kevin Keegan in 1978 and Luís Figo in 2000.

Friends and rivals are full of praise for Ronaldo and his talents. 'Cristiano has had a great year and he deserves the prize', says Messi after the presentation. 'Congratulations to Cristiano on his second Ballon d'Or and to Messi and Ribéry for an incredible 2013', tweets Gerard Piqué. Real Madrid president Florentino Pérez declares: 'He deserves it. For his talent, his desire to succeed and improve every day, and for his self-sacrifice, it's only right that Cristiano has won. The team and I are so proud that they have recognised a footballing leader who always strives to be the best. He is an example to everyone, particularly youngsters.'

'It has been emotional. We were all relieved when they announced Cristiano's name', reveals Sergio Ramos. And Portugal national coach Paulo Bento says: 'It's a just reward for an incredible year for an incredible player. Cristiano is a talented footballer and a consummate professional.' Portuguese Prime Minister Pedro Passos Coelho says: 'Ronaldo makes our team and our country great.' And President Aníbal Cavaco Silva congratulates Cristiano on behalf of the nation: 'You are the first Portuguese to receive such an honour. The trophy is a reminder of your exceptional sporting ability, your determination and your footballing achievements', he writes.

Indeed, CR7 is the first Portuguese to have won the Ballon d'Or twice, and just the third to have won it at all, after Eusébio in 1965 and Figo in 2000. And as he admits in his speech, it has not been an easy ride. He was not the book-ies' favourite going into the new season – at that point Ribéry was leading the pack. The Frenchman and Bayern Munich number 7 had swept the board, winning the Bundesliga, the German Cup, the Champions League and the UEFA Super Cup. By the end of the year he would also have the FIFA Club World Cup under his belt. On top of that he had been named UEFA's player of the 2012–13 season. Meanwhile Messi had won La Liga with Barcelona and scored 42 goals in 45 matches. He was the top goal-scorer in the Spanish championship, and the holder of the European Golden Boot. Cristiano, by comparison, had not won a single title – both he and Real had lost out during the end of Mourinho's reign. But though the season was over, there was still time to redeem himself before the end of the calendar year. During the final four months of 2013 he does his best to up his game. He takes advantage of Messi being out injured to move ahead in the race for the trophy, and in a dramatic turn of events he casts doubt over all talk of a Ribéry win.

It all begins on 15 September 2013, in the royal box at the Bernabéu, where Cristiano signs a contract with Real to take him through to 2018 and become the highest paid footballer in the world – with a salary of 21 million Euros a season, according to various sources. With his contract up for renewal he had been at something of a crossroads, and had fuelled plenty of gossip about his next move. Some incredible offers had surfaced from other clubs, and there had been particular interest from Manchester United. Cristiano was not thrilled about the uncertainty, just as he wasn't particularly excited about the signing of Welshman Gareth Bale for 91 million Euros (according to Real), or 100 million Euros (according to Spurs), and his 11 million Euro salary. Cristiano's new deal restores order in the Real salary stakes, recognises his value and contribution to the team, determines his future and puts an end to any question of the Portuguese's unhappiness, which he revealed to the world in September 2012.

Perhaps it's the new contract – recognition that he is the best. Or perhaps it's his increasing professional and personal maturity. Either way, from September onwards Cristiano is on fire. On 17 September, two days after the contract is signed, he scores a hat-trick at Galatasaray to flatten the Turks in a spectacular 6-1 victory. Ten days earlier on 6 September he had crushed Northern Ireland with three magical goals in fifteen minutes, taking Portugal one step closer to the Brazil World Cup. It is his hundredth cap, and his hat-trick takes his tally for the national team to 43, leapfrogging Eusébio in the list of the country's highest goalscorers of all time, and putting him just four goals behind top-of-the-leaderboard Pauleta.

On 25 October Blatter compares Messi and Ronaldo in a talk at the Oxford Union Society. 'Leo is a good boy. Every father and mother would like to have that at home. He's very good, he's very fast. He plays well, as if he is dancing. The other one [Ronaldo] is like a commander on the field of play.' Blatter stands to attention, imitating a soldier, and the audience laughs. 'One spends more on his hairdresser than the other, but I can't say who is the best. The shortlist for the Ballon d'Or comes out next Tuesday, and then it will be decided', he continues. 'I like both of them. But I prefer Messi.'

The little joke goes viral and Ronaldo is none too pleased. But rather than issuing a statement, he responds on the pitch with a hat-trick against Sevilla, and celebrates his first goal with a military salute, delighting all those who didn't care for the FIFA president's tone.

Meanwhile, his incredible run continues. Between 1 September and 19 November he scores no fewer than 34 goals across all competitions, including five hat-tricks. And that last date in particular marks his spectacular perfor- mance for Portugal against Sweden in Solna in the return leg of a World Cup qualifier. Cristiano had not been on top form in the first leg in Lisbon, although he did score a deci- sive header to make it 1-0 at the final whistle. But his per- formance in Sweden is particularly memorable. He sends Portugal through, puts paid to the Scandinavians' World Cup hopes, and wins his duel with Zlatan Ibrahimović in one fell swoop.

But Cristiano demonstrates that he is more than just a prolific goal-scorer. He is a mature and versatile player and a shrewd interpreter of the game. Three runs from 100 feet, three sprints towards Isaksson's goal, three powerful shots – two with the left, one with the right – culminating in three crucial goals to flatten the opponents. The first goal already leaves Sweden needing three for a comeback. Ibra's two goals have the fans in Solna revved up, thinking he can pull off the impossible. But Ronaldo's second silences them, and by the third the Swedes are well and truly sunk. And if there were any Portuguese fans who had previously accused him of not giving it his all, Cristiano's performance is enough to convince them he is putting in just as much effort for his country as he does in Madrid. His hat-trick takes him level with Pauleta's record, making him Portugal's newest hero.

And it's not over yet. On 10 December at the Parken Stadium, in the final Group B Champions League match against Copenhagen, CR7 sets a new record by being the first player to score nine goals in the group stages. And he narrowly misses making it ten, as goalie Wiland successfully blocks a penalty. By the end of the year he has racked up

69 goals in 59 matches, an average of 1.16 per game and a new personal best. He has netted 38 in La Liga, fifteen in the Champions League, six in the Copa del Rey and ten for Portugal. He has certainly upped the stakes in the 'best in the world' debate.

His stock is on the rise and he is fast becoming the favourite for the Ballon d'Or. FIFA had extended the voting period until 29 November, so his performances for Portugal may well have swayed the voters, and he is top of the polls in all the various sports pages across Europe. It seems he might be in with a chance of knocking Messi off the top spot and overcoming the disappointment of the past four years. The previous year, after Real went out of Europe in the semi-finals, coach José Mourinho revealed: 'Cristiano is so focused on the Ballon d'Or, it affected his concentration.' But this time it is within his reach.

A few days before the Zurich gala, Portugal suffers a great loss. At 3.00am on 5 January 2014, Portuguese football legend Eusébio da Silva Ferreira dies of a heart attack in Lisbon, aged 71. The government declares three days of national mourning for the 'Black Panther', who rose to fame with Benfica and the national team in the 1960s. 'Always eternal #Eusébio, rest in peace', tweets Cristiano, alongside a picture of himself with the legendary goalscorer. Eusébio has been a fundamental influence on CR7, offering him advice at crucial moments throughout his life, such as signing with United, his father's death, and the day of his presentation at the Bernabéu.

The Black Panther has undoubtedly been a role model for Cristiano, and he dedicates the two Liga goals he scores against Celta Vigo on 6 January to his hero. 'I dedicate these two goals to you Eusébio but in fact you were the one who scored them. You'll always be in my heart', he tweets. And he thanks the Spanish footballing world for the love shown to his fellow countryman, as a minute's silence is held at the Bernabéu before the match. 'This is a special day and I want to thank everyone, especially the whole of Spain for the way you have honoured Eusébio. For the Portuguese to feel the kindness of the Spanish is very important. Eusébio was very important to my country, and he helped me so much when I joined the national team. He is a shining example to all players.'

He pays tribute to the footballing legend once again on 13 January. In an evening overflowing with tears, the Ballon d'Or gala marks a shift in Cristiano's public image. His display of emotion transforms him from the superstar referred to so often in the press as arrogant, egotistical, proud or cocky, into a mere mortal. The real Cristiano is visible that night, the child from Madeira who cried almost every day during the early years at the Sporting academy. The man who has said repeatedly that he continues to cry 'out of happiness and sadness. It's good to cry. Crying is part of life.' And how could he not cry when his son comes up on stage? Or when he sees his mother in floods of tears in the audience? There is no doubt he is completely caught up in the moment in Zurich, just as Eusébio was in his day.

He has shown a new level of maturity, he has opened his heart, and in so doing has conquered hearts in Portugal and beyond. And the love of a nation is far more important than a golden ball. Everyone back home has witnessed his transformation – from fans hooting their car horns after the announcement, to the pundits and journalists who concede their admiration. 'Cristiano Ronaldo is a great example to Portuguese society – a man with ambitions who never gives up. He always believes he can succeed', declares daily newspaper *Diário de Notícias*.

Further proof of his country's new-found love comes just a week later, on 20 January in the Sala das Bicas ballroom at the Belém National Palace in Lisbon, where President Cavaco Silva names Cristiano a Grand Officer of the Order of Prince Henry (a Portuguese national order of knighthood), 'for his contribution to Portugal's international reach'. The presentation had been planned for 7 January, but has been postponed following Eusébio's death. The event attracts more national media attention than President Obama's visit in 2010 – live TV broadcast, live online streaming, and 220 journalists present. Cristiano is accompanied by Portuguese Football Federation president Fernando Gomes, national coach Bento, Florentino Pérez and Emilio Butragueño from Real Madrid, Aurélio Pereira, one of his first coaches, and his agent Jorge Mendes. His family is unable to attend due to prior commitments. Ronaldo takes along the Ballon d'Or trophy, and symbolically dedicates it to the people of Portugal. 'The award is a huge source of pride and an incentive to keep working hard and keep representing Portugal across the world. It drives me to be even more determined', he tells broadcaster RTP. 'I hope I will enjoy more successes both individually and with my teams. What I love most is playing football, and I want to keep enjoying myself while also adding a beautiful page to the history books. Without detracting from any of the trophies I have won so far, the dream is to be crowned world champion with Portugal. It's a big challenge, one that every team dreams about. I hope we can make that dream come true.'

Chapter 29

La Décima

And there he was with his legs spread wide on the pitch of the Estádio da Luz in Lisbon. Top off, hands on hips, a roar like the Incredible Hulk from Marvel's comic strip, his ripped biceps, pectorals and abs tensed to the max. Cristiano Ronaldo had just scored the last goal in the 2014 Champions League final from a penalty. Poor Thibaut Courtois, Atlético Madrid number 1. Goalie to the left, ball to the right. It was a goal which made no real difference as it came in the 120th minute when the score was already 3-1 to Real Madrid. And yet CR7 celebrated the goal in this way, namely taking off his shirt and posing for the TV, photographers, viewers and fans all over the world. He celebrated the goal as though it was the most important of his career, as though it was Alcides Ghiggia's winning goal against Brazil in the Maracanazo of 1950. A little excessive considering that the other team had already been crushed and defeated, and given that the CR7's performance was not his best due to troubles with his left knee.

Moreover, the hero of the final was not Ronaldo but Sergio Ramos who in the 93rd minute, when the *colchoneros* looked like the cup was theirs, mustered up a header from a Modric corner: scoring a goal which took the match to extra time and enabled the win. When all was said and done, a spot-kick hardly merited the festivities which Ronaldo was displaying on the pitch, muscles and all. The reason for all this showing off? The iconic image was pre-planned. He needed it for his film: *Cristiano Ronaldo: The Movie*. A feature-length film by Paramount. Why not make the most of such an opportunity to mix utility with fun?

More fun, more true, more spontaneous and, why not, more childish was the celebration the kid from Madeira had put on at the Allianz Arena in Munich. After having netted the third goal against Bayern, just like a kid at primary school who has just started to count using his hands, he put his two hands in the air: both hands together, then the right hand again – fifteen fingers for his fifteen goals in Champions League in 2013–14. He had just beaten the record shared by Lionel Messi and José Altafini, the ex-Milan forward of the 1960s. He was as happy as a child finding the present he wanted under the Christmas tree from Santa.

Leaving celebrations to one side, these two matches in Lisbon and Munich provide a snapshot of Cristiano Ronaldo's 2013–14 season. The footballer who, apart from showing his six pack, cried about winning the tenth European Cup ('*La Décima*') that Real Madrid fans had wanted to win for twelve years. The previous occasion had been on 15 May 2002, when Real beat Bayern Leverkusen at Hampden Park in Glasgow thanks to a magical volley from Zinedine Zidane. In Ronaldo, here was a champion who could lift the trophy for the second time, six years on from when he did it in the Luzhniki stadium in Moscow on 21 May 2008 wearing the red shirt of Manchester United. Now he would do it in the white shirt of Madrid. Here was the Portuguese player who won in Lisbon, the city which had seen him come of age. He made it in the stadium where ten years earlier he had cried with anger and sadness when in the Euro 2004 final he lost with Portugal to Greece. And here was the insatiable goalscorer who scored seventeen Champions League goals in a single season, a record for the tournament, despite playing only eleven of the thirteen matches. This took his overall tally for the competition to 68 – a figure which took him close to the 71 goals of Raúl González, also of Real Madrid and the record goalscorer in the competition's history.

The voracity of Cristiano Ronaldo was one of the keys to success in the competition for Real. It was a real domination: eleven victories, a draw against Juventus and a sole defeat against Borussia Dortmund in Westfalen. Forty-one goals scored, almost double the tally of the second highest scoring team, Atlético Madrid with 26. Real had outplayed the Bundesliga teams, knocking out Schalke in the last sixteen with a tennis-like score of 6-1 (the same scoreline by which they had beaten Galatasaray in Group B), then Borussia Dortmund in the quarter-finals and Bayern Munich in the semi-finals – these being the two finalists from the 2013 Champions League. And now in Lisbon Real had beaten Atlético, the champions of La Liga for 2013–14. A perfect result, about which there is little more to be said.

The best match and the most unexpected result of this run had been Bayern Munich–Real Madrid on 29 April 2014. The Whites had arrived in Munich with a 1-0 advantage from the first leg at the Santiago Bernabéu. Everyone was expecting that Pep Guardiola and his team, who had won the German league, would be unforgiving and able to run rings around the *merengues*. This view was completely reasonable seeing as Real had never left the Allianz Arena on top. None of the Real camp had forgotten that two years ago, the Germans had beaten them on penalties to deny them a place in the final. Sergio Ramos, the man who had moon-balled the deciding penalty, definitely had not forgotten. The player from Andalusia clearly remembered what that miss meant.

Sometimes football can provide poetic justice for players caught up in the ebb and flow of matches. Ramos, the defender, had fate on his side as he managed to beat Manuel Neuer with two top goals in the space of four minutes (15th to 19th), headers from a Modric corner and then a Di Maria free-kick.

Bayern were on their knees. They were a team that did not appear to be involved in the match or to be engaged in play; a team that did not threaten their opponents – it was a surprise for all concerned. Bayern were completely outplayed. The Whites were solid in defence and lethal in attack. Real dominated. The 'BBC' (Bale, Benzema, Cristiano) counter-attack in the 33rd minute put the score beyond reach: Benzema to Bale who streaked upfield taking his marker with him. Into the area: a square pass, which Ronaldo hit on the run, sending the ball between Neuer's legs. 3-0. CR7's hands went up to show it was his fifteenth goal in the Champions League. In the 89th minute came goal number sixteen from a Ronaldinho-style free-kick. The players in the wall jumped expecting the curler; instead the ball was hit deftly across the floor and caught everyone by surprise, including the German goalkeeper. Cristiano had now scored 250 goals with the white shirt on his back. Too many to show all of them with his ten digits ... For Guardiola, the philosopher, and the Bavarians it was total humiliation; for the Spaniards, absolute euphoria. *El Pais* stated clearly what it thought: 'An Imperial Madrid'. A Real team which would add another trophy to its collection on 24 May in Lisbon – after the Spanish Cup final, which Real were to win on 16 April in the Mestalla, Valencia, 3-0 against Barcelona.

Carlo Ancelotti, when appointed coach for Real, had said in the Bernabéu that the Champions League was the main objective, and now he had won it. It was his fifth after two with Milan as a central midfielder (1989 and 1990) and two more with the same club as coach (2003 and 2007). However, Carletto had failed in La Liga. Real let down its sails when anything was still possible and the league would be decided on the last day of the season on 17 May 2014 between Barcelona and Atlético Madrid. In the Nou Camp, a header from the Uruguayan Diego Godín, took the score-line to 1-1, just what *Cholo*'s (Diego Simeone's) men needed. The score gave the *colchoneros* the Spanish title, eighteen years after they had last won it.

Cristiano Ronaldo ended the season as *Pichichi* (top goalscorer) for the second time, with 31 goals in 30 league matches (51 in 47 in all competitions). The European Golden Boot was his, shared with Luis Suárez, the Liverpool number 7, now number 9 for Barcelona. CR7 could have overtaken the Uruguayan forward in the 38th and final match of the season but against Espanyol he did not play. During the warm-up, he felt something pull and decided not to risk it. From the beginning of April, his body had started to give him warning signs. The doctors who examined him diagnosed tendinitis in the left knee and serious inflammation of the muscles. They recommended complete rest because they feared the problems could get worse. They feared that he could miss important matches at the end of the season. They said that his body was on the edge. Ronaldo only took on board some of the advice. He rested for three Liga matches (against Real Sociedad, Almeria and Celta Vigo). He had to miss out, begrudgingly, on the final of the Spanish Cup, where he could be seen consoling Leo Messi after the match. He tried to prime his legs for the match against Dortmund but it did not work and he only made the bench. He played the matches against Valencia and Osasuna in pain and the Champions League semi-final and final with the inflammation niggling him. He was not running on all cylinders. For the first time in his career, his seemingly indestructible chassis had failed him. His body had let him down. He was not expecting it and it gave him a nagging concern that something could go wrong from one moment to the next. He had pushed his engine to the limit and beyond; he had gone against the doctors' and physios' advice. Cristiano was always hungry for the fight, for the win; he always wanted to score. The World Cup was coming up and he could not miss out.

Chapter 30

The last goal

The dream of the World Cup was not to be. It was over as soon as it had started. It was the only goal in Brazil for Cristiano Ronaldo and it was a sad end to a great season.

Some attributed it to the curse of the Ballon d'Or: many champions who have been awarded the coveted prize invented by *France Football* have failed to win, perform at or even qualify for the World Cup – starting with Alfredo Di Stefano in 1958: his Spain team failed to reach the tournament in Sweden. In 1962, Chile, Omar Sivori, the Argentine who had chosen to play for Italy had to head home after losing to Italy in the 'Battle of Santiago'. In 1966, Eusébio, the 'Black Panther', arrived at the English World Cup with Portugal, one of the favourites. He had an excellent tournament: he scored nine goals and was the top scorer, but Portugal only came third. In 1970, Gianni Rivera had won the Ballon d'Or ahead of Gigi Riva but in the final at the Azteca Stadium in Mexico City it was Brazil that, against Italy, won the Jules Rimet Cup, the trophy being held aloft by Pelé, Carlos Alberto and Jairzinho. In 1974, Johan Cruyff had won the Ballon d'Or twice on the trot and the Dutch 'total' football looked invincible but in the World Cup in West Germany he came a cropper against the hosts, led by the 'Kaiser' Franz Beckenbauer.

The list of the curse of the Ballon d'Or includes Karl-Heinz Rummenigge who in 1982 lost the final with

West Germany against Paolo Rossi's Italy. Michel Platini at Mexico '86; Marco van Basten at Italia '90. Roberto Baggio, the *codino divino* (the 'Divine Ponytail'), who at USA '94 merited his title of best player in the world but fluffed the deciding penalty against the Brazil team of Romario and Bebeto. Ronaldo 'O Fenomeno' who in Paris in 1998 fell ill, allowing Zinedine Zidane's France to win. There was Michael Owen in Japan and South Korea in 2002 and then Lionel Messi in South Africa, who, under the tutelage of Diego Maradona, played five matches without scoring a goal and was sent packing in the quarter-finals in Germany (4-0).

The examples of the curse of the Ballon d'Or are many but it is only a myth. The truth was that in the case of the number 7 of Portugal and Real Madrid it was his left knee and inflamed muscles, the heavy schedule and the tiredness after a long season which were the telling signs.

On the eve of the World Cup, CR7's participation in the tournament was touch and go. It was Paulo Bento, the Portuguese coach, who admitted it: 'We do not have a definitive date for when Cristiano will be back at training. The first thing is the fitness of the player. We need to let him relax' – this with not more than two weeks to go to the first match against Germany. CR7 was in the hands of Antonio Gaspar, Portugal's wizard physio, who was responsible for getting him on the pitch. Cristiano's muscular problems kept his teammates, the team staff, the fans and an entire country on tenterhooks. The national squad could not turn up in Salvador de Bahia without its captain, emblem and leading scorer, who had scored 49 goals in 110 matches. The Brazil World Cup needed him. Along with Lionel Messi and Neymar Junior, he was one of the special ones.

On 15 June, Cristiano Ronaldo gave a press conference before the match against Joachim Lowe's disciples to clear any doubt. He would like to have been at 110 per cent but he was only at 100 per cent – but it would be enough to help the team. When they asked him how he had reacted to the rumours that he would not make it to the World Cup, he curtly replied: 'I am used to these unfortunate statements from people. If I am not fit, I am the first to tell the coach that I cannot play. If I feel something is wrong, which I don't, I will not put my career on the line. First me, then football. I am fine. I would have liked to have played without pain but it is not possible. From when I started playing football, I cannot remember a match without pain. It is part of the job.'

He was convinced that this was the best moment of his career. He was motivated and wanted to do well, even if he did not need to prove anything to anyone at the World Cup. He just wanted to put the icing on the cake for a fantastic year. It was not completely true because if Cristiano wanted to put himself on a par with the Black Panther, Eusébio, he would have to give his all; he wanted to take his team to the top of the world. He believed it was possible. He thought it was Portugal's year. He thought there was a good vibe in the camp and would do anything to make it continue. Regarding his German rivals, he stated that they were one of the favourites to win but he had faith that the run of bad luck that Portugal had had against the Germans – not winning for fourteen years – would end on 16 June 2014. The recent example of the Champions League was also comforting. Real Madrid had not beaten Bayern Munich for a long time, but now they had done so. He hoped this was a sign of things to come. Destiny.

But fate was not on their side. At the end of the 90 minutes of ordinary time, it was the German Chancellor, Angela Merkel, sporting a red jacket, who was smiling. She visited the changing rooms to greet *Der Mannschaft* and have a photo taken with the players. She was happy to have flown to Brazil to watch the first and decidedly convincing match of her nation's team. The mood in the Portuguese changing rooms was doom and gloom. Portugal had been battered by Germany and let in four goals: a hat-trick for Müller plus a goal from Hummels. After 45 minutes, the Portuguese were down by three goals, a lead which meant the Germans could control in the second half without breaking into a sweat, while taking off key players to rest them and enabling their centre forward to score the first hat-trick of the World Cup.

The first few minutes of the match did not make the onlookers think that this fate would befall Cristiano & Co. The match seemed balanced with Portugal able to press on and create chances thanks to Veloso, Meireles, Moutinho and Ronaldo. A mistake from Lahm and the ball ended up at CR7's feet; he shot with his left, on target. Neuer, the goalie, blocked and pushed the ball away from goal. It was the first chance for the Portuguese. It was looking good. But then Özil, on the right, combined with Müller and Götze and the first German goal was on the scoreboard. Götze entered the box; João Pereira could do nothing else but bring him down. Penalty to Germany. Müller put the ball in the net from the spot. Impeccable. 1-0.

The Portuguese boat was starting to show a few holes. After half an hour, a splendid header from Hummels off a Kroos corner and Pepe was beaten: goal. 2-0. Pepe, who was on edge due to the mistakes in defence, defended a ball from an attack from Müller; there was a hand and the German went down. The Real Madrid defender seemed to believe Müller was play-acting. A head-to-head ensued and the referee gave a red card to the Portuguese player.

Portugal were down to ten men. Germany scored the third before half-time.

In the second half, it was one-way traffic. The German fans could smell victory and started to celebrate and think about the next match. The Portuguese had to defend. The Pepe sending-off was compounded by injuries to Hugo Almeida and Coentrão. Paulo Bento stated that CR7 was fit and able to play but everyone could see that the tendinitis prevented him from giving his all. He was in pain. Joachim Lowe, over the moon after the match, pointed out that the key to success was their taking advantage of the spaces behind the two Portuguese wingers. Cristiano and Nani attacked but did not come back and defend.

Against the United States, who in their first match had beaten Ghana 2-1, it was already effectively a final. The match was on 22 June at Manaus. It was hot and sticky, so much so that Néstor Pitana, the Argentine referee, called a time-out 30 minutes into the game so they everyone could cool down. Ronaldo had a new haircut. A 'Z' like Zorro on the side of his head – a war cry for a crucial match, and a look which grabbed the attention of the social media world. Klinsmann's Yankees were not intimidated and nor were the US fans, who booed Ronaldo for the entire match. Cristiano was not on his best form and his off-peak fitness was clear for all to see. Not even a shot on goal. But in the last minute he switched flanks and finally found the right place to put the ball so that Varala, the Oporto player, could equalise for 2-2. Portugal had been saved by the bell in the 95th minute. A single point was not the desired result and Portugal had one foot in and one foot out of the World Cup. In the last match, CR7's team would have it out with Ghana. However, a draw between the USA and Germany could make any effort by Portugal pointless. In the days leading up to the last match of Group G, the outcome of the Germany–USA match and whether it would be fixed was all over the ether. The match was tight but in the end the Germans came through and beat the Americans 1-0.

The evening before the Portugal match against the Black Stars, a big point of focus for the media in light of Germany's win over the US, was chaotic to say the least. The Ghanaian players had threatened to go on strike if they did not receive their World Cup match bonuses. The players got their way. An armoured truck turned up at the Ghana camp and each player received $225,000 in cash. The African problems did not end there. Sulley Muntari and Kevin Prince Boateng were asked to leave the World Cup. The Milan player had allegedly punched a member of the Ghana staff and the Schalke 04 player had insulted James Kwesi Appiah, the coach. Despite this, on 26 June in the Estadio Nacional in Brasilia, the Ghana team had the upper hand. They did not need to pull back a big goal difference like Portugal. With ten minutes to go to the end of the match, the score was 1-1. Ghana were a step away from the last sixteen. Time for Ronaldo to make his mark, luckily for Portugal – and, as it turned out, for the USA. CR7 had been close three times: a cross/shot from the right that had clipped the crossbar, a central header which Dauda managed to deflect, and a missile free-kick. He had claimed a penalty for a shoulder barge in the box by Boye but the referee was having none of it. In the 80th minute, he found his scoring boots. Dauda parried a high ball into the path of Ronaldo who from a few metres out drilled the ball into the back of the net: 2-1. The captain had scored but he did not celebrate. He looked at the clock. Was there time to overcome the negative goal difference that the Germans had saddled them with? The chances came, and they fell to

Ronaldo: three to be precise. Normally he would not have missed them but this time the ball did not want to go in. It ended 2-1 to Portugal. Both Ghana and Portugal were out. Germany and the USA were through to the knockout stage. Beto, the Portuguese goalkeeper, was in tears both from the physical pain and from being knocked out. CR7 was man of the match but it counted for nothing because his team was out of the World Cup. Ronaldo commented later in the post-match press conference: 'We are leaving with our heads held high. We tried to do our best but football is like this.' He would not take questions. CR7's teammates did not criticise him like the press did after the match. Nani, taking responsibility for everyone, said: 'It was not Cristiano's fault but that of the whole group. We have missed a great opportunity.'

On the night of 26 July, Portugal returned home to Lisbon. For the first time since 2002, the team had not made the knockout stages. Ronaldo, for the third time, could not realise his dreams. He has taken part in three World Cups, namely Germany (2006), South Africa (2010) and Brazil (2014). He has played 1,202 minutes, thirteen matches, and scored three goals. Not great for a star of his importance. By the time of the next World Cup, Russia 2018, he will be 33. Who knows …

Chapter 31

Unstoppable

YEEEEEEESSSSSSSSSSSSSSSSS!! Cristiano Ronaldo yelps with delight. He has just got his hands on his third FIFA Ballon d'Or award in Zurich and he celebrates as if he's scored a trophy-winning goal. The roar is for his teammates' benefit – it's his battle cry. He's unleashed it before, during training and some matches, although tonight it's as though they're hearing it for the first time, and it certainly provokes a reaction on social media.

It is 12 January 2015 and nothing can ruin Cristiano's night – not even the knowledge that he wasn't Sepp Blatter's favourite for the award, nor Michel Platini's. Nor was he the top choice of presenter Thierry Henry, who reads out his name in a rather impassive tone. The FIFA and UEFA presidents preferred Bayern Munich goalie Manuel Neuer, who helped Germany win the 2014 World Cup, while Henry favoured his old Barça teammate Messi. But even without their backing, Ronaldo has received 37.66 per cent of the vote, more than his two rivals combined. Messi has just 15.76 per cent and Neuer 15.72 per cent.

Unlike last year, Cristiano manages to avoid the tears. But he is still highly emotional, taking a long pause before speaking. 'I dedicate this to my son, my family, my mother,' he says finally. He goes on to thank the team and the Real Madrid staff, making particular mention of manager Carlo Ancelotti. 'It has been an incredible experience working with the coach,' he enthuses. 'He has won everything. What can I possibly say about him? He's on another level. He is an extraordinary man. He deserves everything.' Later he adds, 'I don't want to tread water, I want to do as well as Messi. He hasn't thwarted my dreams, rather he has inspired me.' Leo is his reference point, the mirror he holds up against his own achievements. Even his four-and-a-half-year-old son admires his father's biggest rival. 'He watches your matches and he talks about you,' Cristiano tells the Barça star when they meet before the ceremony – an encounter that leaves Cristiano Junior speechless.

Junior and his grandmother have accompanied Cristiano to Zurich, although partner Irina is absent. They have been together for five years and she always joins him at these sorts of events. The press whips up a frenzy about a suspected break-up, but the couple make no comment.

Tonight there is no need to hide his ambition – or what his critics like to call his lack of modesty. He makes no apology for who he is, acknowledging unashamedly that he wants to be immortalised in the history books. He already has three Ballon d'Ors, the same as Johan Cruyff, Michel Platini and Marco van Basten. But at the very least he wants to equal Messi's record of four. His agent claims he wants another two. 'Cristiano is the perfect machine,' declares Jorge Mendes at the end of the ceremony.

Right now the stats are in his favour. Real Madrid won four trophies in 2014 (the Champions League, the Copa del Rey, the UEFA Super Cup and the FIFA Club World Cup) and he scored 61 goals in 60 matches (38 in 28 in La Liga, thirteen in twelve in the Champions League and five in nine internationals). But the figures mask another reality: the Portuguese has now spent many years pushing his body to the limit. He is about to turn 30 and every day he faces a ferocious battle to keep himself at the top of his game.

In fact, the start of the 2014–15 season saw CR7 burdened with injuries. An inflamed right patellar tendon had kept him from giving his all at the end of the previous season and during the Brazil World Cup, and now he had to follow a strict regime to get fit for the new season. Real had even been prepared to sacrifice his place in the team for the Super Cup against Sevilla on 12 August at Cardiff City Stadium, but Cristiano had no intention of missing that match. In the event, not only did he get his way, he scored two goals to give his team their first title of the season, and their second UEFA Super Cup.

Next up was the Spanish Supercup against Atlético Madrid at the Santiago Bernabéu on 19 August. It had been nearly two months since the two teams met in the Champions League final, and revenge was on the agenda for Diego Simeone's team. Real went ahead in the 81st minute with a goal from James Rodríguez, but Raúl García got the equaliser in the final moments of the match. The visitors had made a good impression. The Whites, on the other hand, had looked uncertain. All would be decided at the Calderón, but would Cristiano be playing? The Portuguese had pulled a muscle in his left leg, and hadn't been able to play in the second half of the home leg. It was starting to look like 2013–14 all over again.

On 22 August he was not in the starting line-up as the rivals battled it out for the title. Atlético's goal took him by surprise just as he was settling down to watch from the dugout. Barely two minutes had elapsed since kick-off and it was to be the only goal of the match. Ancelotti sent him on in the second half for Toni Kroos, but there was nothing he could do, and the *Atleti* emerged victorious.

Everyone was in agreement: Real Madrid had been unconvincing. Clearly, neither the team nor its star player were 100 per cent on form. But that didn't stop Cristiano from amassing more trophies in the coming weeks. On 28 August, Platini presented him with UEFA's Best Player in Europe Award for the 2013–14 season. The European journalists of the jury had been seduced by his goalscoring prowess and had awarded him 24 points, five more than Manuel Neuer and fifteen more than Dutchman Arjen Robben. The Portuguese had been a finalist every year since the award's inception in 2011, but had never won it. Now he was in the victors' club alongside Messi, Andrés Iniesta and Franck Ribéry. 'Thank you so much to my teammates,' he said at the presentation ceremony. Without them I wouldn't have won this trophy – an important personal achievement. I hadn't won it before and now I'm very happy.'

It had been a golden year for Cristiano, at least in terms of recognition. He had cemented his place in the team thanks to a change in attitude as much as his scoring record. He had ditched his individualistic style and had taken on more of a leadership role, despite not actually being captain. But he was still not completely fit, and this kept him off the pitch for several weeks. First he missed Portugal's qualifier against Albania for UEFA Euro 2016, which ended 1-0 to the Albanians, and then the clash with Real Sociedad at Anoeta, which Real Madrid lost 4-2 despite being two goals up in the first fifteen minutes. This fiasco, coupled with the departures of Xabi Alonso to Bayern and Ángel Di María to Man United put the Whites in the eye of the storm.

And Cristiano could not extricate himself from the debate. 'I have very clear views on it, but I can't always say what I think because it would be front page headlines tomorrow and I don't want that,' he said on 1 September

2014. 'If I were the one making the decisions I might do it differently, but everyone has their own opinion and everyone's free to say what they want. If the president thought it was best to sign some people and let others go then we have to respect his decisions.'

His comments were made during a publicity appearance at the Jarama racecourse alongside Jenson Button. After going for a spin with the 2009 Formula One champion, he admitted he was 'shit-scared' during their high-speed manoeuvres.

Back to football: CR7 was hit particularly hard by the departure of his close friend Di María. The media claimed he tried to convince him until the last minute to stay, but it didn't work. The Argentine would later acknowledge that Ronaldo was 'always there for him'.

Cristiano's comments about the team caused a furore, which he tried to quell over the following days via his Twitter account. 'My remarks have been misinterpreted. Yesterday I heard what my president had to say and I am behind him 100 per cent.' And in case there were any lingering doubts, he posted another tweet praising the Whites' latest signings, which included the Colombian James Rodríguez and Germany's Toni Kroos: 'Our new teammates are fantastic! We have an incredible squad! Let's do it! C'mon Real!'

That settled that debate ... at least for the time being. But CR7 also revealed another item of interest that had nothing to do with football. For years he had remained silent on the identity of Cristiano Junior's mother. Now he offered an unexpected detail: she is Portuguese, not American as previously rumoured. He would not say anything further, although by now it is known that it was his mother Dolores who went to collect her newborn grandson from a Florida clinic in 2010 while Ronaldo was playing in the World Cup in South Africa. The Aveiro family matriarch apparently learned of the birth when Cristiano called and allegedly told her: 'I'm having a son and I want you to help me bring him up and take care of him, as you have always done for me and my siblings. No one will ever know who her mother is.' No more news on that front ... for now.

Finally, on 13 September, almost a month after the UEFA Super Cup, Ronaldo was back on the pitch – coincidentally, in another derby with Atlético Madrid. He scored but the Whites lost 1-2. The fans didn't hide their anger, and their piercing whistles were heard across the Bernabéu. But memories are short in football, and Real were to rocket back into the stratosphere in a matter of days with three consecutive triumphs. The first was in their opening Champions League match against FC Basel, where Bale, Ronaldo, James, Benzema and an own goal from Suchý made it 5-1. The second was on 20 September against Deportivo La Coruña in a historic Liga match. Cristiano was the first to score, beating the opposing goalie with a header from more than twelve yards. He stayed sitting on the ground as, one by one, his teammates came rushing over to congratulate him. It was his first ever goal at the Riazor ground and nothing could wipe the smile off his face. And he went on to score two more goals as Real ran amok, a hat-trick that cemented what the team medics had already confirmed: his injury troubles were behind him. The scoreline at the final whistle was a resounding 2-8 – the Whites' most impressive away result in their La Liga history.

A few days later Ronaldo was on fire yet again, this time in front of his home crowd. He scored four against Elche (5-1 at the final whistle), and reclaimed his place as top scorer in La Liga. He was let off the hook having given away the penalty that enabled the visitors to take the lead. Bale got the equaliser and then Cristiano took over from there. His first goal came from twelve yards out, the second from a header, his third from the penalty spot, and the fourth came after a rapid counterattack. They were not his best goals – neither particularly elegant nor technically brilliant – but there was no doubt that he was now king of La Liga. No one else even came close.

'Trying to stop Cristiano is like when NBA players used to practise trying to stop Michael Jordan, and he still kept on netting 30 points a game,' said Elche coach Fran Escribá after the match. And Ancelotti made no attempt to hide his pride: 'He has a unique sense of movement – he is always in the perfect position.' And, as the Real manager pointed out, that was despite the fact that he was playing as a pure number 9 against Elche. 'He doesn't like that because he has his back to the goal,' explained Ancelotti. 'He prefers to play on the wing so he has the goal in his sights.'

The Portuguese had scored eight goals in three matches. True, they were against more modest teams, but the next few fixtures proved that it was not just a lucky streak. On 27 September Real Madrid faced Villareal. They won 2-0 thanks to goals from Modrić and Cristiano, although the most memorable moment happened not on the pitch but in the sky. A group of Man United fans known as 'United Reel' had sent a small plane to fly a banner over the stadium reading 'Come home Ronaldo'. In certain circles it was suggested that the stunt was orchestrated by Ronaldo's agent Jorge Mendes in a bid to force Real to sell him back to the English club where he played from 2003 to 2009, but this rumour went unconfirmed. Everything died down after a few days, but the rumour mill continues and the story will no doubt resurface in the future.

For now there was no indication that Cristiano wanted to

leave Real Madrid, and it was clear that the club would be even less willing to see him go. In just about every press conference the coach reiterated how happy he was to have him in his team. 'He is the best footballer I have ever worked with in my career,' insisted Ancelotti. If at first everyone focused on his ego, they had now changed their tune. CR7 was totally committed to his teammates and all the staff at the club. The press even made mention of the gifts he gives the staff every year, like at the end of the pre-season summer tour in American when he surprised each of the physios and technical staff with an iPhone 5S. The year before it had been an iPad, and before that a laptop. And when Real won their tenth Champions League trophy he bought a car for each of the three physios who had helped him get back to full strength so that he could play in the final. But the biggest gift went to someone outside the club. In March 2014 Cristiano had been so affected by the story of Erik, a ten-month-old suffering from a brain abnormality that caused him to have up to 30 seizures a day, that he paid £60,000 for the little Real fan's brain surgery.

Indeed, CR7's public image had changed so much that he was able to get away with a 'Ras Tas Tas' dance after scoring the first goal against Athletic Bilbao at the Bernabéu on 5 October. His interpretation of the catchy Colombian salsa move, made popular by James Rodríguez during the World Cup, only lasted a few seconds, but in another time Ronaldo would surely have caused a storm in a teacup with his celebrations – just ask Barça star Neymar what rained down on him after he broke out some flashy moves in a match against Rayo in the same week. Controversies aside, the most important thing was the scoreline: 5-0 to Real Madrid. And Cristiano went back to the dressing room with another hat-trick under his belt.

Now it was time for him to turn his attention to his country. In a friendly against France he had everyone on tenterhooks after being substituted in the second half and being captured by the TV cameras putting ice on his left knee. But it was a false alarm. A few days later the Portugal captain scored a winning header against Denmark, bagging three crucial points in the bid to qualify for Euro 2016.

And his goal tally was to keep on rising. On 18 October Real Madrid were back to crushing their opponents. This time it was 5-0 against Levante. Ronaldo scored two and Ancelotti was starting to run out of adjectives to describe his star player. 'It is impossible to ask more of Cristiano,' he said at the press conference. And the number 7 was at it again days later in a Champions League match, scoring the first in the Whites' 3-0 victory over Liverpool. The next *Clásico* against Barça, scheduled for 25 October at the Bernabéu, was looming. But first …

A football-shaped meteor has fallen somewhere on earth. Cristiano receives a call: 'The boots have arrived.' He leaps into them and he is transformed. He is a superhero capable of galactic speeds. He can leap from building to building like Spider-man. He has the city at his feet. After a few circuits around the globe he lands on the pitch at the Bernabéu. And all thanks to Nike. The global sports giant had spared no expense in riding the media tidal wave with their latest advert in the lead-up to one of the most hyped matches in football. Ronaldo and Messi were to go head to head in their first duel of the season. Would the Portuguese's new boots bring him luck?

Judging by the result, the answer was yes – despite the fact that Neymar put the visitors ahead after just four minutes. But the Blaugrana could only hold the advantage for half an hour. Just before half-time Cristiano levelled the scores with a penalty, following a handball by Gerard Piqué. The Whites came back after the break with their batteries recharged and unleashed two more to seal their victory and move one point behind their eternal rivals in La Liga.

Three days later it was time for Spain's Liga de Fútbol Profesional 2013–14 awards. Cristiano took home three: Best Player, Best Goal and Best Striker. And at the beginning of November European Sports Media presented him with his third Golden Shoe trophy in recognition of his 31 goals in 2013–14 (the same as Luis Suárez, then of Liverpool, though the Uruguayan took three more games to reach that tally). And in case anyone still had any doubts, Ronaldo made it crystal clear at the awards ceremony that he was exactly where he wanted to be: 'We will have to talk to Florentino Pérez to renew for a few more years. The truth is I am extremely happy, along with my family and in my personal life … All I want is to win, and I hope to finish out my contract with Real Madrid at the age of 33, and then we'll see if the president still wants me here.'

Pérez made it clear that he was every bit as happy with their ongoing union: 'We have an extraordinary squad with a magnificent coach. And we have a worthy heir to Alfredo Di Stéfano: Cristiano Ronaldo, current Ballon d'Or holder, who has already won his third Golden Shoe and who is already a Real Madrid legend.'

A week later Cristiano would have two more prizes in his trophy cabinet: the Pichichi award for being La Liga's top goalscorer, and Best Player, both awarded by sports newspaper *Marca*. But the recognition extended beyond his achievements on the pitch. According to Forbes, he had become the second-highest paid sportsman in the world. In just one year he had moved up from ninth place into the runner-up position thanks to $80 million-worth of income and endorsements in 2014. He was second only to American boxer Floyd Mayweather, who brought in $105 million. Leo Messi was two places and $13 million behind Cristiano.

The two rivals came face to face once again on 18 November in the Portugal–Argentina friendly at Old Trafford. Cristiano had recently become the highest goalscorer in European Championship history with a total of 23, including qualifying matches and finals tournaments. His header during Portugal's 1–0 win over Armenia on 14 November had helped him overtake Denmark's Jon Dahl Tomasson, the previous record holder. Already Portugal's top goalscorer of all time, Ronaldo now had 52 goals in 117 matches for his country.

But neither CR7 nor Messi had a stellar night in Manchester. In fact, they were both only on during the first half. But Cristiano's fans didn't seem to mind: he received continual applause from those who had watched him play at Old Trafford for six years. And in case there was any doubt about their loyalty, they threw the odd boo in the Argentine's direction. In the end Portugal managed a 1-0 victory thanks to a goal by Raphaël Guerreiro.

Back home in Madrid Cristiano was ready for the next round of fixtures – and the goals kept coming thick and fast: two against Eibar, one against Basel, three against Celta Vigo, one against Ludogorets and two at Almería. The Whites had now won every game since 16 September when they first took on Basel, making 20 successive victories: twelve in La Liga, six in the Champions League and two in the Copa del Rey. They had netted 74 goals in that time – nearly four per match – and had only conceded ten. Twenty-five of those goals were scored by Cristiano.

Against that backdrop, Real Madrid touched down in Morocco to compete in the Club World Cup. They went straight into the semi-finals against Mexico's Cruz Azul on

16 December. It was a fairly uncomplicated match that the Spaniards were able to seal with a convincing 4-0 victory, though Ronaldo did not make it on to the scoresheet. Four days later, they faced Argentine team San Lorenzo in the final. It was an ugly game, but simple enough for the Whites to navigate, despite their opponents' relentless defensive tactics, which led to them racking up 24 fouls and four yellow cards. Real's two goals were scored by Sergio Ramos and Gareth Bale – just like in the Champions League final in Lisbon. Their 2-0 victory earned them their fourth trophy of 2014, and their first Club World Cup. But for the second match in a row Cristiano had made no impression on the pitch. San Lorenzo's tough defensive line-up left him no space to play his usual game.

In the end, his most camera-worthy moment came after the match, when he went up to collect the trophy. Waiting to shake the players' hands were Sepp Blatter, Florentino Pérez, the Crown Prince of Morocco Moulay Hassan ... and UEFA president Michel Platini, who a few weeks earlier had declared that the 2015 Ballon d'Or should go to a 'world champion' – in other words, if it were up to him he would give it to Germany's Manuel Neuer. His comments had ruffled feathers in the Madrid camp, Ronaldo's in particular. So now, when Ancelotti stopped to exchange a few words with Platini just in front of him, the Portuguese took advantage and stepped straight past him to shake hands with the rest of the dignitaries. The European football head honcho noticed and looked rather disconcerted, but CR7 carried on as if nothing had happened, ignoring him completely.

The Club World Cup was the final fixture before the festive break, and at the start of the holiday Ronaldo headed home to Madeira for the inauguration of a statue that had been put up in his honour. More than three metres tall, and sculpted out of 800 kilos of bronze, it didn't exactly resemble the player, but that wasn't the most noticeable thing about it. What caused a stir among the commentators was the rather disproportionate 'asset' with which the sculptor had endowed his subject. The man in question, however, was immune to all the fuss, simply commenting that 'the statue is more beautiful than I am. It's very good. I love it.'

From Madeira, he headed off to Dubai with Cristiano Junior and Irina, posting photos online of their luxurious vacation. But the player's mother and siblings were noticeably absent. Given what a close-knit family they are, the rumour mill went into overdrive. What was happening in the Aveiro clan? Was there perhaps some conflict between the model and the mother? It was too soon to tell.

Dubai was not just a holiday for Cristiano. He was there to receive yet more trophies at the Globe Soccer Awards: Best Player of the Year and the *Marca* Fans' Favourite Player of the Year. In fact, the gala was almost entirely a tribute to Real Madrid. The players raked in the gongs and the club was named Best Club of the Year. The event was something of a reunion for all the big names in football, so it was inevitable that CR7 would run into Platini. They were seen exchanging a few words on the stage, although out of earshot of everyone else. Perhaps they were burying the hatchet? Moments later, a Real Madrid TV camera followed him backstage. Radiating happiness, he celebrated his latest trophies in his usual manner: with a roar of triumph.

'It would be a dream if 2015 is as good as 2014, or better,' he would later say. But the following day in Dubai, Real Madrid lost their first match in three months, against AC Milan. Though Ronaldo scored, it finished 2-4 to the Rossoneri. It was only a friendly, but it was to prove a bad omen for the Whites.

Chapter 32

Highs and lows

The dream is crushed. In five short days everything that could possibly go wrong has gone wrong.

On Sunday 17 May at 8.45pm, Cristiano Ronaldo enters the dressing room tunnel with wounded pride. His team have demolished Espanyol 1-4 in Barcelona, thanks to his hat-trick. But it's a hollow victory. The Whites needed to win but they also needed Barça to choke against Atlético to keep the title race open. Real have done their bit ... unfortunately so has Messi. The Argentine has netted an incredible goal at the Calderón to see his team crowned champions with one match of the season still to go. The two matches finish at the same time, and while the Blaugrana get started on their celebrations, the Whites are left to lick their wounds.

It's their second disappointment in less than a week. The first came the previous Wednesday, when they were knocked out of Champions League by Juventus in the semi-finals. In the first leg in Turin on 5 May, Real had buckled under pressure and lost 2-1. Cristiano scored the visitors' only goal with a header from a cross by Dani Carvajal. And the Whites missed out on a chance to make history: they have only won once at Juventus' stadium, and that was 53 years ago. Eight days later on 13 May Ancelotti's men tried to strike back against the Italians. And for 57 minutes the final was in their sights. They were dominating possession, and in the 23rd minute Cristiano put them ahead, converting a penalty after a foul on James Rodríguez. The Bernabéu erupts with excitement. Real's 'BBC' (Bale, Benzema and Cristiano) kept things buzzing with more chances in the next few minutes than in the entire first leg.

But what at first seemed like it would be a walkover gradually started to look like an uphill struggle. Soon after the start of the second half, former Real Madrid striker Álvaro Morata hit a shot past Casillas to make it 1-1, putting an end to the hopes and dreams of his old team. And despite continued attempts from the Whites, the scoreline would not budge. Real Madrid were out of Europe. To rub more salt into the wound, Barça were through to the final and in Berlin on 6 June would win their fifth European Cup. With better performances it could have been Real Madrid's eleventh.

No Liga title, no Champions League and no Copa del Rey. It has been a bittersweet season for Ronaldo. His individual successes, like the Ballon d'Or, can't quite make up for his disappointment over the lack of team trophies. Real Madrid are left with just the European Super Cup and the Club World Cup, both of which were won in the first five months of the season.

It was in January that everything shifted. It was a challenging time, both on and off the pitch.

In the first few weeks of 2015 everyone was talking about the player's private life following his split from Irina Shayk. It had been love at first sight when they met during an Armani photoshoot, although break-up rumours always circulated throughout their relationship. It was now clear why she didn't join him at the Ballon d'Or gala, and why he didn't mention her in his acceptance speech.

Their separation after five years together was all over the front pages, and not just in the tabloids. The sports papers were also bogged down in the details of what happened between one of the most idolised – and bankable – couples in the world.

Portuguese daily *Correio da Manha* claimed that it was CR7 who ended things because they hardly ever saw each other and he supposedly 'wants a woman who is always by his side'. Once again there was talk of an allegedly uneasy relationship between Shayk and the player's mother and sisters. It was even claimed that the break-up had been caused by Shayk's reluctance to attend her mother-in-law's 60th birthday. 'Dolores Aveiro is convinced that Irina was not the right partner for her son,' claimed *Correio*. 'She would prefer someone who is willing in the future to assume the role of mother to little Cristiano, but that wasn't a priority for Irina.' And, of course, they all wanted to dig up dirt on Cristiano's supposed infidelities. He opted to remain completely silent on the matter, only releasing an official statement on 20 January via Associated Press to confirm the split: 'After dating for five years, my relationship with Irina Shayk has come to an end. We believed it would be best for both of us to take this step now. I wish Irina the greatest happiness.' He would say nothing further about the matter, nor would he comment on any of the supposed new romances that were already rumoured in the media.

At first, his ex adopted the same approach, communicating only via her agent: 'All negative rumours regarding Irina and Ronaldo's family are completely false and have nothing whatsoever to do with their break-up.' But on 11 February Irina herself hinted that the separation may not have been as amicable as previously thought. 'I'm looking for a man who is honest and faithful,' she told *E! News*. It was unclear if this was a swipe at CR7. A few weeks later she was even more explicit in an exclusive interview with

¡Hola! magazine in which she said she felt 'ugly and inse-
cure' while with Cristiano. Once again she emphasised the
importance of faithfulness and concluded that she thought
she had 'found the ideal man … but no'.

The *Sun* claimed to have the inside track on the mean-
ing behind Irina's comments. It alleged that the Portuguese
had cheated on Irina with at least twelve different women.
It claimed that she had supposedly discovered various messages that he had sent to girls in different countries, that he
had denied it, and that she had decided to break things off.

With no confirmation either way, that might have been
the end of the matter, if it weren't for the fact that Portugal's
Best Player of All Time – as he was named in January by his
country's football federation – just didn't seem to be himself on the pitch right now. Suddenly, without warning, after
a fabulous first half of the season, Ronaldo's performance
levels plummeted, and so did his team's form.

The first few weeks of the year saw a string of defeats
and disappointments for Real Madrid. First they lost 2-1 to
Valencia in La Liga, then they were knocked out in the last
sixteen of the Copa del Rey – again at the hands of Atlético,
just like in the last Spanish Supercup. In the first leg at the
Calderón Cristiano was on the bench due to muscle problems. It ended 2-0.

Minutes before the return leg kick-off, when the Whites
had hopes of a comeback, Ronaldo showed off his third
Ballon d'Or trophy to the Bernabéu crowd, to a deafening
ovation. He was joined by James Rodríguez with his FIFA
Puskás Award for the best goal of 2014, as well as Sergio
Ramos and Toni Kroos who had been named in the FIFA/
FIFPro World XI.

But the match was to end 2-2, and after Real's elimination, the look on Cristiano's face could not have been more

different. 'Thank you to the fans, on behalf of the team I want to apologise to them,' he said in the press zone. But he also tried to play down the significance of the occasion. 'We were unlucky. The Copy del Rey was the least important of the tournaments. La Liga and the Champions League are more important this year. Sometimes it's better to take one step back in order to take two steps forward,' he explained, confident that it was just a hiccup. He went on to talk about his fitness, which had been in doubt – despite the fact that he had scored Real's second goal against Atlético: 'Life is not just about goals, being 100 per cent fit all the time is impossible. I'm not a superhero.'

CR7 might be human like the rest of us, but he fights every day to appear otherwise. 'If I can play more than 60 games a season, year after year, it's because I take care of myself. I sleep well, I eat well. Even in those areas I strive for perfection. Otherwise you can't maintain that pace,' he told *France Football.* 'At the moment I'm trying to improve my left foot, my acceleration and my free kicks. That's an area where I've had less success. I know I'll get it back. I just have to have the humility to recognise that things don't work without a lot of practice. I'm guided by hard work.' The interview, published on 21 January, revealed a more intimate and personal side to the player. He insisted that the word 'leader' did not represent who he really was. 'I think every player on the pitch is a leader in his own way, everyone has a different role,' he said.

And of course, as expected, Messi's name came up again. He acknowledged that he is motivated by the Argentine, 'just like all those players who make you up your game, because you push yourself to be better than they are. All competition is a motivator.' And he is sure that competitiveness also motivates the Flea. 'It's good for him, it's good for me and for all players who want to grow. Messi has four Ballon d'Or trophies, I have three. All that stuff is good for the world of football.' He said that right now he was calm and he was not yet focusing on 'what next year will bring'. And of course, he confirmed he was happy at Real Madrid now that he was in 'the best dressing room' he had ever experienced in his career.

In case there were still any lingering doubts about his loyalty to the club, his agent confirmed a few days later that he would 'almost certainly retire at Real Madrid'. And that is a long way off, because Jorge Mendes is convinced that Cristiano will keep going until he is 38 or 39. But not everyone was won over by the agent's optimism. Some asked whether he had been more subdued since his separation from Irina, and whether it had affected his game. Dolores flatly denied it. 'My son is happy,' she insisted. But a few days later it was clear that something was going on with CR7. Real were playing Córdoba in their 20th league match of the season. After struggling for a large part of the match, they managed to beat the home team 1-2, although it was still a weak performance. Worst of all, Cristiano barely made an impression. Nothing came out the way he wanted. And in the 83rd minute he imploded. Unable to score after a pass from Toni Kroos, he took out his frustration in the worst possible way, kicking and then slapping the Brazilian Edimar. Earlier he had already knocked José Ángel Crespo during the struggle to reach the ball after a corner. And now, after his attack on Edimar, he hit Deivid Rodríguez and Crespo again when they rushed over to condemn his actions.

The referee was in no doubt: it was a red card. Ronaldo didn't even bother to protest the decision, heading straight for the tunnel. The whistles from the crowd were deafening as he left the pitch. He seemed to respond by touching the team shield on his shirt, a gesture interpreted by some as a final act of defiance. But a few minutes later he apologised on social media. 'I apologise to everyone, particularly to Edimar, for my rash actions.' Córdoba had seen the worst of Ronaldo. It's not something that happens often, but this side of him has surfaced a few other times. In his first season at Real Madrid he received a red card for elbowing Málaga's Patrick Mtiliga, who ended up with a fractured nose. In the final of the 2013 Copa del Rey it was for kicking Atlético's Gabi Fernández in the face, and during the 2013–14 season he got a red card after clashing with Athletic Bilbao's Ander Iturraspe.

His actions in Córdoba got him banned for two matches. At first there was talk in the press of a punishment of up to twelve games, but the Portuguese had two things in his favour: he was not a persistent offender, and he had apologised immediately after the incident. 'The moment he was sent off in Córdoba, he showed remorse for his actions. That's not easy for Cristiano,' said teammate Íker Casillas. 'He's in the spotlight and everyone always focuses on him. Making amends is the right thing to do and for that we support him. We cannot condone this type of behaviour, we are role models for millions of spectators, so let's focus on Cristiano as the positive, ambitious player that he is.'

He was out of the team for the games against Real Sociedad on 31 January and Sevilla on 4 February, both of which were victories for the Whites. On 5 February, the day after his ban was lifted, it was his 30th birthday. He spent a quiet day with his son, avoiding any grand celebrations, just concentrating on getting back on the pitch. Birthday parties would have to wait until after one of the most hyped Liga clashes of the year, the derby with Atlético Madrid.

Meanwhile the press marked his birthday with column inches and radio segments dedicated to his achievements – and the challenges ahead. They analysed his transformation into more of a goalscorer than in his early days, more of a number 9 than a number 7. They praised his stats, more impressive each year, and his thirst for goals. They also noted the injury problems that seemed to have held him back, made worse by the wear and tear of recent years, but which the club insisted were not a big deal.

Finally on 7 February he was back on the pitch at the Vicente Calderón, where Real had the wind knocked out of their sails by the *Atleti*. Cristiano could only manage one shot at goal during the entire match. And for 90 minutes he endured mockery and insults from the stands, with the Atlético fans incessantly mimicking his yelp of delight when he won the Ballon d'Or. Cristiano's frustration mounted and he even had an altercation with a ballboy for not giving him the ball. The final scoreline said it all: 4-0. It was the worst defeat for the Whites since the 5-0 thrashing that Guardiola's Barça gave them under Mourinho in November 2010. Plus it was their sixth consecutive defeat by Atlético.

'That was the worst match since I took over,' admitted coach Ancelotti. CR7 made no attempt to hide his disappointment either: 'It was a shitty day, but we have to think positively because we are still number one.' What did he think was missing? 'Everything. We had no drive, we had no attitude. We weren't at our freshest – mentally or physically. We played really badly, in every position, from top to bottom. We need to just forget about this as quickly as possible, because Real cannot be losing 4-0 to any team in the world. It's happened, and now we have to pick ourselves up and carry on, there's still plenty to play for in La Liga.' He acknowledged that many players had been worn out by their recent fixtures, although he didn't really think it an excuse. 'In my opinion, we are much better than Atlético, but we have to prove it on the pitch. We will definitely win La Liga again,' he concluded confidently.

The humiliation at the Calderón left many Whites fans deeply hurt, and they were therefore unable to shrug off what was Cristiano's biggest slip-up since arriving at the club. Just hours after the defeat, he headed out for his big 30th birthday celebration at one of the city's most exclusive restaurants. The party had already been organised and he decided not to cancel. Unfortunately someone decided to leak some pictures of him and most of the squad singing karaoke on stage and having a good time – too much of a good time, by the fans' reckoning. The indiscreet person in question was Colombian musician Kevin Roldan – friend of James Rodríguez – whose posts only added fuel to the fire: 'Thank you for hiring me as the headline performer at your 30th birthday. It's an honour that you enjoy my music. It's going to be a very special night, I hope you enjoy the show. We're going to tear it up in Madrid tonight,' wrote the Reggaeton star just before the party. And after the event he uploaded video and photos showing the player wearing a huge carnival-style hat.

Twitter erupted with vitriol and the hashtag #LaFiestaDeLaDeshonra ('shameful party'), which became a trending topic for the whole of the following day. The club couldn't explain why Cristiano – usually so fiercely private – hadn't taken more steps to keep the details of his ill-timed party under wraps. Even Casillas, Sergio Ramos and Ancelotti stayed away, perhaps conscious of how the whole spectacle could look. Jorge Mendes immediately tried to rectify the situation in a radio interview, saying that the footballer was 'distraught over the defeat' and that everyone at the party was trying to cheer him up. He also insisted that the party had been planned more than a month in advance, that it couldn't have been cancelled, and that the star 'didn't want to be rude to those who had come'. Finally, he claimed that the CR7 was considering suing Kevin Roldan, the only person who seemed to have benefited from the scandal. 'There is no such thing as bad publicity,' declared the musician. 'The controversy has brought me new followers, downloads and visits to my site. Everything is a blessing from God.'

In the Real Madrid dressing room you could have cut the tension with a knife. According to the press Cristiano was annoyed with Casillas and Ramos. It was alleged he thought they fuelled the controversy by privately voicing their disapproval to journalists. He supposedly couldn't understand their position given that they also went out after the defeat, and the goalie celebrated his girlfriend's birthday that same night – albeit in a more discreet setting. But more worrying for the club was the friendship that had been forged between Ronaldo and Alberto Garrido, the organiser of his big night out. The PR guru had been on the scene a lot more since the player's split from Irina. CR7 was going out more, and Garrido had been charged with getting him into some of the best clubs in the city without anyone even knowing he was there. The two of them, along with James Rodríguez, seemed to be joined at the hip. It was the first time that the player's health-conscious image had been questioned.

And while the press were going into overdrive, Florentino Pérez decided to intervene. The Real Madrid president interrupted the team's first training session after the Atlético defeat and spent two hours reminding the players what they represent and what is expected of them. But he was there to motivate more than criticise, and he called for unity and hard work. Judging by their performance on 14 February at the Bernabéu, his words must have sunk in, as they beat Deportivo La Coruña 2-0. It wasn't not a stellar performance, but convincing enough. For Cristiano it was something of a trial by fire. He spent most of the game far away from the action; the most involvement he had was to assist in the second goal, but it was his first time out in front of the home crowd since his party and it was a relief to see that they welcomed him as always, and that for the most part they were still loyal to their biggest star.

Four days later he scored one of Real's two goals in their victory over Schalke 04 in the last sixteen of the Champions League. 'Cristiano is back,' declared the coach, adding, 'It was never a problem that he didn't score in two games. He is always growing, as is the whole team.' His next test was against Elche in La Liga on 22 February, where Real netted another two, one by Cristiano. They were top of the table with a four-point lead over Barça – but their advantage was to evaporate all too quickly. On 1 March against Villareal they couldn't extract more than a 1-1 draw (Ronaldo scoring the goal), and then they lost 1-0 to Athletic Bilbao, slipping down below Barça. Everyone was in agreement: neither Real Madrid nor Ronaldo was playing to their full potential.

At least they were through to the Champions League quarter-finals after knocking out Schalke on 10 March, albeit with rather more effort than should have been necessary (3-4 to the Germans on the night; 5-4 to the Spaniards on aggregate – making them the first team in Champions League history to make it through to the next round after conceding four goals at home). But Cristiano lost his cool over the protests from the stands at the Whites' mediocre performance. Even the slightest whistle set him off. This time he offered no apology, instead deciding not to speak to the press until the end of the season.

Against this tense backdrop Real Madrid arrived at the last big *Clásico* of the season, at the Nou Camp on 22 March. As always, the atmosphere had been heating up for several days, with comments from both sides. Former Barça star Hristo Stoichkov had not minced his words in favouring Messi over Ronaldo: 'You can't compare a legend to a player at the end of his career,' he said. And he predicted that 'if Barcelona win, La Liga is theirs'. This would prove to be correct.

During the first half of the match the visitors dominated possession, but Barcelona were the first to score, with a goal by Mathieu in the nineteenth minute. After that CR7 had various chances, but he could only convert one. Nonetheless it was a great goal, a fabulous pass from Benzema prodded into the net by Cristiano. The Whites kept the pressure on after the break, but without managing to score, while Barça caused them ever more difficulty. Luis Suárez eventually took advantage of a pass from Dani Alves to make it 2-1. This time Real had lost with honour, although Cristiano appeared to make another vulgar gesture on the pitch, grabbing his groin after the referee gave him a yellow card. To be fair, he had endured yet another round of chants mocking his now infamous roar. And the fans' latest was 'Cristiano doesn't drink water', to replace their earlier 'Cristiano is a drunk' chant (by now deemed defamatory and banned by the league's governing body) which they had sung in reference to his party.

What was left of the season turned into a race to catch Barcelona and, for Ronaldo personally, to overtake Messi as top goalscorer. On 5 April it was clear that the individual award, at least, was within his reach. Real Madrid destroyed

Granada with a 9-1 thrashing, the Portuguese scoring five, of which the first three were within eight minutes of each other. He celebrated with renewed energy, and at last there were smiles after the final whistle. It was the first time he had ever scored five in a match; the press marked the achievement by dubbing him 'the cannibal'. He collected the ball, signed by all his teammates, conscious that this feat was something only the best of the best can ever achieve. Just six players in Real Madrid history had done it before him: Alday, Alsúa, Muñoz, Pepillo, Puskás and Morientes. And he was now the eighth-highest goalscorer in the history of La Liga with 214. Three days later he scored his 300th goal in a Real shirt in their 2-0 win over Rayo Vallecano. It's an incredible tally, but for Ronaldo it is just motivation to keep on going.

On 23 May, as French magazine *So Foot* revealed that he had donated €7 million to victims of the Nepal earthquake, Cristiano was crowned Pichichi of La Liga with 48 goals, and the top goalscorer in Europe yet again. Two individual titles that just weren't quite enough. Next season would bring fresh challenges and a new coach – Rafa Benítez. The former Liverpool and Napoli boss was now confirmed as successor to Carlo Ancelotti, the man who had been there to support Ronaldo during this intense year of highs and lows.

Facts and figures

Name: Cristiano Ronaldo dos Santos Aveiro

Nicknames: CR7, CR9, Cris

Date of birth: 5 February 1985

Birthplace: Funchal in Madeira, Portugal

Nationality: Portuguese

Parents: Jose Dínis (died 6 September 2005) and María Dolores

Sisters: Katia and Elma

Brother: Hugo

Son: Cristiano Junior

Height: 186 cm

Weight: 85 kg

Position: Winger

Shirt number: 7

Clubs

Andorinha (1993–1995)

Nacional (1995–1997)

Sporting Lisbon (1997–2003)

Manchester United (2003–2009)

Real Madrid (2009–present day)

Sporting Lisbon

Debut with first team: 14 July 2002, friendly against
Olympique Lyonnais

League debut: 7 October 2002 against Moreirense FC

First goal: 3 August 2002, friendly against Real Betis

Appearances:

League: 25   Goals: 3

Cups: 3   Goals: 2

Europe: 3   Goals: 0

Manchester United

Debut: 16 August 2003, Premier League match against
Bolton Wanderers

First goal: 1 November 2003 against Portsmouth

Appearances:

Premier League: 196   Goals: 86

Cups: 38   Goals: 17

Europe: 55   Goals: 16

Real Madrid

Debut: 21 July 2009, friendly against Shamrock Rovers

La Liga debut: 29 August 2009 against Deportivo de La Coruña

First goal: 29 July 2003, friendly against Liga Deportiva
Universitaria de Quito

Appearances (up to 24 May 2015):

Liga: 200   Goals: 255

Cups: 34   Goals: 24

Europe: 66   Goals: 64

Portugal national team

Debut: 20 August 2003, friendly against Kazakhstan

First goal: 12 June 2004 against Greece in the opening match
of UEFA Euro 2004

Appearances (up to 24 May 2015):

Caps: 118   Goals: 52

Tournament participation

UEFA Euro 2004

FIFA World Cup 2006

UEFA Euro 2008

FIFA World Cup 2010

UEFA Euro 2012

FIFA World Cup 2014

Club titles

With Manchester United:

Champions League (2008)

Premier League (2007, 2008, 2009)

FA Cup (2004)

League Cup (2006, 2009)

World Club Cup (2008)

Community Shield (2007)

With Real Madrid:

Copa del Rey (2011, 2014)

La Liga (2011–12)

Spanish Supercup (2012)

UEFA Champions League (2014)

UEFA Super Cup (2014)

FIFA Club World Cup (2014)

Individual titles

Ballon d'Or (2008, 2013, 2014)

FIFA World Player of the Year (2008)

European Golden Shoe (2008, 2011, 2014, 2015)

PFA Players' Player of the Year (2007, 2008)

PFA Young Player of the Year (2007)

Sir Matt Busby Player of the Year (2004, 2007, 2008)

Bibliography

De Calò, Alessandro, *Il calcio di C. Ronaldo ai raggi x* (Milan: *La Gazzetta dello Sport*, 2010)

Oldfield, Tom, *Cristiano Ronaldo: The £80 Million Man* (London: John Blake Publishing, 2009)

Ortego, Enrique, *Cristiano Ronaldo: Sueños cumplidos* (Madrid: Editorial Everest, 2010)

Ronaldo, Cristiano and Brandão, Manuela, *Momentos* (Lisbon: Ideias et Rumos, 2007)

Magazines
FourFourTwo, London
France Football, Paris
Don Balón, Barcelona
Guerin Sportivo, Bologna

Newspapers
Spain
El País
El Mundo
La Vanguardia
Marca
As
Sport
Mundo Deportivo

UK
The Times
Guardian
Independent
Daily Mirror
Daily Star
Daily Telegraph
The Sun
News of the World (now defunct)

Portugal
Diario de Notícias
Público
Jornal da Madeira
Correio da Manhã
A Bola
Record

Italy
Corriere della Sera
La Repubblica
La Gazzetta dello Sport
Corriere dello Sport

France
L'Équipe

Yearbooks
Guía de la Liga 2010 (*Marca* Magazines)
Guía de la Liga 2011 (*Marca* Magazines)
Guía de la Liga 2012 (*Marca* Magazines)

TV channels
Spain
RTVE
Antena 3
Telecinco
laSexta
Intereconomía TV
Real Madrid TV

Portugal
RTP
SIC

UK
Sky Sports
MUTV

Documentaries
Planeta Ronaldo (SIC)
Cristiano Ronaldo al Límite (Castrol)

Radio
Spain
Cadena SER
Cadena COPE
Onda Cero
Radio Marca

UK
BBC Radio

Websites

www.fifa.com

www.uefa.com

www.realmadrid.com

www.manutd.com

www.sporting.pt

www.twitter.com/cristiano

www.twitter.com/cr7web

www.facebook.com/Cristiano

www.cronaldo7.es

www.ronaldofan.com

www.ronaldoweb.com

www.cristianoronaldo.com

www.cr7.es

www.ronaldoattack.com

Acknowledgements

I would like to thank Diego Torres, Manuel Pereira, Ian Hawkey, Simon Flynn, Sheli Rodney, Laure Merle d'Aubigné, Roberto Domínguez and Roberto Baldinelli.

Dedicated to Elvira, Lorenzo, Olmo, Alda and Tullio.

ALSO AVAILABLE

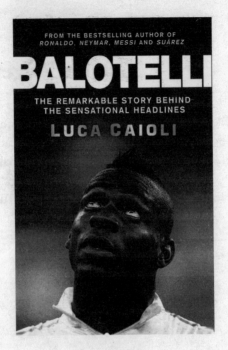

FROM THE BESTSELLING AUTHOR OF
RONALDO, NEYMAR, MESSI AND *SUÁREZ*

BALOTELLI

THE REMARKABLE STORY BEHIND
THE SENSATIONAL HEADLINES

LUCA CAIOLI

BALOTELLI

Mario Balotelli has a reputation like no other in football. Since exploding on to the scene at Inter Milan in 2007, he has won league titles in both Italy and England, moving between Europe's elite clubs.

Yet for all his undoubted talent, he is better known for his off-field antics – not least his infamous run-ins with both the police and Manchester's firefighters. Once described by José Mourinho as 'unmanageable', match-winning performances at the highest level have continued to convince clubs such as AC Milan and Liverpool to give him a chance.

With exclusive access to friends, teammates and coaches, acclaimed football biographer Luca Caioli talks to the people best placed to explain the mystery that is Mario Balotelli.

ISBN: 978-184831-913-4 (paperback) / 978-184831-914-1 (ebook)

MESS!

MORE THAN A SUPERSTAR

LUCA CAIOLI

2016 UPDATED EDITION

FROM THE BESTSELLING AUTHOR OF
RONALDO, *NEYMAR* AND *SUAREZ*

MESSI

Lionel Messi is the greatest footballer of our time: a magician with
uncanny ability to beat defenders, find space and score goals.
At the peak of his powers during Barcelona's 2015 treble win – a
decade on from his first Spanish title – the four-time Ballon d'Or
winner has again eclipsed his rivals and proved emphatically
that he has no intention of surrendering his crown just yet.

Messi is Luca Caioli's classic portrait of modern football's star
turn, now fully updated to include all the action from 2014/15.
Featuring exclusive testimony from those who know him best,
including coaches, teammates and even Messi himself, it offers an
unrivalled behind-the-scenes look at the life of a football superstar.

ISBN 978-190685-091-3 (paperback) / 978-190685-092-0 (ebook)

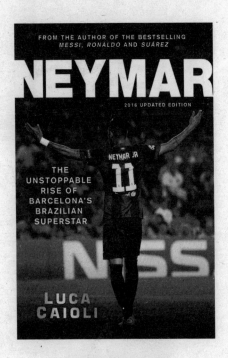

FROM THE AUTHOR OF THE BESTSELLING
MESSI, *RONALDO* AND *SUÁREZ*

NEYMAR

2016 UPDATED EDITION

THE
UNSTOPPABLE
RISE OF
BARCELONA'S
BRAZILIAN
SUPERSTAR

LUCA
CAIOLI

NEYMAR

From an early age, Neymar Junior was identified
as a future great of world football.

Since then there have been both highs and lows, with his early
triumphs at Santos sometimes overshadowed by the controversies
and disappointments of his early days at Barcelona and at the
Brazil World Cup. But his pivotal role in Barça's spectacular 2015
treble has reconfirmed him as one of football's most devastating
attacking forces and he now stands on the brink of greatness.

Fully updated and drawing on exclusive interviews with those
who have known and worked with him, *Neymar* paints a
compelling picture of the life and career of a global icon.

ISBN: 978-190685-095-1 (paperback) / 978-190685-096-8 (ebook)